DRAGONS ON THE ROOF

Unravelling Vietnam

By the same author

Hanoi of a Thousand Years

Secrets of Hoi An, Vietnam's Historic Port

Hue, Vietnam's Last Imperial Capital

ABOUT THE AUTHOR

Carol Howland is an experienced travel writer, a former feature writer for a national magazine and a contributor to more than a dozen British newspapers. Following a mid-career foray into stockbroking, she edited two finance magazines, but never lost her passion for travel. Early in her career, she wrote and revised guidebooks and more recently, returned to travel writing. Enthralled by the country, she has published four books exploring Vietnam's cultural heritage. She now lives in France.

'Carol Howland has written four travel books, that had they been written and read by the intelligentsia of America before the Vietnam War, would have made the US pause and take stock of the state of affairs in this small, now well-known country.

'The author's meticulous research into the customs, traditions and cultural history of Vietnam are a mind opening revelation to the uninitiated traveller. She explores the exotic venues of an historically turbulent culture that is vibrantly alive and growing in spite of today's conflicts among the powerful nations of the world.

'Reading her series of books on Vietnam, *Dragons on the Roof, Hanoi of a Thousand Years, Hoi An – Vietnam's Historic Port, and Hue – Vietnam's Last Imperial Capital,* is a deeply rewarding experience. Without even mentioning the Vietnam War, she leads the reader on a journey through the cities and countryside of this beautiful Asian country and the mysterious mindset of the proud, persistent and independent people of Vietnam. Her descriptions of the ancient civilizations in the early years and how the country developed through Taoism, Confucianism, Hinduism, Buddhism, and Catholicism leave the reader with an astounding wealth of information to synthesize in order to appreciate the varieties of experience one can expect when visiting this country.

'From the tale of the two Vietnamese Trung sisters who repulsed the An Chinese in 40 AD through the expulsion of Kublai Khan, the Japanese in WWII, the French Colonialists, and infamously, the US, to the beautiful flower gardens, architecture, cuisine of the rich and poor, to the type of jewellery worn in the imperial court of Hue, she writes in great detail of the marvels of manners and grace still apparent in the Vietnamese people.

'First published in Hanoi by Vietnam's publisher of foreign language books, her books celebrate Vietnamese culture, a remarkable series of books that elucidate the many faces of Vietnam. Her wit, insights and thoroughness permeate the writing and bring joy, excitement and expectation to the would be traveller and historian. Read them, go to Vietnam, and follow her suggestions to have a really rewarding experience in Vietnam!'

Ken Embers, Vietnam representative for Globalism; Director of English Programs and Projects for Vietnam Children's Libraries International; Captain, helicopter pilot, Vietnam 1968-69.

'Like a military reporter, Carol Howland embeds herself with her subject. However, her strategy is less military than empathy and Howland has not only the gift of insight but the gift of friendship: she leaves her subjects like a long lost pal, a priceless asset in this big hearted but still endlessly enigmatic country.'

Peter Howick, Columnist, *The Evening Herald,* Dublin

DRAGONS ON THE ROOF

Unravelling Vietnam

CAROL HOWLAND

MYNAH BIRD BOOKS

Published by Mynah Bird Books 2018
1 Regents Court, 10 Balcombe Road
Branksome Park, Poole, Dorset BH13 6DY

First published 2008 by The Gioi Publishers,
46 Tran Hung Dao Street, Hanoi, Vietnam

ISBN – 13: 978-1-9998436-0-1
ISBN – 10: 1999843606

This book is dedicated to Vietnamese scholar, Huu Ngoc, whose works were so inspiring, and to the memories of Phan Van Thiet, Nguyen Phuoc Bao Hien and Duc Thinh, who have since died.

CONTENTS

9

PART IV – HANOI IN WINTER

INTRODUCTION

Words don't cost anything,
Therefore it is up to us to choose them
so as to give satisfaction to others
– Vietnamese proverb

It happened at Halong Bay.

From the deck of a cruise ship at dawn, the misty harbour lay spread out like an oriental scroll, the paint still glistening wet. Distant figures under conical hats poled slim, curved boats as delicate as curled leaves, tiny silhouettes against the jade water.

To the east, huge black peaks reared abruptly from the sea, their vegetation still swathed in the semi-darkness before sunrise. Layer upon layer of these dark behemoths roamed the horizon, a giant labyrinth beckoning towards the South China Sea, perhaps to the edge of the world.

The beauty of the scene brought a tightening in my throat. Even then, I felt a strange yearning to melt into that misty landscape and to wander unnoticed through this mysterious, oriental land.

A few days later, midway down the country, that same yearning welled up in me again, this time at Thien Mu pagoda, just upriver from Vietnam's former imperial capital, Hue. Looking out over the Perfume river through the lacy, red petals of a flamboyant tree – the scene so picturesque that it might have been a too pretty picture – I had the overwhelming feeling that this was not the last time I would gaze out over the Perfume river. I felt a curious longing to find a spot overlooking this river, somewhere nearby, and to stay here, maybe for a year. *A Year on the Perfume River* – yes, I liked the sound of it.

Then further south at Nha Trang, arriving in early morning at the busy fishing port where sunlight burnished the huge square fishnets to shimmering gold; where boats with red, white and blue sails bumped one another like dodgems and the voices of commuters on the river bank railed at the small ferryboats in their impatience to get across, the same longing caught in my throat.

What I fancied was a meandering wallow in the rich culture of a country whose history stretched back to primitive stirrings. Even the brief shore excursions of the cruise assured me that Vietnam revelled in just such a deep, rich heritage. Abounding in myths of dragons and fairies, sacred turtles, magic swords, heroic generals and cunning battle strategies, Vietnam's foundations lie buried in the unwritten legends of pre-history. The country's recorded history – the past two thousand years – unfurls like a tapestry of warring clans and dynasties, flowering in the last few centuries in a sophisticated court life, a highly developed theatre, in classical music and poetry – until the merciless twentieth century. It set my curiosity spinning. How had these people survived so many wars – in the twentieth century alone against the Japanese, the French, the Americans and most recently, their old enemy, the Chinese? More urgently, even during the space of the cruise I could see the country changing fast, moving rapidly from a deeply spiritual ethos to a rampant consumer society. I wanted to tap those spiritual values, their myths and legends *now* – before they disappeared altogether. So my quest would be – if I could pull off my return for an extended stay – to delve deeply into Vietnam, to slip behind the tourist facade and find out what had made these people so resilient, how they had survived all the wars, what held them together.

Beware of impulses in the dead of night. One night during the cruise, I even contemplated jumping ship. Well, why shouldn't I have an extended grand adventure? I had been financially responsible, paper-clipped to an editorial desk in London for far too long. I had no husband, a grown up daughter and a recently estranged lover. Why not rob the savings and have a year-long literary fling? Total distraction. Now or never.

But why was I reacting so strongly to an unknown country at first sight? Why does one fall in love with a person, much less with a country, and so completely as to up sticks and move there for a time? The eddy of emotions set me thinking.

Apart from the allure of Vietnam's captivating beauty, perhaps it was the past resurfacing, calling me back. Years ago, I had wanted to visit the forbidden, far side of the Truong Son mountains, the east coast of the Indo-China peninsula. Why forbidden? Because I found myself next door in Cambodia with a war on the far side of the mountains.

12

It all began at university where I read *The Tale of Genji* –
possibly the world's first novel, written by an eleventh century
Japanese court lady – and fell into a passion for Japan.
Extramurally, I read Japanese literature and history and
contemplated a second degree in Oriental languages.

Then I met and hastily married another student, who on
graduation joined the American diplomatic corps. For his first
posting, he was given a choice of continents. I cajoled him into
choosing Asia and so we found ourselves – not in Japan – but
posted to Cambodia during the early skirmishes of what gradually
turned into the Vietnam War. Throughout our time in Cambodia,
most weekends were spent in the *Deux Chevaux,* (a tiny, French,
corrugated tin can, estate wagon on wheels), bouncing through
the flat and dusty, or monsoon-drenched countryside, over split-
log bridges in search of lost Khmer temples. From Phnom Penh
we visited Bangkok, but it was suggested that diplomatic staff not
visit Saigon, or if they did, not to drive. So, we never went.

These were tense times. Towards the end of the two-year
posting, we lived with packed suitcases under the bed and one
night at midnight, made a test drive at ninety miles an hour to
Sihanoukville to see how long it would take to reach the coast. As
a wife I was never privy to intelligence, but it did filter out that
the Viet Cong were making sporadic incursions into Cambodia in
the Mekong delta.

With hindsight, it is easy to see in what idealistic innocence,
if not stupidity and arrogance, the US blundered into a conflict
that on reflection, considering the devastating defeat suffered by
the French at Dien Bien Phu (1954), America was highly unlikely
to win. But back then, it was a religious war: American
democracy pitted against Communism.

The official US line ran that democratic South Vietnam – in
reality an unpopular pro-Western Catholic regime in a Buddhist
country – was fighting against domination by the Communist
North. And so they were. The North's propaganda ran that the
Vietnamese were once again fighting foreign invaders, a
nationalistic theme that plucked a steel string in the Vietnamese
psyche, still reverberating from the Indo-China War with the
French, moreover, that has resounded for two thousand years, had
the US powers that be in Washington, bothered to study
Vietnamese military history.

As a result of having lived in Cambodia during my impressionable youth, whenever I visit South East Asia, it feels like returning to a second home.

In fact, getting to Vietnam had been something of a coup. As a travel writer for British newspapers, I had been trying to arrange a commission to support a trip to Vietnam for several years. It was only when I encountered the managing director of a cruise line at a drinks party that suddenly, it fell into place.

Early in the cruise I had wondered how the Vietnamese would respond to Westerners, especially Americans, who had brought them so much death and grief. Well, mercifully, although they have not forgotten for a moment the pain and suffering, thirty-odd years later the Vietnamese are busy getting on with their lives in a dash to catch up with Western consumer societies. Westerners are very welcome. The Vietnamese recognize that foreigners bring much-needed money, investment and jobs and they don't blame Americans for the past sins of their government. In fact, the Vietnamese welcome to foreigners, long prevented from penetrating their Communist domain, is so effusive sometimes that it is almost embarrassing.

About mid-cruise I decided that I was going to come back somehow – and to stay for as long as possible. To be sure, it was an impulsive decision, an emotional response to the beauty of the country, curiosity about the people, their history and culture, but also the notion that perhaps in this far-flung country, I might leave my old life behind and lose myself. One of the appeals of travel is to leave one's self at home and to arrive, a new person in a new place. Somerset Maugham refers to the travelling stranger as 'the gentleman in the parlour.' Sometimes it works for a little while, until the old self catches up, having taken a later plane.

Back in London I looked again at the impulsive decision under a sodden wintry sky. I wondered if I were emotionally fit enough to set off alone on such a long jaunt. How would I cope, a fifty-something woman travelling alone, devoid of family and friends, what's more in a Communist country, if not hostile, a country whose government is still readjusting from wars and reunification, a country only gradually relaxing its vigilance over every activity of its citizens. And tourists.

To be sure, I have often travelled alone. My twenties were spent writing budget guidebooks. I am accustomed to living abroad, having transplanted myself from Cambodia (alas alone), briefly to Japan to study Japanese, then from New York where I worked on magazines, to the sun in the Bahamas. When the Bahamian government changed and foreign workers were no longer welcome, instead of returning to New York, I moved off to Mexico where a real job never quite materialized, then to England where I got stuck into journalism.

But would I be allowed an extended stay? I had read about Vietnamese bureaucracy and several books by other authors, who had either kept their writing projects concealed or who had been firmly and expensively escorted every step of the way from one official reception to the next. That was not what I had in mind. Nevertheless, I decided to try the official approach, first.

In a rush of enthusiasm, I wrote to the Vietnamese embassy in London. What I hoped to do, I explained, was to write a book about the Vietnamese people and their culture – not the politics, not the wars. Enough had been written by those who were there and lived through it. My objective would be to dig beneath the surface, to get to know the Vietnamese and try to unravel some of their cultural mysteries.

The only way to stay longer than a tourist visa allowed, I was told, was to obtain a business visa. This entailed sponsorship by a company in Vietnam. I knew no one in Vietnam. The nice man at the embassy asked if perhaps I might help with editing an English language newspaper in Saigon. Knowing the rudeness of saying *no* in the East, I agreed, asking if the newspaper would be able to send me pages so that I could do the editing at night from wherever I might be travelling. The man at the embassy gently explained that Vietnam's infrastructure was probably not quite ready for that. He kindly suggested that I approach the Foreign Ministry in Hanoi and gave me an English-speaking contact.

When finally I got through to the man, the response was cordial, but according to the rules, journalists must be attached either to a publication or a broadcasting authority, or have a set itinerary of no longer than six weeks and be escorted by a guide at the journalist's expense the entire time. I did not think I would need a guide (minder) every minute and certainly did not want to be restricted to a set itinerary. He then passed the problem parcel on to the Ministry of Culture.

At the Ministry of Culture it was suggested that I might be sponsored by a publishing house that formerly had been part of the ministry, publishing not only history and political tracts, but also books on Vietnam's culture. Sponsorship did not mean that I would be employed, nor that anything I wrote would be published by this publisher. I dared not ask if it would be scrutinized (it wasn't). No contracts, no exchange of money, no promises. From what I could gather over a crackling line six thousand miles away, it merely meant that the publishing house would sign the necessary form for my visa.

Six weeks after my return from the cruise, I had the visa.

PART I

HANOI IN SUMMER

HELLO VIETNAM!

A hundred things heard are not worth one seen
– Vietnamese proverb

On the first of April, I set off. That seemed appropriate.

Blinking my way down the steps of the plane in brilliant tropical sunlight, the heat hit me like a wall of fire. The Vietnamese have numerous apt expressions for the heat. 'Heat that bursts the heavens' feels about right.

The bus ride to the terminal is scorching. Long queues inside. The immigration officer looks like a scowling middleweight boxer having a really bad day. He scrutinizes my business visa printed in blood-red ink for an agonisingly long time, then stamps it hard, apparently furious that he can't send me straight back on the next flight. So much for a smiling welcome.

Bags on trolley, I heave it through the doors of the departure lounge to a roaring pack of taxi drivers, their arms thrusting over a barrier that restrains them from pouncing on arriving passengers. Never have I been so glad to see my name in print – on a placard held high by a chap with the name of my hotel embroidered on his yellow shirt. After an overnight flight, just this once I am relieved to have a minder. Welcome to Vietnam.

Not having slept on the plane, I am ready for the big sleep. The hotel has thoughtfully popped a bottle of sparkling *blanc de blanc* on ice. At 8 a.m. London time, 3 p.m. Hanoi time, it seems a bit louche to open it. I do anyway and as I lie waiting for sleep, take up the musings that occupied me during the long flight.

Conflicting emotions churn around my sleep-deprived brain: excitement, anticipation, fear. What madness gripped me to leave a job as editor of a magazine in London and commit myself to a year in an Asian country where I know not a soul? Have the enigmas of the country and my impulsive enthusiasm carried me too far? Well, this time I've done it, I'm here.

In the several weeks between the cruise and my second departure, I had read the creation myths and legends of the Hung kings, handed down orally over two thousand years, myths that are slowly being confirmed by archaeologists as a fairly accurate reflection of Vietnam's pre-history.

Originally, Viet was the name of an ethnic group. Nam meant south – of China. The Viets were just one of several ethnic groups who lived south of the Yangzte – in the foggy pre-history before the Chinese empire was united – in the area that is now southern China and northern Vietnam.

It was with some admiration that I learned that these Viets, who became the Vietnamese, had repeatedly seen off their huge encroaching neighbour, China, in the tenth, twelfth, thirteenth, fifteenth, eighteenth and most recently in the twentieth centuries, and that despite Chinese domination for more than a thousand years (179 BC to 938 AD), the Vietnamese had stubbornly retained a strong sense of their cultural identity. Moreover, the Vietnamese had seen off Kublai Khan's marauding hordes three times: in 1257, 1284 and 1287. These were one tough, indomitable, intensely nationalistic people.

I had begun to fill in a thumbnail sketch of Vietnamese history. With independence from the Chinese in the tenth century came fierce rivalry between feudal lords and later, civil wars between the dynasties of the North and the South – that wasn't new to the twentieth century. From independence in the tenth century right up to the French Indo-China War, viewed romantically, Vietnam's history flows like a flamboyant pageant of royal courts and oriental intrigues worthy of Machiavelli. Plus the wars, there were always wars.

With China to the north, the Truong Son mountains to the west and the South China Sea to the east, eventually there was only one direction to go – south. The great migratory march southward started in the eleventh century. By the seventeenth, the Vietnamese had reached the Mekong delta, expanding their rice culture and developing their economic and military power along the narrow coastal plain, pushing the Chams further south and other ethnic groups into the mountains where they remain to this day (see historic appendix). I am plunging into the historic heartland of the Viet civilization, the Red river valley and Hanoi.

18

A SWORD AND A PAINT BRUSH

Where the fatherland is, there also is the hero
-- Vietnamese proverb

Awake at dawn, to my surprise I find the streets full of people moving in one direction. I follow them and find myself at a crowded lakeside, women strolling arm in arm, chatting on benches, a man doing *tai chi*, another stretching his legs against a tree, a group of elderly women waving wooden swords to music from a ghetto blaster. A boy lopes past with a football – before breakfast? Hawkers call out, selling snacks. The open air Bon Mai cafe serves me coffee to the drone of cicadas under the trees.

Hoan Kiem (Lake of the Restored Sword) is the extended, leafy sitting room of Hanoi, the spiritual heart of the city. Apparently, in former times the lake was much larger, so vast that it was used by mediaeval kings to review their naval fleets. Now, it is only covertly linked to the Red river (Hong Song).

I sit sipping my coffee, watching all Hanoi parade past rather like an early morning *passegiata.* At the far end of the lake, mist hangs over a red, arched bridge, which Hanoians playfully call 'the perch of the rising sun.'

The tiny stone Turtle Pagoda that squats on a green tuft of an islet in the middle of the lake, I soon discover, serves as the icon for Hanoi on VN-TV weather forecasts.

One by one, the shops opposite start to open, bursting with silk paintings, woodblock prints, lacquer ware, inlaid boxes, basketry and carved statues. Art galleries, clothes shops, Fanny's ice cream parlour, the cafe Lac Viet and a couple of restaurants on balconies peeping through the treetops, line the west bank.

North of the lake, squeezed into a triangle, is the medieval quarter known as the Thirty-Six Streets. Here, guilds serving the royal court arose along the eastern wall of the imperial Citadel. Most of these narrow streets, as higgledy-piggledy as a fist full of joss sticks accidentally dropped, originally were named after the crafts practised in them: Silk Street, Noodle Street, Hemp Street, Cotton Street, Sail Street, Coffin Street, Mat Street, Bowl Street, Medicinal Herb Street, Votive Offering Street, Grilled Fish Street.

19

Hanoi first became the capital in 1010 when the founder of a new dynasty, Ly Thai To, moved his capital north from Hoa Lu. Exploring the fertile delta of the Red river, the emperor had a vision – of a golden dragon flying across the sky – doubtless, a harbinger of prosperity. It must have been summer when Hanoi is so hot that celestial visions are only a little less likely than hallucinations of Hades. Naturally, the new capital had to be called Soaring Dragon (Thang Long). Six hundred years later when the Nguyen (pronounced more or less, Win) dynasty moved the capital south to Hue, Thang Long was ignominiously demoted to Hanoi, city by the river.

Of Thang Long's original royal palaces, the Citadel, nothing remains, hardly surprising in a capital that over the centuries has found itself the target of expansion by the Chinese to the north and the Chams to the south, whose kingdoms clustered around Danang in central Vietnam and further south. But Thang Long's first citadel must have been impressive. A seventeenth century visitor to the ruins penned this in his diary: 'The palace alone occupied an area with a perimeter of six or seven miles (9-11 km). The paved marble courtyards, the doors and ruins of the apartments testified to its former magnificence and caused people to regret the destruction of one of the most beautiful buildings in Asia.'

In the eighteenth century, the Trinh lords who effectively ruled through the weak Le dynasty, possessed another fine palace. One of the fathers of traditional medicine in Vietnam, who used the self-deprecating pen name, the Lazy Old Man (Lan Ong, 1720-1791), wrote not only a description of his professional visit to the Trinh palace to treat a sickly young prince, but he was so impressed that he composed a poem as well to express his delight and wonder:

'When we arrived at the rear entrance to the palace, the mandarin who had summoned me acted as my guide. We passed two gates in succession and took an alley to the left. I raised my head to take a look: in trees and shrubs all around, birds were chirping, rare flowers were blooming and heavenly scents were wafted by the wind. Criss-crossed balusters lined the verandas. Messengers carrying orders shuffled back and forth. At each gate, guards controlled people's comings and goings, demanding presentation of (stone) tablets, serving as guarantees of safe-conduct.

'I was eventually allowed to enter (the palace). We followed a veranda in the west and came to a large building, on both sides of which royal palanquins painted red and gold stood in attendance. In the centre of a platform was a gilded royal bed with a pink hammock hanging over it. In front of the bed and on each side stood tables laid with uncommon objects. I cast a furtive glance at them and moved with my head bowed. We passed through a door and arrived at a large, tall building, its beams and pillars painted red and gold. I whispered a question to the mandarin who had summoned me. Here is his answer.

"'We just crossed the great palace named Picking Up the Coniza (sic). The building with a second storey is called the Crimson Palace and is reserved for the crown prince, who is in the habit of drinking tea there, hence its nickname, the tea room. In fact, it is the medicine room, but because people are shy of uttering this word, they prefer to call it the tea room."

'After the meal a eunuch went running to invite in the great chancellor and bade me to follow the latter. The great chancellor, for fear that I might get lost, ordered me to follow in his steps. When we arrived at the set place, he pushed aside the brocade hangings and we entered. Inside, it was dark and I could not make out any other door or opening. Hangings succeeded hangings, each preceded by a lit candle which allowed one to see one's way. After passing beneath four or five sets of tapestries, we came to a room in the middle of which stood a gold-bedecked bed. On the bed sat the little prince, a child of five or six years old, clad in red silk. A large candle was planted on a bronze stand, giving out some light. Close to the bed was a dragon-sculpted royal armchair, lacquered red with gold ornaments and a brocade cushion. Behind a silk hanging embroidered with gold and silver thread, a group of palace maids were huddled together. I vaguely saw their painted faces and pink garments. The room smelled of flowers and incense. I surmised that his highness had just left the armchair and retired behind a tapestry so that I could feel at ease when taking the pulse of his little son.'

This was his poem:

Guards carrying golden spears stand at the thousand gates
Under the southern skies, this is the most respected place
Multi-storey painted palaces and buildings rise
towards the sky

Pearl blinds and jade balusters shine under the rising sun
Flowers continuously emit delicate scents
In the royal gardens the voices of parrots are heard
To the commoner that I am, these enchanting places
have so far been unknown.
I remain speechless, like a fisherman
straying to peach blossom stream.
(tr Huu Ngoc)

The end of Thang Long as the capital came in 1805 when from the new capital, Hue, the first Nguyen emperor (Gia Long) ordered that the palaces of his family's enemies, the Trinh, be torn down and replaced by a fortification in the style of the French military architect, Vauban. Of Gia Long's later, nineteenth century fortress, only one watchtower and one gate remain.

Most of Hanoi lies on the west bank and numerous lakes remind one that this is a river delta. The largest of these lakes is prosaically called West Lake (Ho Tay), around which modern villas and the tree-line-breaking tower of a new international hotel have shot up in recent years. Two legends explain West Lake's origin.

In one, an eleventh century monk who had rendered services to the emperor of China, was allowed to bring back a large quantity of bronze with which he cast an enormous bell. When the bell tolled, the sound carried so far that the golden calf, hearing the bell, mistook it for the call of his buffalo mother and rushed south to find her. In his headlong stampede, the giant calf turned up great mounds of earth, creating a deep hollow that eventually filled with water: West Lake.

The other legend concerns the slaying of the nine-tailed fox. In this legend, the dragon king, Lan Long Quan of the pre-historic Lac people, the shadowy ancestors of the Viets, flooded the evil fox's lair, creating West Lake – the fox had been molesting maidens. Oh yes, dragons go right back to the creation myth of the Viet people.

As sunlight filters through the lacy leaves of the flamboyant trees and the branches of the willows dip their fingers in the cool surface of the water, the trees, the lake, the arched bridge and the temple assemble themselves in a delicate oriental water-scape, the image of Hanoi that will forever remain in my memory. No wonder Hanoians are drawn to their lake like a cool, silvery magnet.

With a name like Lake of the Restored Sword, there had to be a story. In fact, it was the very first Vietnamese legend I heard, just one of the beguiling tales of heroes, fairies and wronged maidens in the folklore of this land of myth, poetry and song that subsist – for the moment – just beneath the surface of daily life. The legend of the restored sword, Vietnam's version of excalibur, goes like this –

Having ruled Vietnam for a thousand years from 179 BC to 938 AD, once again in the fifteenth century, the armies of the Chinese (Ming) surged south and reconquered the Viets. During this second, mercifully brief period of Chinese rule (1407-1427), the Chinese systematically attempted to eradicate local Viet culture, breaking stone stelae in temples and destroying Buddhist pagodas. Entire libraries of Buddhist works compiled over the previous four centuries of independence were burnt or seized and carted off to China. The Vietnamese found this Ming domination particularly bitter.

According to legend, the dragon emperor of the waters (Lan Long Quan again), decided it was high time to intervene. At that time there lived a fisherman, who one night to his astonishment, lifted his net to find that it held a sword. Taking this as a sign, a bit later he joined the volunteers to fight against the Chinese. One day the commander-in-chief, General Le Loi, called at the fisherman's hut and noticed the gleaming sword standing in a corner. Engraved on the metal were the words, 'By the will of heaven.'

A day or two later in a forest, General Le Loi noticed a peculiar brightness at the top of a banyan tree and climbing up, found a sword hilt inlaid with jade. It was then that he remembered the strange sword in the fisherman's hut. Sensing the supernatural, he carried the sword hilt to the fisherman's hut and not to his surprise, found that the sword fitted perfectly.

The fisherman gladly relinquished the sword to the general and from that time on, Le Loi's troops won battle after battle, the strength of his army seemingly magnified tenfold. Before long, the Vietnamese were liberated from the Ming.

As a result of his victory, Le Loi was crowned king. Sometime later, one day while boating on the lake in the heart of the capital, suddenly the sacred golden turtle rose to the surface of the water, approached the royal boat and spoke: 'Please be so kind as to return to my master, the emperor of the kingdom of the waters, the sacred sword that he has entrusted to you.'

Standing in the boat, Le Loi felt the sword begin to quiver, so he threw it into the lake. The golden turtle dived, surfaced holding the sword in his mouth and dived again. Since then, the lake has been known as lake of the Restored Sword.

Historically, it was indeed General Le Loi who defeated the Ming in 1427, who taking the throne, established the Le dynasty. Curiously in 1965, when America was escalating the war, a giant turtle was caught in Hoan Kiem lake and its 550-pound preserved body is still displayed as a talisman in the temple of the Jade Mountain (Ngoc Son) on an island in the lake. Biologists estimate that the turtle was around five hundred years old, its birth neatly coinciding with the fifteenth century legend of Le Loi.

I meander round the lake towards the bridge and buy a copy of *Vietnam News,* the English language daily, from an open air news-stand in front of the heavy, institutional post office buildings, one for domestic, one for international post. A smart young woman approaches, hoping to exchange Vietnamese *dong* for dollars (everybody hoards dollars or gold). At the street entrance to the red bridge, professional photographers perch on plastic stools waiting for customers from the provinces, who use the famous bridge as a background – Ho was in Hanoi!

Young boys pester persistently, touting postcards and books on Vietnam's painful history.

'You want postcards?'

'No, thank you.'

'Why not?'

'I don't use postcards, I write letters.'

'Why you not help me?'

In exasperation I buy from one boy and a swarm of young boys surround me, complaining at the injustice of my having bought nothing from *them.* A few beggars hold out a hand or a straw hat. Weeks later, one evening at the door of the post office, my feet become ensnarled in the legs of giggling little boys, determined to prevent me from leaving without giving them some money.

I cross the red arched bridge to the temple of the Jade Mountain (Ngoc Son). The island where the turtle is displayed has served several functions in the history of the capital. The Trinhs, one of the powerful clans who came to control the throne, built their 'country villa' here in the fifteenth century. A Buddhist pagoda followed in the nineteenth century. The present temple is dedicated to deified warriors and a couple of scholars, one of them La To, the patron saint of physicians.

Two elderly men sit beneath the flowering trees playing chess as though posed for a photograph; another sits reading. Young girls who should be studying, rush up, smiling shyly, wanting to practise their English. Ironically, since the end of the Vietnam War, English has been the required language in schools. The scene is so tranquil that I envy the Trinh lords their villa; surely the island is Hanoi's ultra-prime position.

I wonder through the lakeside shops, then the Thirty-Six Streets, dazzled by the colours in Silk Street, by the jade jewellery in Silver Street, by the paper dollars in Paper Street – the Vietnamese burn fake paper money in pagodas at *Tet* (New Year) ceremonies to ensure prosperity in the coming year. The heat is so enervating that I retreat to Fanny's ice cream parlour. Plenty of time for side-walk cafes when I get my bearings. That night I discover Le Bistro in an old, high-ceilinged French colonial villa and rather wistfully, wish I were not alone. At this moment, as entrancing as the city may be, a year in Vietnam stretches a worryingly long time ahead.

HANOI STREETS

Next morning feeling somewhat apprehensive, I puff up the stairs to the sixth floor, thatch-roofed 'boardroom' atop the The Gioi building to meet my 'sponsors' for the first time. The Gioi (pronounced Tay Zoi), modestly translates as World Publishing. At the meeting is a daunting line-up of the director and the entire editorial staff. The chief English editor, Tran Doan Lam, acts as interpreter and I later learn that he acquired his doctorate and impeccable English in Russia.

The meeting starts very formally, a gathering of twenty serious faces, me explaining phrase by phrase with pauses for interpreting, the kind of book I hope to write.

'I want to explore Vietnamese culture, to discover the beliefs, myths and ancient history that have made the Vietnamese how they are – no recent wars, no politics.'

What I do not say is that the real impetus, the very real urgency to write the book now, is to capture the traditional culture and those ephemeral spiritual values that are being overwhelmed and rapidly swept away in a tsunami of Western consumerism. With more than two-thirds of the population under thirty, seemingly hell bent on motorbikes, pop music and making money, the mindset of the country is changing fast, before my very eyes and I fear that Vietnam's rich culture may die with the older generation.

As understanding reaches director Mai Ly Quang – whose second language is French, his third is Russian – a broad smile spreads over his face.

'You have found the right address.'

It is a scene of mutual relief. From that moment on the people at The Gioi cannot be more friendly, kind, helpful and generous with their time and advice. In fact, the illustrated books on Vietnamese culture published in English by The Gioi, the foreign language publisher of Vietnam, prove to be such a trove that I find it difficult to leave Hanoi.

26

That afternoon I move into the (paying) guesthouse attached to The Gioi in Tran Hung Dao Street, a board avenue in the former French quarter lined with tall *cay sau* trees. I soon learn that a good many streets in Vietnamese cities are named after this popular general, Vietnam's most venerated military hero. He is also commemorated in the island temple of Hoan Kiem lake and for good reason. It was he, who in the thirteenth century saw off three successive waves of Kubla Khan's Mongolian hordes.

A great strategist and stirrer of the people, and doubtless a military historian, Tran Hung Dao repeated the strategy of the earlier tenth century general, Ngo Quyen, who had the wit to apply the local knowledge of a wily old woman to defeat the Chinese in 938, thus gaining the Viets' independence from the Chinese after more than a thousand years of domination.

The strategy worked like this. On the advice of the old woman who lived on the bank of the Bach Dang river near Haiphong, General Ngo Quyen placed wooden spikes in the riverbed pointing up river. As the tide rose, the large Chinese junks sailed up river in pursuit of the much smaller boats of the Viets. When the tide turned and the Chinese wanted to sail back down river to the sea, their galleons became impaled on the spikes. The Viets ambushed, setting fire to the Chinese junks, forcing the Chinese to flee overland into the ambush of the waiting Viets.

Hanoi's History Museum holds a three-dimensional tableau of General Ngo Quyen's original watery victory in 938, showing the tiny wooden and thatched sampans of the Viets, pitted against the much larger junks of the Chinese, as well as some of the actual ironwood spikes dug up in 1953 by people working on a dyke (at Yen Giang). It was this tenth century liberator, General Ngo Quyen, who in 938 established the first capital of the newly independent Viet nation at Hoa Lu, south of Hanoi.

The same strategy worked very well a second time, three centuries later for General Tran Hung Dao, against a different enemy. When the tide turned and the aggressors tried to retreat – 40,000 troops aboard a fleet of 400 ships – the Mongolians found their boats impaled on huge, iron-tipped spikes implanted in the riverbed. For centuries, always from an inferior position of strength, whenever Vietnam has triumphed militarily, always it has been by using cunning strategy.

Vietnam will never, ever forget the threat of China.

My room is furnished with a small desk, wardrobe, fridge and television (VN-TV only, which transmits CNN a day late with Vietnamese voice-overs). It might be a room in a college dormitory, but for the air conditioning, the floral curtains and the Vietnamese style bathroom – the shower sprays the entire floor, leaving it wet. So whenever I enter the bathroom, I wear flip-flops.

Hanoi is hot and heavy with humidity. Having arrived as springtime is blasting into summer, I learn to go out either before nine when the heat gets a stranglehold on the city, or in the evening after sunset. April often coincides with the third month of the lunar year for which the Vietnamese have an appropriate saying: 'Old dogs hang out their tongues in the heat of the third month.'

I quickly come to measure the heat by the number of showers I take. A one-shower day could only be in winter. A two-shower day is a cool day in spring, say 29 C (85 F) – with 90 per cent humidity, which adds a bit of steam. A three-shower day, before breakfast, on returning from any morning outings and another before supper, is an ordinary hot day, say 33 C (91 F). A four-shower day, one first thing, another at midday, another before dinner and a last shower before dropping into bed, becomes quite normal, even with air-conditioning when the temperature frequently tops 39 C (100 F).

The cicadas offer a fairly reliable aural thermometer. You can easily tell whether they are simply warm and drowsy, gently exercising their legs of an evening, or have reached a pitch of white-hot hysteria.

The sounds of construction are everywhere and Vietnamese building practices would give Western health and safety officials apoplexy. Outside my window, I watch as builders wearing flip-flops tile a steeply pitched roof. To protect their materials, they tie ropes around the chimneys to secure the baskets of wet cement and tiles. The roofers themselves walk slowly at angles up and down the roof wearing no safety ropes at all. One day it rains and I glance out to see that several tiles have come loose and slid down the roof. Another afternoon, I look out to see a chap walking blithely along the ridge line of the roof as though he were crossing a room – four storeys up! As I close the curtains – I can't bear to watch – he laughs.

Another new take on life is Hanoi's sacred lunchtime, not to be confused with a lunch *hour*. Traditionally, it started at eleven-thirty and went on until it was deemed, not quite so hot: half past two, three, even half past three. Most offices now start lunch at twelve.

Then after lunch is the siesta, wherever people happen to find themselves: head down on their desks (rarely), more often laid out across the tops of their desks or on the floor (no carpets). I have even seen a man asleep on his motorbike, one arm under his head on the handlebars, lying balanced on his side along the narrow double-seat, one arm dangling as the traffic whizzed past three feet away. One day I passed a snoozing bicycle repairman on a street corner, lying curled up like a shrimp on his three-inch high wooden bench.

Having experienced a week-long heat wave, I begin to understand. If it is impossible to get to sleep until well past midnight – most people don't have air-conditioning – and they wake at five as offices start at seven, it is not unnatural to collapse for a nap in the heat of the day.

One of the first questions any newcomer to Hanoi must address, unless he steps into a taxi, is how to cross the street. The only accepted rule of traffic is that it moves on the right, sometimes. From there on, it's a free-for-all with subtle expectations. Never has the expression 'go with the flow' been more appropriate. Generally, traffic flows fairly slowly, not much faster than a bicycle. Bicycles and motorbikes weave in and out like a school of fish or swarming insects, equipped with screeching horns and growling motors.

To turn left, bicycles and motorbikes line up on the left side of the street – even if it is a two-way street – and then shoot off anticipating the light changing to green, hopefully before oncoming traffic crosses the junction to flatten them. Well, that's the theory.

To pass, hooting cars and motorbikes move towards the centre of the street. Rarely does a bicycle, motorbike, or cyclo (short for the French *cyclopousse,* a bike with a passenger chair in front) move over to the right to make way. So to overtake, cars have to cross the centre line and move into the left lane for a full frontal confrontation with oncoming traffic. Amazingly, approaching traffic obligingly moves over to the side to create just barely enough space in the middle of the road for the passing vehicle to skin through.

As for priorities, at first I think that bicycles and cyclos have it, on the grounds that they are more vulnerable and in the case of cyclos, harder to stop. Then I decide that 'might makes right,' as cars almost physically nudge cyclists and motorbikes to the right side of the road, until I watch a motorbike slowly and deliberately pull in front of a bus at the extremity of a three-point turn, making the bus wait to complete his turn until the motorbike has passed by.

Women carrying heavy loads dangling from shoulder poles do receive a certain deference on crowded pavements, unless a motorbike zooms up a ramp off the street onto the pavement to park. Motorbikes stop for no man, woman or child, giant, genie or god. Not even angel-faced, winsome young girls or homey matrons on motorbikes ever glance to either side as they mount a pavement, blaring their horns. Leaving the pavement is the same. They simply launch into the street traffic, often from inside a house, look straight ahead and *go*. Passing traffic and pedestrians must avoid *them*.

Once I was frightened out of my wits by motorbikes zooming up from behind – on the pavement (sidewalk) – as they made an illegal turn.

Into all of this, introduce the hapless, innocent, law-abiding and cautious Western pedestrian. The unwary foreigner can get an awful fright, stepping off the curb as the light turns green, to be charged by a stampede of growling motorbikes, streaming full throttle around the corner through the pedestrian crossing. As a pedestrian, it is easy to find oneself standing on the curb, waiting to step off, because the number of right-turners, then left-turners, make stepping into the street altogether too hazardous – until the light has turned red again, and again, and again. Maybe the wise pedestrian should carry one of those tiny plastic stools and a book. I even heard about the wife of one expat on contract, who arrived and tried to cross a street, found she couldn't, walked straight back into the hotel, packed her bags and left, never to return.

From day one, I watch the locals.

Standing at a corner, a Vietnamese pedestrian may casually glance at the traffic light – or not – before stepping nonchalantly off the curb into the buzzing traffic. He then ambles slowly and steadily across the street without looking left or right. Bicycles and motorbikes magically part to let him pass, cars steer around him – nobody seems to slow down. He leads a charmed life. Perhaps it is best not to look, on the theory that if you look straight ahead and keep walking, drivers will know where you intend to go, whereas if you glance at them, they won't have the faintest idea what is in your infernal foreign mind.

At night, to give pedestrians a little extra thrill, cyclists do not carry lights. Nor are the streets very well lit. So a bicycle can mow you down, quite unannounced. Conversely, it can be downright terrifying in the near darkness, facing a dense line-up of motorbike beams bearing down upon you from across the street you have in mind to cross. I comfort myself with the notion that few accidents occur because Hanoi traffic travels at such a gentle pace, until I pick up the English newspaper and read the statistics. At least the police are patrolling Hoan Kiem lake after midnight to stop the macho motor-bikers from racing round the lake.

From 15 December 2007, wearing a safety helmet became compulsory for all motorbike and bicycle riders throughout the country, a move provoking much grumbling as the helmets were expensive at $10 and hot to wear. I am waiting for some bright spark to invent a battery-operated, air-conditioned safety helmet. Then everyone will have to have one to be chic and sporty.

I wish someone would build a monorail.

A TEMPLE TO LITERATURE

A man without education is an uncut gem
– Vietnamese proverb

A few days after arriving in Hanoi, I am introduced to Ngoc, a pretty university student who is studying languages and international affairs. Daughter of a government official, her ambition is to become a diplomat. Ngoc's English is excellent and she volunteers to show me around Hanoi. Our first excursion, she feels, should be to the Temple of Literature.

The Temple of Literature? Can you imagine, a Church of Saint Shakespeare?

Next morning Ngoc, neat in a puffy-sleeved blouse tucked into her black jeans and a straw hat with a rolled brim set square on her head like a tiny Peruvian Indian, installs me on the back of her motorbike. At the four-pillared gate to the Temple of Literature, Ngoc points out two seemingly inconsequential stone stelae, 'Commanding all who would enter to dismount (from their palanquins) and show respect – including the emperor.'

This is the first indication that scholarship has long been held in such high esteem in Vietnam.

'In higher esteem even, than royalty,' Ngoc assures me.

While Britain was still wallowing in the dark ages – two centuries before the founding of Oxford, one century before Bologna University – Vietnam was busy establishing a university. Van Mieu, literally the Temple of Literature, 'first opened its doors in 1070 as an altar to Confucius,' under Emperor Ly Thanh Tong. Six years later, it became the Royal College for the Teaching of Royal Princes to Rule. Considering that an emperor might have more than a hundred wives or concubines, naturally there would have been quite a few young princes to educate. Only one year later, Van Mieu began to admit the sons of mandarins and from that time on became known as the College for the Sons of the Nation (Van Mieu-Quoc Tu Giam).

Somewhat later, the college expanded further, this time admitting those who had succeeded in passing regional examinations, thus creating very early in the country's history, a meritocracy of social mobility through education, at least for those whose families were wealthy enough to allow a son to immerse himself in books for a few years as a financially unproductive member of the family.

Although no longer a university, the Temple of Literature remains an oasis of quietude in the bustle and cacophony of Hanoi's busy street life. A central path, symbolic of the Confucian Middle Way or Golden Mean, divides the walled temple complex of five successive courtyards. No doubt the grandiose names of the gates and the inscriptions throughout were meant to inspire the neophyte scholars towards high intellectual attainment, rather like the portraits of illustrious alumnae that throng the halls of British and American universities.

To a Westerner, Confucianism appears to be not so much a religion as a system of ethical conduct, including a wealth of received knowledge to be passed on. The number five has special significance.

There are five essential elements: metal, wood, water, fire and earth.

There are five basic virtues: humanity (benevolence), righteousness, civility, knowledge and loyalty.

There are five commandments: Against murder, theft, lust, lying and drunkenness.

There are five sorrows: life, old age, sickness, death and separation – Confucius knew a thing or two, five centuries BC.

There are five cardinal relationships: king and subject, father and son, husband and wife, between brothers and between friends.

The five Confucian classics are: *The Great Study, The Golden Mean, The Analects (Conversations Between Confucius and His Disciples* and *The Works of Mencius (The Upper Book* and *The Lower Book).*

Plus the five additional works: *The Odes, The Annals, The Book of Change, Rites and Ceremonies* and *The Spring* and *Autumn Annals.*

In front of the Great Portico, a two-storey stone gate under a double tile roof, Ngoc begins my tutelage on the subject of dragons, pointing to the image of a flying dragon.

'Symbol of good luck, royalty, and later, of the mandarinate. Eventually, the dragon also came to signify the rank of the doctoral degree, *tien si.* The image of the descending tiger, coming down from the mountain to help humanity, serves as a symbol of strength and power. The tiger signified the rank of bachelor degree, *cu nhan.*'

The inscription in Chinese characters over the main entrance translates as: 'Among the doctrines of the world, ours is the best and is revered by all culture-starved lands.'

No wonder there was a head-on clash with the French!

Another modest inscription reads: 'Of all the temples devoted to literature, this is the head; the perfume of culture floats throughout the millennia.' Hanoi's Temple of Literature was considered to be the veritable fountain of Vietnamese erudition.

Old frangipani and banyan trees spread their shade over the first two grassy courtyards where although the Temple of Literature is no longer a university, students still sprawl with their books, studying for upcoming exams. Bright pink lotus blossoms float amongst a carpet of green lotus pads in the rectangular lily ponds to left and right of the central path, exactly symmetrical and perfectly balanced, as everything must be in a Confucian environment.

Two carp perch nose-down on the roof ridges of the gate leading to the second courtyard: 'Paying obeisance to a flask of nectar from heaven' – doubtless, the nectar of Confucianism. 'The carp symbolise students on their way to becoming mandarins,' Ngoc explains.

'Legend has it that the carp that succeed in passing through a natural stone arch known as the Gate of Emperor Vu in the Hoang Ho river during the violent tides of the third lunar month, become dragons. Successful mandarin examination candidates are likened to the carp that have passed through the arch.'

In another version, fish aspiring to dragon-hood have to swim up three waterfalls, a process that takes a thousand years. In this version, the carp represent a symbol of the common people, swimming up from the grass roots of a pond by way of three levels of examinations (local, provincial and royal) to the status of mandarin.

Smaller gateways at the far extremities of this wall bear more inscriptions in Chinese ideograms: 'Accomplished Virtue' on the right, 'Attained Talent' on the left. As every student had to be able to read Chinese ideograms, *chu nom,* to be admitted to the college, these inscriptions would have admonished them daily. Nowadays, only a few scholars devote themselves to the old *chu nom* texts, tenuously preserving a link with the country's rich, traditional literature.

At nine in the morning the cicadas are already sawing away in heated competition with the frogs. On the far side of the second courtyard stands the rather glorious two-storey, red lacquered Constellation of Literature Pavilion (Khue Van Cac).

'This pavilion is considered to be rich in the complementary symbolism of *yin* and *yang,* the union of contrasting parts, according to the cosmic Great Primary Principle.' It is also extremely, orientally picturesque. The pavilion bears the inscriptions: 'Just as the Khue constellation shines in the sky, the humanities shine everywhere' – a sentiment to warm the hearts of Western humanities academics, who may sometimes feel underrated. The opposite, parallel inscription reads: 'The deep waters of the royal college perpetuate the fountain of the doctrine.' Quite so.

Two smaller gates lead from this courtyard. The one on the right, called the Crystallisation of Letters, refers to literary expression that is profound and full of feeling. That on the left refers to the Magnificence of Letters, paying homage to ideas that are well and beautifully expressed. Like many a student before me, I make sure I pass through both gates, hoping the glorious phrases will have some osmotic effect.

In the Garden of the Stelae, the square pond known as the Well of Heavenly Clarity has lost its heavenly clarity. Despite the humid heat, I am not in the least bit tempted to leap into its greenish froth. Two lines of stone stelae, each stele solidly planted on the back of a stone turtle, symbol of longevity, list the names, native places and ages of the successful doctoral candidates from 1442 to 1779. The earliest turtles, I notice, hold their stone heads high, noses in the air. The later, less snooty turtles merely poke their heads out of their shells and rest their weary chins.

The oldest stele dated 1442, erected by order of Emperor Le Thai Tong, bears a noble inscription: 'So the erection of this stele will be of great help, a warning to the wicked and an encouragement to honest persons: knowing the past and looking to the future helps to foster the dignity of scholars and to consolidate the state.'

Having grown up in a country that rarely attracts the erudite or even the wise to political leadership, I especially appreciate the following sentiment: 'Virtuous and talented men are the life breath of the nation.' The message on the stele of 1592 expresses a rather wistful hope. 'Heaven has ushered in an era of renewal: The world has opened a period of cultural restoration.'

35

Ngoc explains that Van Mieu represented far more than just an educational establishment of learning for learning's sake, however much learning was lauded. Those who passed its bachelor and doctoral degrees were awarded posts as mandarin commensurate with their academic achievements. For centuries it was literally the college for training the nation's rulers, its administrators, its civil servants. Had Ngoc been born a century earlier – as a boy – she would have studied here.

For candidates who passed all four examinations, the final question was set by the emperor himself and it was he who decided the order of merit for the doctoral candidates at the top of each class.

Students of all ages studied together. A decree of 1185 set the lower age limit at fifteen; there was no upper limit. The length of study varied. Examinations were usually held every three years, sometimes as infrequently as seven.

The multi-stage examination process lasted several months. The first was to pass a regional examination, held triennially. Successful candidates then walked to Hanoi from wherever they lived in the country, carrying their sleeping mats, brushes and ink stones in order to sit the four-part *thi hoi* examination. It is thought that the examinations in Hanoi were held on the site of the National Library, as suggested by the street name, Trang Thi (Examination Street). With 450 to 6,000 candidates sitting, the examination area would have needed to be extensive. I wonder if they erected thatched roofs to protect the poor examinees from the rain and sun? If the culmination of the examinations was in the third lunar month (usually April), the capital would have been quite chilly and drizzly at the beginning, and steamily hot by the end.

At the first doctoral examination, only three candidates passed; at the second, seven; at the third, the success rate rose to twenty-three.

Part I of the examinations was over the Confucian classics.

In Part II, the candidate had to write as though he were the emperor, discussing matters of state.

In Part III, the candidate was asked to compose two different genres of poems on given topics. The *tho phu* was a poem of twenty-eight characters, divided into four lines of seven characters. The *phu* was a prose poem of eight, seven-character lines.

In Part IV, the candidate was asked to comment on how to handle problems facing the country, drawing from his knowledge of

Confucian classics and the history of previous dynasties. It comes as no surprise then, that many of the most brilliant statesmen were also fine poets. One such was Nguyen Trai, the moving spirit and strategist behind the victorious fifteenth century battle against the Chinese led by General Le Loi. Nguyen Trai is still honoured as one of Vietnam's greatest statesmen and in addition to his involvement in matters of state, he also found time to serve as a royal examiner.

The Call of the Roll, the publication of successful candidates on the third day of the third lunar month, was a glorious event for the literati. Upon the successful, the emperor bestowed favour, mandarin ranks, mandarin bonnets and robes. He feted them with a banquet in Quynh Lam Palace and when they returned to their native villages, they travelled in state on horseback, with footmen bearing banners to herald their approach and footmen carrying fringed parasols to protect the new doctors from the sun, as can be seen in many paintings and tableaux in mosaic and lacquer.

Only 2,313 candidates were awarded the title of doctor between 1070 and 1779, most in their twenties and thirties. The youngest ever was eighteen, the eldest sixty-one.

Another tile-roofed structure, the Gate of the Great Synthesis, some say the Gate of Great Success, leads to a fourth courtyard, the Courtyard of the Sages.

'The side gates laud the beauty and value of Confucian doctrine as its influence echoes throughout the world. The Gate of the Golden Sound evokes the first peal of a bell; the Gate of Jade Resonance reflects the last reverberation of a gong.'

Classes were held in two buildings alongside the Courtyard of Sages. In the grounds beyond were six dormitories (destroyed by bombs), each holding twenty-five rooms. There was even a print shop for school texts.

In the Courtyard of Sages where chess games using human chess pieces still take place during *Tet* (New Year) celebrations, a topiary incense jar, perhaps representing Confucian nectar, is guarded by two long-legged, leafy topiary cranes, their bodies covered in tiny white flowers. On the steps of the Great House of Ceremonies, where formerly the emperor would have passed to make his offering at the altar of Confucius and the new doctor laureates would have knelt to express their gratitude, two girls pose for photographs wearing *ao dais* (pronounced ow as in now, zai as in eye) – long side-slit tunics over flowing trousers, the national costume.

Golden dragons curl around the thick red lacquered columns, flicking their tails amongst clouds. Two lanky bronze cranes, the birds of transport between heaven and earth, stand balanced on the backs of bronze turtles on each side of the altar, eternally poised for take-off. A gracefully draped, carved and lacquered wooden 'tapestry' hangs above the altar. The scent of burning joss sticks rises in a wisp of smoke towards the rafters as a couple of contemporary students light joss sticks to invoke the spirit of Confucius to help them through their coming exams.

Inscribed over the altar are the words: 'Teacher of thousands of generations.' The tinkling sound of traditional Vietnamese music drifts from the Sanctuary building just behind the House of Ceremonies, its rooftop ridge line ablaze with jubilant dragons making obeisance to the moon – the carp have succeeded in becoming dragons.

Inside the House of Ceremonies, it was not long ago that the giant, jolly red statue of Confucius and his four disciples, two on each side, naturally, came out of hiding in a warehouse where they resided during the early years of Communist rule. The opening of Vietnam to International tourism may have contributed to an official softening towards religion, resulting in the return of many religious statues to Vietnam's altars. The brightly painted statue of Confucius looks quite pleased and happy to be back, the palms of his hands not quite touching as though he were about to clap.

A tableau honours the fourteenth century scholar, Chu Van An (1292-1370), rector of the national university for forty years, whose name has come to be revered as an embodiment of integrity and devotion to scholarship: 'The father of education in Vietnam.' One of his short poems demonstrates the subtlety of expression in those distant times and from the far side of the world, hints of a pre-Wordsworthian sentiment.

Spring Morning

In the hut in the mountains one is free the live long day
A clump of bamboo leaning o'er screens from cold mountain air
Green grows the grass and the sky reels in joy
Late lingers the dew in the cups of scarlet flowers
The man alone with the lonely cloud clings to the mountain side

His spirit like water in old wells lies still, unshaken by any tremor
As the sweet pine logs sink to ash the pot for tea stops boiling
A murmur of birds from the deeps of the ravine bring him back from
the light sleep of Spring.

(tr Huu Ngoc)

Westerners might refute whether classical literature provides a proper preparation for governing a nation, but the system of Confucian ethics based on central control served both China and Vietnam for many centuries as a framework for the society of the day – and central control remains.

Ironically, it was the Confucian Nguyen dynasty that ended Van Mieu's function as the nation's first university. Having moved the capital to Hue with their ascent to power in the early nineteenth century, they also 'moved' the Temple of Literature. The last examinations at Hanoi'sTemple of Literature took place in 1919.

That night over a book on Confucianism, it begins to dawn on me just how deeply embedded in the Vietnamese psyche the thirst for learning and poetry is. If every civil servant had to prove himself a poet, it is hardly a wonder that even today, every Vietnamese considers himself or herself to be a poet.

A WOMAN WITHOUT A HUSBAND

Royal edicts yield to village customs
– Vietnamese proverb

A day or two later, I am reading a Vietnamese legend, suddenly to realise that the annual festival must be about now. I ring Ngoc and we set out for it next morning.

Immaculate conception is hardly exclusive to Christianity. In the legend of Giong, the hero was born to an earthly mother and a very unearthly giant. The legend goes like this –

Long ago, before history was written down, a woman lived in a village in the Red river delta, the cradle of Viet culture. One day she went into her garden to gather aubergines and found a giant footprint. Naturally, out of curiosity she placed her own foot in the footprint. Not so naturally, as a result she became pregnant. In due course, she gave birth to a baby boy, who she named Giong.

The poor woman suffered dreadfully as an unmarried mother. She was ostracised and driven out of her own and the neighbouring villages, Dong Vien and Dong Xuyen. But the villagers of nearby Phu Dong felt sorry for her and took her in, allowing her to set up home in their village. Yet despite her devoted care and feeding, the baby seemed to languish, lying listless in his cot. At the age of three, he still could not speak.

Now as it happened, this was during the reign of the sixth Hung king in the prehistoric state of Van Lang, one of the early names for what has become Vietnam. Van Lang was under attack by An (Chinese) invaders. The desperate king sent an envoy to tour the villages, appealing to the people to rise up and defend themselves. As the entourage passed through Phu Dong, to everyone's amazement, hearing the commotion, baby Giong sprang to his feet and with his first words ever, begged his mother to invite the king's envoy to come to their house. When the envoy came and repeated his appeal, with great perspicacity the tiny tot replied: 'Please sir, request his majesty the king to provide me with an iron horse, an iron hat and an iron whip. I will wipe out the enemy.' Well, you can imagine the envoy's astonishment, not to mention his mother's, but as the situation was so desperate, the envoy carried the child's message back to the king.

Meanwhile, little Giong started eating with such gusto that his poor mother could no longer afford to feed him. And once again, the whole village rallied round, contributing rice and aubergines for the little boy. When the royal envoy returned to the village with the iron horse, the iron hat and the iron whip, little Giong stretched out his arms and legs and grew and grew until he became a colossus. He seized the iron whip, placed the iron hat on his head and with a loud cry, leapt onto the horse. The horse let out a hysterical whinny and galloped off towards the enemy.

As Giong's horse snorted fire over the invaders, the young warrior beat them furiously with his whip and they scattered, helter-skelter. When the whip broke, Giong uprooted a bamboo tree and continued to thrash the enemy with a rod of bamboo. When at last the An had been vanquished, Giong rode off to Mount Soc Son where he stopped, removed the armour, hung it on a tree, then galloped off on his horse into the clouds, never to be seen again.

The story of Giong particularly appealed to me because the village of Phu Dong still exists and every year in the fourth lunar month, it commemorates the legend of Giong's victory with a three-day festival, re-enacting the events of two thousand years ago.

At six, Ngoc and I on the back of her motorbike, set out north-east of Hanoi along Highway 1. Crossing Chuong Duong and Cau Duong bridges, we turn right, travelling downstream along the Duong river on a very stony road for two and a half miles (4 km) to Phu Dong. When you have travelled twenty-four miles (40km) on a motorbike in the space of a morning, you know you have travelled twenty-four miles (40 km).

It is not yet seven when we arrive. Already, food stalls and kiosks hawking religious beads, lacquer boxes, plastic toys, fruit, flowers and joss sticks have been set up. A crowd mills around the courtyard of the temple complex and the banks of the village pond. Little boys rush up to say hello, then scatter. A man pushes a stalk of sugar cane through a grinder and a young girl stands on a scale, simultaneously having her height measured.

Women carrying trays stacked with offerings of fruit move towards the temple. Ngoc tells me that the Dong Festival is very important to people from Phu Dong. Many who no longer live here will have made the festival an occasion to return home for family reunions and to worship. Then Ngoc enlightens me as to the difference between temples and pagodas. 'Temples are dedicated to heroes or heroines of legends or history; pagodas are for the worship of Buddha, sometimes also Confucius and others.'

Here at Phu Dong, both the temple and the pagoda are very old. The carved and lacquered fretwork between the pillars has mellowed to a deep ochre. The temple is dedicated to Giong and a huge, cheerful-faced statue of the hero dressed in red looms over the altars where flowers and food have been laid out like a harvest festival. We enter the dark temple, heavy with the scent of joss sticks, to the reedy sound of an ensemble: a two-string fiddle, oboe, flute and drums.

A double file of village men approach the altar ceremoniously, wearing royal blue silk tunics over white trousers and slippers of red brocade with turned up toes. Their square black hats decorated with gold braid have turned-up corners like lamp shades. Ngoc whispers that they represent Giong's victorious troops paying tribute to their commander. An honour guard of younger men wearing red tunics and black trousers lines the central aisle of the temple.

The pageantry and ritual, Ngoc explains, is an attempt to recreate the scene of victorious triumph. A few minutes later a 'tiger' prances into the temple towards the altar and performs a dance. Quite where he figures in the legend is unclear. Perhaps the great Giong even commandeered the wild beasts. To one side of the temple stands a life-sized, white lacquered horse under a glittering saddle, Giong's magical stead. Outside, a group of matronly women wearing yellow-sequinned tunics, assemble in two lines: the vanquished Chinese troops. A few minutes later, an honour guard of young men forms a procession under red-fringed parasols, bearing covered tributes for Giong. A glimpse into an older world of pageantry.

In a pavilion beside the temple, people sit on low wooden beds covered with straw mats, chatting, pouring cups of tea and fanning themselves. A few men play chess. Ngoc explains that the younger women with shaved heads wearing brown tunics are nuns. The older women, also wearing brown dresses, are not nuns, but village women who have joined a religious organisation of Buddhist women followers called *vai,* attached to a specific pagoda. Something like a churchwoman's guild, perhaps.

In the pagoda behind the temple, carved, life-sized, pot-bellied guardians stand to each side of the entrance, one of whom has collected wads of *dong* notes tucked up his wooden sleeves. The beams and pillars have been carved and lacquered, the altar area stretching back through several ranks of Buddhas. Likewise, a tray on the altar is piled high with *dong*. Behind it, a narrow, semi-circular passageway contains three dark, carved grottoes, full of small statues of Buddha, 'Buddhas en route to enlightenment,' whispers Ngoc. It pleases me immensely that there is also a temple dedicated to Giong's poor mother and her statue looks quite happy.

The origins of the Kien So pagoda at Phu Dong go back into very early Viet and Buddhist history. The pagoda was already old in 829 when a Chinese monk, whose religious name was Vo Ngon Thong, came to Phu Dong and founded the second order of the Thien Tong (Zen) sect in Vietnam. On arriving at the pagoda, Vo Ngon Thong took up the position that he was to maintain for many years, seated all day long, staring at the wall, meditating and saying nothing. The only person who realised that he was an eminent monk was Cam Thanh, the monk who devotedly served him. Finally, just before Vo Ngon Thong died, he spoke to Cam Thanh, saying: 'Before he died at the age of ninety-eight, my master Nam Nhac Hoai Nhuong recommended to me' – and then at last, he put into words the culmination of his years of silent meditation, or in his case, the thoughts of his master before him whose thoughts, presumably, he felt it impossible to improve upon:

'All things come from the mind,
Without the support of the mind, nothing can exist.
If one reaches the bottom of the mind,
One will meet no obstacle.
If one does not meet a higher mind,
One had better keep silent.'

There is no record of whether Cam Thanh felt the sting of this insult. He organised his master's burial and had a tower built in his honour on nearby Mount Tien Son. Well, what else could he do?

FACING THE MUSIC

Thirty years old,
Springtime for the boy,
Autumn for the girl
— Vietnamese proverb

One morning I consult an authority on Hanoi, author of The Gioi's guidebook to the city, Pham Hoang Hai, about where I might hear traditional Vietnamese music. Is there a music conservatory? Hai becomes very animated.

'Today, tonight, there is a concert, just near here.' He sends me footing up the street to 51 Tran Hung Dao to the Chuong Trinh Culture Centre, to check out time and ticket availability.

To my astonishment, at nine in the morning the musicians are already packing up, having finished their rehearsal. One of them gives me a photocopied programme and tells me to come along with a friend at eight that evening, explaining that the programme will serve as a ticket. The concert will be given by the Traditional Folk Music Club of Hanoi.

That evening, a Swede, also staying at The Gioi's guest house, and I are ushered to the second row of the drawing room, complete with crystal chandelier in what once must have been a grand French villa. I wonder whose it was. We are the only Westerners in the room. A very hot gentleman in a black suit reads a very long speech in Vietnamese and we all applaud the end of it. From that moment on, it is pure aural pleasure.

Two young women in flowing pink and blue *ao dais,* a man in a green satin brocade tunic, black trousers and a pillbox hat; and two young men wearing sequinned red and orange velvet jackets and green trousers, dazzle with their costumes before playing a note. The Vietnamese love bright colours. So do I.

At the first notes, faces at all levels appear at the open doorways as the overflow crowd stands in the corridor to hear. I feel guilty that we have been given two of the best seats, but am soon lulled into fantasies of being entertained by royal court musicians. Carved garuda birds support a horizontal sixteen-string instrument *(dan tranh).* Two young women play the lute *(dan ty ba)* and a thirty-six-

44

string instrument with mallets *(tam thap luc)*. One man plays the long-necked guitar *(dan nguyet);* a 'mandarin' plays a bamboo flute.

The metallic string music feels as cooling as a waterfall with a warm, murmuring overlay of bamboo flute. As many of Vietnam's stringed instruments have derived from China, naturally the music sounds vaguely Chinese, but to my ear, rather more soothing.

Next to appear are two pretty singers wearing peasant costumes: red and green sashes over long diaphanous maroon tunics and black trousers. Another girl passes round a tray of what look like large chestnuts, slit open like flower petals. Not knowing quite what to do with them, we sit clutching them for the duration of the performance.

The peasants are followed by what instantly becomes my favourite Vietnamese instrument, the monochord *(dan bau)* – a one-string instrument with a narrow rectangular sound box and a vertical wooden, curled 'pig's tail' that the musician vibrates with one hand, sending out a plaintive, soulful tone, vaguely reminiscent of the cor anglais. There is wild applause at the end of every piece, each musician handed a bouquet of flowers wrapped in cellophane.

Then stage hands move in three enormous bamboo xylophones *(lem trung)*. Unlike horizontal Balinese gamelans, these are much larger, the pipes strung vertically, short tubes at the top. Sounds of the *lem trung* would soothe a raging beast.

The *lem trung* players are joined by a wonder boy, dressed head to toe in white satin, playing a bamboo piccolo, its tone at first sweet liquid, then full of piercing trills like bird calls. He would have received a standing ovation had our chairs not been so tightly packed that no one could stand up.

Next, a straw mat is laid and an elegant matron in a stylish, sparkling black *ao dai,* seats herself on the mat – I admire her effortless agility. Her accompanist is a young man with a long-necked, three-string guitar. She croons in a low alto register, tapping a wooden knocker, the guitarist weaving a cross-melody around the song line. A distinguished, elderly gentleman joins her, tapping a tiny drum. The variety of sounds he produces is quite amazing.

To my consternation, the audience keeps chattering, which I suppose they have done throughout, but as this performance is so intimate, it seems as rude as the opera crowd in Venice, who titter throughout performances. The Vietnamese singer seems unperturbed. The next singer, wearing a stunning yellow and turquoise *ao dai,* is accompanied by two horizontal stringed instruments, lacquered drums and cymbals. Various techniques of plucking evoke more watery cascades. While I love the instrumental music, the Vietnamese voice has a back of throat nasal quality and I have to say, I prefer it when they don't sing.

Then the xylophones return, each joining in like a fugue, the tempo accelerating until at full frenzy, the flute whirls over the top.

In Vietnam there is a long tradition of special songs for blind singers to sing while begging, so I am not surprised when a blind singer is led in by one of the musicians. He sits on a tiny, low stool, operates a toe-tapping knocker and plays a four-string guitar.

Disproving what I just said about singers, a young soprano appears and sings what might easily be the Vietnamese equivalent of *Songs of the Auvergne.*

She is followed by a female dancer, who kneels with a tray on her head. As the tempo quickens, she rises, turning and smiling, her finger movements reminiscent of Indian, Thai or Cambodian dancing. At the end she presents each of us in the front rows with a small red triangular packet wrapped in cellophane – something else to hold.

When the performers all line up together for a final bow, the audience rushes to the stage with more bouquets. It is heartening to see that this lovely traditional music is greeted with such warm, enthusiastic support.

A few days later in the same venue, the heading of the programme reads: Great Singer Hans Dieter Bader – Master Class.

This time it is the piano accompanist who presses me with copies of the programme on the morning of the concert. Once again, my Swedish friend and I are placed in the front row – sitting next to Great Singer Hans Dieter Bader himself, who beams throughout the concert at his protégés.

A master class, this is not. Obviously, any criticism and instruction have taken place in private beforehand to save oriental faces. This is a full blown recital ranging from Handel to Offenbach.

The evening dresses of the singers are wildly extravagant – rented, I wonder? – and the suits of the male singers would have thrilled a pop star. Perhaps they *are* pop stars. Vietnam has a long tradition of singing: village love-song competitions between boy teams and girl teams. Every morning, songs waft out over the neighbourhood loudspeakers while I am having breakfast; every evening, Vietnamese television transmits a programme of traditional Vietnamese romantic ballads. Three nights a week, there are concerts of popular love songs in this venue and now, of course, karaoke is popular as a night out for the young.

It must be said that one does not instinctively associate European opera with Vietnam. But there is a conservatory of music in the Western classical tradition and I am delighted to learn that there is also a relatively brief tradition (in the Vietnamese scheme of culture) of performing European opera here as well. In fact, the beautiful Hanoi opera house, built by the French in the early twentieth century, has been recently restored to its full elegance.

Tonight, fourteen youngish singers perform familiar arias and songs by Puccini, Mozart, Weber and Wagner, surprisingly well. All the same, there is something vaguely risible about listening to a diminutive Vietnamese tenor throw his heart into Leoncavallo's *Pagliacci*. In the finale, Herr Bader mingles his tenor voice with those of the Vietnamese singers in a spine-tingling *tutti* performance of Flotow's *Letzte Rose* and I feel that my European musical roots have been truly refreshed.

One of the pleasant facets of life in Hanoi is the unexpected musical events. Come a rainy Sunday, I take myself off to visit the Ho Chi Minh Museum. So has most of Hanoi. Never on Sunday, particularly never on a rainy Sunday, if you want to read the tiny English captions under the photographs.

From a central dais, a colossal statue of the father of his country raises a hand in greeting to the crowds in the foyer of this slightly baffling edifice of floating stairs and marble platforms. Children of ten or eleven approach with, 'Hello, how are you?' before shyly skittering away again.

Disregarding kings and queens, Britain lacks such a beloved paternal figure. Churchill? Well, maybe. The scene brings back memories of visits to the Washington and Lincoln Memorials and to Jefferson's home at Monticello. We file past a reconstruction of Uncle Ho's humble thatched childhood home and peer at his school records. Poor chap, he came number two in his class and I feel sorry for him, having to suffer this ignominious lack of academic privacy in a country where scholarly achievement is so highly esteemed.

Upstairs, a handwritten sign reads Concert, with an arrow. The sound of plucked strings drifts through the swinging doors and following my ears, I come to a small room where a few chairs have been set up. Four young women, each wearing a different ethnic costume, motion to sit down. To my delight there is a new instrument, a row of huge horizontal bamboo pipes, which the musician plays by clapping her cupped hands at the end of each pipe. It makes a breathy tone somewhat similar to Peruvian pipes and derives from one of the ethnic hill tribes.

Between numbers, one of the musicians hands out tiny cups of green tea. To mark the end of their performance, they play *Auld Lang Syne,* hand one member of the audience a red rose and in jest, plop a straw peasant hat on my head. For the privilege of listening, we are invited to buy a CD or a tape of their music, or there is a wooden box on the table for donations.

Let it not be said that one's cultural life in Hanoi is not varied. A week later in the Children's Theatre in Ly Thai To Street, there is a concert by the Hanoi Symphony Orchestra. The solo cellist is Professor Bui Gia Tuong, director of Performing Arts and professor at the Music Conservatories of Hanoi and Ho Chi Minh City.

As I inquire about tickets at the door, his charming wife Hao introduces herself. She was a dancer, she tells me – in the army – and they were separated for most of the first ten years of their marriage while he studied in Russia under Rostropovich. In 1982 and 1986, he sat on the jury of the Tchaikovsky International Competition in Russia and it was at her husband's invitation that Rostropovich visited Vietnam a few years ago. The concert is conducted by Le Phi Phi, born into a musical Hanoi family, who after graduating from Hanoi Conservatory, studied conducting at the Tchaikovsky Conservatory in Moscow under Nikolaev.

The very young orchestra is about a hundred strong and the entire cello section has studied under Professor Bui Gia Tuong. The first performance of *The Song of the Huong River,* a suite for cello and orchestra by Vietnamese composer Hoang Duong, is easily accessible to the Western ear, a subtle blending of two musical traditions that would bear many a pleasant listening. The professor plays with warmth and passion and my heart goes out to him and to the conductor, who both perform wearing the jackets of their evening dress despite the heat, while male and female members of the orchestra are stripped to white shirt sleeves and blouses.

48

The second selection, Saint-Saens's *Cello Concerto,* the professor plays with great sensitivity and verve. At the interval I am introduced to him and we converse haltingly, me in French at his wife's suggestion, he in English about the programmes soon to be performed. On hearing that I am from London, he tells me how much he likes Elgar. The professor joins us for the first two movements of Dvorak's *New World Symphony,* tapping his fingers on the chair arm.

A rush of bouquets follow the finale. Then the musicians pack up and go home – by motorbike.

I hang around as violinists and woodwinds sling their instrument cases on straps over their shoulders and fire up. When a trombone player places his instrument vertically in front of him, resting on the handlebars, held in place by his knees, I remember a cartoon exhibition that featured lots of motorbike accidents and wonder how on earth he is going to see where he is going. But the prize for panache goes to the cellists, who sling their vulnerable instruments in soft cases on straps over their left shoulders, climb aboard and set off in convoy, perhaps for protection.

What the bass viols did, I will never know.

Apart from the occasional concert, ignoring karaoke, discos and Vietnamese films, evening entertainment, if varied, is a bit thin in Hanoi, unless you are a bar fly. So most nights I read or mindlessly watch VN-TV soap operas. My young Swedish friend will soon leave, having finished his project.

WITH DUE RESPECT TO SCHOLARS

Spoken words fly away
– Vietnamese proverb

Prolific writer and scholar Huu Ngoc – his family name is Nguyen, dropped from his pen name – has generously found time to invite a group of foreign writers and editors to visit as he elegantly puts it, 'some suburban Hanoi villages endowed with scholarly traditions.' Happily, I have been invited to come along.

Huu Ngoc's formal introduction can hardly be improved upon: 'The substratum of Vietnamese culture is the Viet rice culture born in the delta of the Red river (first millennium BC) and named the Dong Son culture (Bronze Age). Onto this were grafted Chinese culture and to some extent Indian culture, which gave birth to the Vietnamese traditional culture.'

Historically, the hierarchy of respect in Vietnam started at the bottom with musicians and singers and ranged upwards through traders, peasants, physicians and monks, with mandarin and scholars at the pinnacle of society, nearest the emperor. To Vietnam's long tradition of scholars, add the ingrained Confucian respect for age and aged scholars have long been much venerated – up to the present when the acquisition of a Mercedes and mini-hotels has begun to replace the acquisition of learning.

In the Vietnamese intellectual scheme, long before the Temple of Literature was ever thought of, the earliest scholars were Buddhist monks. In the second century AD, a monk named Mau Tu, who lived in a remote village near Hanoi (Luy Lau, Ha Bac province), wrote one of the first books on Buddhism in Han, the old Chinese script. Clearly, Ly Hoac Luan was no intellectual slouch. The title of his tome translates as *Truth – Illusion - Metaphysics,* a reflection of the sophistication of Buddhist thought in the second century.

It is thought by some that Buddhism may first have arrived in Vietnam as early as the third century BC, as it is recorded in India during the reign of the Emperor Asoka, that Buddhist missionaries were sent out to Europe and the Orient, including South East Asia. Even the names of the two missionaries sent to Myanmar and

Thailand are known, Uttara and Son. Chinese documents of the period attest to the existence of an Asoka Tower near Haiphong (Ne Le Citadel in Giao Chi, present-day Do Son), so these missionaries may even have reached the coast of what is now Vietnam.

Another theory is that Mahayana Prajna Buddhism was brought to Vietnam by traders from India by sea, via Java and Champa. What is certain is that during the thousand years of Chinese domination from 179 BC to 938 AD, many scholarly monks from Vietnam travelled to China, India and Indonesia.

With the ousting of the Chinese in the tenth century, there was a renaissance of indigenous Viet culture. Popular folk tales, legends and the stories of Viet military heroes were compiled. The writing of a national history was begun and in the eleventh century, the founding of the Temple of Literature.

Buddhist and Confucian scholarship and the civil service were closely intertwined. Scholarly monks have frequently served as advisers to emperors, and many mandarin have retired to country pagodas as scholarly monks to labour over Buddhist texts.

During the eleventh century renaissance of the newly independent Viet nation, the Ly dynasty built several libraries to house Buddhist scriptures. These libraries were deliberately burnt, along with much Buddhist architecture in the fifteenth century by the Chinese Ming during their twenty-year domination, 1407 to 1427.

What remained after the defeat of the Ming was pretty well finished off by Le Loi, following his victory in 1428 – strengthened by the divine sword, courtesy of the golden turtle of Hoan Kiem lake. On taking the throne, according to the custom of the day, the done thing was to obliterate the previous dynasty. Le Loi therefore endeavoured not only to eliminate every relative and official loyal to the earlier Trinh lords, he went a bit overboard and also tried to eradicate the cultural achievements of the Trinh. These major upheavals in the fifteenth century, first by the Ming, twenty years later by Le Loi, ensured the victory of Confucianism over Buddhism and disrupted Viet culture for several centuries.

At 7 a.m. we set off in a minibus, a mixed group of French, English and Vietnamese speakers. From the noisy, rush hour streets of central Hanoi, it is only a few minutes to the quiet countryside. Straight roads slice between avenues of eucalyptus and casuarina trees spiked by the occasional coconut palm. Here the sunlight beats down, pure and untainted by city pollution on the gold, ripening rice stretching across the flat lands of the delta as far as the eye can see. So bright is the sun that the ripe paddies seem to glow. Everywhere, peasants stand knee deep in the paddies, colourful figures wearing conical hats, scything rice, a highly animated pastoral scene, the method unchanged for two thousand years.

The first village we visit is Dai Tu, home of a famous specialist in Sinology and Vietnamology, eighty-something Vu Tuan San, who has co-authored a worthy work, lightly entitled, *Vietnamese Traditional Agriculture Through Old Archives in Chinese and Nom Scripts*. I do not envy him the task. But for a few modern houses, the village, only about five miles (11 km) south of Hanoi just off Highway 1, might be deep in the hinterland.

Vu Tuan San graciously receives us in his modest study behind a pretty flower garden. Scrolls of Chinese script decorate the walls not taken up by books. His sweet-faced wife pours green tea into egg cup-sized china cups.

Through Huu Ngoc as translator, he welcomes us, inquiring from which countries we come and before leaving, he gracefully brushes for each of us, a greeting in traditional calligraphy on red paper, wishing friendship forever between Vietnam and England, France and Canada.

In the centre of the village pond of bright pink water lilies, an enormous gold statue of Ho Chi Minh dominates the temple, built by the villagers to commemorate a visit in 1955 of the highly venerated father of their country. Burning joss sticks are passed round. Each Vietnamese in turn plants his joss stick at the solid feet of the statue and places the palms of his hands together in a prayerful position, raising and lowering them several times in an act of worship. We Westerners dutifully plant our joss sticks with a bit of embarrassed head nodding. The village of Dai Tu, Huu Ngoc tells us, holds the distinction of having had two successful eighteenth century doctoral candidates. To have had one successful candidate from a village would have been exemplary, but to have had two is quite extraordinary when over a period of seven hundred years of examinations, in any one year there might have been only eleven or twelve candidates who received the highest doctoral *tien si* degree. Holders of the *tien si* represented the very cream of the intelligentsia of feudal Vietnam.

From Dai Tu, it is only three miles (5 km) to Huynh Khung village, along narrow roads over which rice has been spread to dry. It is difficult to believe that we are still so near the capital. Obviously, no motor vehicles are expected. Several times the minibus stops so that carts loaded with rice can be pushed by hand to one side of the road to enable the minibus to edge past. Once in an act of camaraderie, Huu Ngoc and the director of The Gioi, Mai Ly Quang, leap down from the front seat and help the peasants push the carts aside, before we shame-faced foreigners in the air-conditioned bus realise what is happening.

At Huynh Khung village, we are led to a small temple where a very old stone stele mounted above an altar is dedicated to Chu Van An, the fourteenth century Confucian scholar mentioned earlier, father of Vietnamese education, who for forty years served as rector of the Temple of Literature in Hanoi.

In the temple dedicated to him in his native village, blue and white china bowls, red lacquer vases and candlestick lamps honour him on the homely altar, an alcove separated from the temple proper by an upper canopy of brocade drapes. Standing before his altar, it is easy to understand how a daily reminder in such an everyday setting of family heroes would serve as a strong incentive to the living to aspire to the achievements of past generations.

Not only does ancestor ancestor worship supply ample role models, it provides a more attainable and perhaps more coveted goal – to be remembered and venerated by one's own kith and kin in one's own village – than say, burial in remote Westminster Abbey.

As it is the first of June, Children's Day in Vietnam, with great pomp we are marshalled into the *dinh* (village hall), where primary school children in funny costumes entertain their parents with dances and banging drums. Then, somewhat perplexingly, we are lined up in front of the children and their parents by the female secretary of the village people's committee and asked to sing.

Merciful heavens. Thankfully, one of our group volunteers, a French Canadian who has trained as a singer, turns what could have become a fiasco into a moving experience. He dedicates *Au Clair de la Lune* to the children and there are quite a few damp eyes in the house amongst the older generation who were educated by the French. Later, he tells us that two elderly members of the audience had been singing along with him.

We walk much of the next two miles (3 km) to Ta Thanh Oai village, shuffling along roads lying deep in hay, stopping to say hello to smiling children, snapping photos of the people harvesting.

The friendly country people wave and motion for us to join them. We pick our way nervously along the narrow dykes between paddies, feeling vaguely uncomfortable as city gawkers.

At Ta Thanh Oai, the village elders with blackened teeth and wispy beards, wearing thick black satin headbands, are still buttoning their red and yellow silk tunics to welcome us officially when we arrive at the temple. One pours out shallow bowls of tea, each served with a fragrant frangipani blossom laid alongside, which ordinarily, they admit sheepishly, would not be allowed inside the temple 'because it is too voluptuous.' Another elder teaches us to smoke a bamboo water pipe.

It had been in this village in the eleventh century that the king, Le Dai Hanh, while marching northward to fight the Chinese who were invading – always the Chinese – noticed the beauty of a local girl fishing for mussels and married her. It is not recorded how many wives he already had.

The village, however, is more famous for its scholars, particularly the illustrious Ngo family.

The patriarch, Ngo Thi Nham, born 1746, passed his doctorate examination at thirty and became a famous general under Nguyen Hue (more of him later). A brilliant strategist, after helping to defeat the 50,000-strong Chinese Qing dynasty army in 1789, Ngo Thi Nham served as a politician, diplomat, writer and advisor to Nguyen Hue, when he became emperor.

As Emperor Quang Trung – men changed their names when they became emperor – Nguyen Hue appointed him historian and rector of the Temple of Literature and he wrote treatises on Buddhism, particularly of the Truc Lam sect, which sought to reconcile Confucianism and Buddhism. There is a famous quotation attributed to him: 'My master faces the world through Confucianism and leaves it by way of Buddhism.'

Unfortunately, Emperor Quang Trung ruled for only four years before he died. Then fortunes turned. When the southern Nguyen family came to power in 1802, Ngo Thi Nham was arrested, beaten to death and his name obliterated from the list of doctors honoured on the stone stelae at the Temple of Literature.

The villagers have erected two tombs side by side, dedicated to father and son, who was also a famous writer. While digging the two tombs beside the temple, the villagers uncovered certain bronze artefacts, a bowl and several arrowheads, dated seven thousand years old. They are displayed in a glass case in the temple dedicated to the two scholars.

A few days later when I show Huu Ngoc the happy-snaps I had taken, he asks me for prints. I think nothing of it until he shows me a scrapbook he has prepared, mounting the prints to send to the villagers to commemorate the occasion.

It was during the visit to scholarly villages that I began to understand the depth of Vietnamese patriotism. It is through the veneration of great men – not necessarily their rulers – that the Vietnamese keep alive their history, their political struggles, their cultural identity. And where the history stops, legends begin, giving the Vietnamese a strong sense of continuity stretching right back to pre-history.

HUU NGOC'S GARDEN PARTY

A living man is worth more than a heap of gold
– Vietnamese proverb

A few days after the outing to scholarly villages, I meet Huu Ngoc climbing the stairs to The Gioi's library, as I did the first time we met, having recognised him from the photograph on the dust jacket of his delightful book, *Sketches for a Portrait of Vietnamese Culture.* A slender man with cropped grey hair, invariably crammed under a beige rain hat, thick glasses magnifying lively dark eyes, one slightly askew, give him the look of maybe an ageing gangster. I believe he is in his eighties.

Huu Ngoc has been a man of many parts. He was born in Hanoi's Silk Street, amongst retired scholars, the son of a clerk working for the French electric company. Having passed through the French lycee system during the colonial period, he left Hanoi in 1939 and worked as a teacher in Vinh and Hue until 1945. Already during his days at the lycee, he had made contact with revolutionaries. In 1946, he started a Resistance newspaper in French, *l'Etincelle (The Spark),* aimed at soldiers in the French army, who included Legionnaires and those drafted from the African colonies into the French expeditionary forces to fight against the Vietnamese. *L'Etincelle* was smuggled into hotels and restaurants used by French forces, even into French military quarters.

Later, he became chief of the army office responsible for re-educating French prisoners of war. When soldiers from Morocco, Senegal, Algeria and France were arrested, they were taught about Vietnamese nationalism before they were released.

From 1958, he served under his friend, Dr Nguyen Khac Vien, as deputy director of The Gioi, the publishing arm of the Ministry of Information and Propaganda, now the Ministry of Culture. Huu Ngoc succeeded him as director of The Gioi in 1978.

In 1964 he and Dr Nguyen Khac Vien started a series called *Vietnamese Studies,* a monthly scholarly journal published in English and French covering many facets of Vietnamese life and culture, of which he became the editor in 1978. The journal has now reached over a hundred volumes. Simultaneously, together with Dr Nguyen Khac Vien, he co-edited an exhaustive anthology of Vietnamese

Literature, translated and first published in French in the seventies. The English version appeared in 1981. Although long out of print, I was lucky to find a copy at Hanoi's History Museum bookshop. A good three inches thick, it begins with poetry from as early as the tenth century and concludes with short stories written during the war years. As I nibble my way pleasurably through the book, I keep longing for far more than one poem or excerpt from each author, so the anthology serves the editors' purpose admirably, to whet the appetite for more Vietnamese poetry and literature.

During the last few years, Huu Ngoc has written books on French, German, Japanese, Chinese, Swedish and American cultures in Vietnamese, as well as numerous tomes on the history and culture of his own native Vietnam, which have been translated into other languages. He also writes a chatty weekly column for *Vietnam News,* the English language newspaper. In short, he is a prolific writer and scholar of the old Asian school, a renaissance man in modern times, who just happens to be living in Vietnam.

Moreover, he acts as a kind of unofficial cultural ambassador for Vietnam. Scholars from many nations seek him out, having read his books and he is always friendly and helpful to them in their research into Vietnam's history and culture. Apart from his many intellectual pursuits, he has taken a lively interest in village life and in the welfare of the Vietnamese people. For several years, he has actively worked with the Swedish-Vietnamese Fund for Promotion of Culture. Through his advice and guidance, more than four hundred grants for projects in Vietnam have been set up: the publication of scholarly works and their distribution to libraries, restoration of pagodas and temples, a multitude of cultural and educational sponsorships. In recognition of this work, he tells me on the stairs that the Swedish Government has decided to award him the Swedish Polar Star Medal, the first Vietnamese to be so honoured. He kindly invites me to come along with his family to the ceremony at the Swedish Residence and asks me to wait in his small monastic study – a wooden desk with books and papers falling out of the open drawer, two low cane chairs and a cane tea table piled high with more books and papers – while he, to my embarrassment when I realise, rushes three shops down the street to have the invitation photocopied.

Departure is at half past four by minibus, which drives round Hanoi picking up relatives: his daughter, two daughters-in-law and their two children each, a son and a couple of colleagues from The

Gioi. When we reach the pavement near his home in a narrow lane off the street, the minibus is full. He helps his elderly wife, wearing a traditional white silk tunic over flowing black silk trousers, her silver hair in a bun, up into the minibus beside the driver. But he, all dressed up and slightly stiff in a smart black jacket, tie and grey trousers in thirty-seven-degree heat, insists on going separately. He must have caught a x*e om,* a motorbike taxi.

His wife politely asks if I speak French. The languages a Vietnamese speaks is a reliable indication of age. The elderly, who completed their studies before Dien Bien Phu in 1954, speak French. The next generation speaks Russian and a few who were sent off to Cuba, speak Spanish. The current young are required to study English at school – much to the chagrin of French tourists – and I have fun exchanging textbook questions and answers with Huu Ngoc's seven-year-old granddaughter.

The walkway under the canopy of the Swedish Residence is lined with baskets of congratulatory bouquets; it is Swedish National Day. Pretty Vietnamese girls in flowing *ao dai* serve cool drinks. One of Huu Ngoc's tiny, adorable granddaughters is all dressed up for the occasion in a pair of gold trainers beneath her frilly dress.

The gathering is made up of family, Swedish Embassy personnel and numerous Vietnamese government officials, who form an open circle around the diminutive figure of Huu Ngoc. I introduce myself to another Westerner, Barbara Cohen, an Italian-American in Hanoi to study Vietnam's ethnography. The Swedish ambassador delivers a touching tribute to the man a couple of heads shorter than him, who has done so much to foster friendly relations between the two distant and quite disparate nations.

Cameras roll, the cameramen move from one angle to another. Flashes flash. The ambassador, his every word translated into Vietnamese, turns to ask Huu Ngoc if he may pin the medal onto his jacket and for an instant, Huu Ngoc appears not to have heard. I wonder what he was thinking about. Having received the medal and a bear hug from the ambassador, he delivers his thank you speech in Vietnamese, although he speaks and writes fluently in both English and French. In turn, the speech is translated into English.

As the diplomatic corps begins to arrive to celebrate Swedish National Day with toasts of champagne and canapés, the family drifts out into the garden and settles on wooden benches beneath the trees with the children. The diplomats remain on the terrace, discussing the things diplomats discuss. Sitting with the family, I am introduced to Huu Ngoc's youngest son, who took a degree at the University of Birmingham (UK) and who now works for the United Nations Office on Population in Hanoi. Although writers, especially travel writers, are accustomed to leading solitary lives, surrounded by Huu Ngoc's warm, extended family, for a moment I feel quite estranged from my own close friends and culture. The moment passes.

Even though I have known Huu Ngoc for a short time, it is deeply moving to have witnessed this diminutive, great scholarly man, receiving some of the recognition he so richly deserves. I am deeply indebted for much of the research on Vietnam's traditions, history and legends to his various books and my gratitude stretches beyond that of a researcher. He writes so well, with such light grace and style that the research has been a pleasure and I thoroughly recommend his books.

Altogether, it is a very special day and a really splendid garden party.

BEHIND THE GREEN BAMBOO BLIND

Money can even buy fairies
– Vietnamese proverb

At first I think they are toys, the funny wooden dolls peering through the windows of souvenir shops in Hanoi. They have cheery, round, painted faces and plump little bodies very untypical of the Vietnamese – and they float! Sometime later, at Thang Long Water Puppet Theatre at the north end of Hoan Kiem lake, I see them fully in action.

The theatre darkens to a glittering, red satin floating palace. Green bamboo blinds serve as curtains behind the watery stage. Drums roll, wooden knockers knock, cymbals crash and a female singer belts out a piercing screech. Before I can wonder how she produces such a noise, presto, shiny gilt dragons pop up from beneath the surface of the water, spewing spouts of water. They bob up and down, dragon-like I presume, swimming back and forth across the watery stage. Quite a flamboyant entrance.

A farmer riding a black and white buffalo emerges from between the green bamboo blinds, ploughing watery furrows. Another farmer appears, flipping water with a tiny basket from one paddy to another, while another, astonishingly, deftly plants sprigs of rice! How do they manage to make floating puppets do that? The puppets, fifteen inches (38 cm) high, are so comical that it is easy to forget that they are being dexterously manipulated from behind the bamboo blinds by strings passed through underwater poles.

In the next scene, lotus pads appear and virtuoso butterflies flit about as a fisherman is chased by an assertive fish. A tidy line of ducks is herded by a Vietnamese hunk, flinging a net, head-shaking worriedly as a tiger swims nearer and nearer. The hunk protects a fair damsel from the tiger, or perhaps it is the fair damsel who chases the tiger up a palm tree. But up the palm tree shoots the tiger, somehow manipulated from below.

Kids from six to sixty love it, no common language required. This is pure slapstick, albeit extremely skilful slapstick. Next, from his boat the fisherman does battle with an enormous, shiny red fish, the victory easily won by the fish. The fisherman falls oars over head into the water and has to swim, very comically, stiff wooden arm over wooden arm, the fish on his back. In a few minutes the fisherman recovers himself, this time fishing placidly with a round basket that he drops by mistake over the head of a pretty pearl fisher. How the audience loves it.

In the next scene, a gang of young boys lark about in the water as boys will, turning somersaults and with incredible expertise on the part of the puppeteers, one boy is tossed onto the shoulders of another, then another to make a stack of three boys!

At the sound of a chime, sparklers go off under water, making sparks and smoke. From the smoke, eight dancing girls emerge, flapping their angel wings. I later learn that this is a scene from a famous Chinese legend in which two students each marry a fairy, a story that has also been incorporated by the Vietnamese into a popular folk opera, *cheo*.

The finale features the four sacred creatures: turtle, dragon, phoenix and unicorn, amidst much smoke and sparklers. The live music – flute, lute, two-string fiddle, a loud horn, drums, gong and a wailing singer – creates a boisterous din throughout.

While the audience is still clapping and rocking with laughter and delight, the bamboo blinds part and ten men and women puppeteers step forward, hip deep in water to take a bow.

You might easily imagine that water puppetry is a recent diversion dreamt up for the tourists, but in fact, it is a traditional folk art – unique to Vietnam – going back for certain to the twelfth century and very probably, much earlier in the rural villages of the North where it originated. An inscription on a stone stele at the Doi pagoda (Tien District, Nam Ha Province) confirms that water puppetry was already in vogue as a court entertainment in 1121 under Emperor Ly Nhan Tong. One can only wonder when it actually began.

Village festivals in Vietnam – the heavy festival season is in April – are lively events including boat racing, wrestling, giant swings, competitive kite flying, bird racing, firecrackers (until they were banned) and water puppetry, performed in village ponds. In a rice culture, ponds are laboriously dug by hand to raise the floor level of houses against the heavy annual flooding of monsoon rains and the water that fills the ponds is used for cultivation and daily use. Naturally, there is a homely proverb: 'When drinking water, remember its source.'

The structures of most water puppet theatres are temporary, erected for festivals. The oldest standing permanent water puppet pavilion, built in the later Le dynasty (1533-1708), is at Thay pagoda (Quoc Oai, Son Tay Province). Another dating from 1775, remains intact at the Dong temple in Hanoi.

Architecturally, water puppet theatres have three parts: a manipulation room behind the bamboo blinds, a stage (the pond water or a water tank) and the audience. Traditionally, performances were given in daylight and the village pond might have tufts of grass, water manioc or clumps of duckweed or water hyacinth growing among the puppets to make manipulation just that bit more difficult.

The puppets are carved from light, durable wood, often from fig trees. They stand twelve to thirty-nine inches (30-99 cm) tall and weigh from two to ten pounds (1-5 kg). The base of the puppet is submerged and fitted with a control mechanism that serves as a float. They are coated with resin from the lacquer tree and painted bright colours from plant resins. The poles are of wood or bamboo and measure from ten to thirteen feet (3-4 m) long. Movements of the puppets are controlled by fine strings made of waxed, plaited hair, coir, silk or jute strung through the poles.

Puppet carving ranks as an important folk art and is similar both in form and subject matter to the carvings found in *dinh* (communal houses) of the seventeenth and eighteenth centuries: fish, frogs, dragons, foxes, snakes.

The characters in water puppet sketches are borrowed from history, legends and myths as well as from daily peasant life – planting rice, catching crabs, fishing, tending ducks, chasing a fox, ploughing – activities with which peasants would readily identify as well as admiring the skill of the puppeteers.

Sometimes snippets of stories from classical opera *(tuong)* or folk opera *(cheo)* are lifted. Such is the delivery of the prince in his palanquin and the severing of Khuon Ling Ta's head from the *tuong* play, *Son Hai*. The *Sich Bich* fire fight is taken from the *tuong* play, *The Three Warring States*.

The *Fairy's Sighting of Tu Thuc* is taken from a *cheo* play based on a legend in which the hero, Tu Thuc, lives with a fairy for three years, then returns Rip van Winkle style to find the world much older and tragically for a Vietnamese, himself forgotten in his own home village. Sometimes scenes and stories get mixed up in the staging to add an element of surprise. Fishing from peasant life might blend into the story of Le Loi sailing on Hoan Kiem lake when the golden turtle reclaims the sacred sword. The scene, *Felling Banana Trees,* can quite unexpectedly evolve into *The Severing of Lieu Thang's Head.*

Sketches run up to seven minutes. The rhyming texts, spoken and sung, identify the stories, poetry or folk songs for Vietnamese audiences. But originally, water puppetry was purely a mime form. Traditionally, water puppetry was practiced as a hobby, although village puppetry guilds have also acted as mutual-aid societies, digging ponds used for rearing fish as well as for performances. Not all guild members perform. However, all guild members contribute rice and money towards a fund to be handed down from generation to generation.

Historically, few women performed. Guild members tended to be heads of families and women were considered not strong enough to manipulate the poles. The women of Thang Long troupe disprove this supposed frailty. More importantly, women were considered poor security risks as it was feared they would divulge how the puppet mechanisms worked to their husbands' families, if they moved as brides to their husbands' villages. Until very recently, guarding professional secrets has restricted the possibility of an exchange of skills.

Although some stories are popular and enacted by nearly every guild, each guild had to reinvent the techniques, resulting in a diversity of forms. In the past, puppetry was learned through imitation and practice, the old teaching the young. Currently, Hanoi has four guilds: Dao Thuc, Nhan Thai, Ha Huong and Thi Lan.

Probably the most universally beloved water puppet character is Teu, the round-tummied, fun-loving, mischievous, jokey master of ceremonies, who makes irreverent comments and jokes, something the Vietnamese throughout their long history of domination – Chinese, feudal, French, Communist – have often been denied.

Of the water puppet troupes, the Thang Long company of Hanoi is best known, having performed nearly round the world. In a tour to the US, members of the troupe were moved to tears at Lincoln Center in New York, when the mayor raised the flag of Viet Nam before an audience of foreign diplomats. In 1997, the troupe toured US universities. It seems ironic that Thang Long got to the University of Kansas in 1998 – before London. So popular are the performances abroad that two stages have been left, one in Europe, one in America.

Yet the company has known hard times. Founded in 1969 with no theatre, just a meeting room in a thatched house, the troupe gave only one or two performances a week, always at a loss.

Le Van Ngo, director of the Thang Long Company, greets me in his top floor office above the theatre, a man of indeterminate age with black hair and lively dark eyes in a serious, kindly face. He admits that he was over twenty before he learned to manipulate water puppets. He had not come from a family of puppeteers, but joined a water puppet troupe as a singer. During performances, he 'saw how much the children liked the puppets and found love for the puppets' himself. It was not an easy life being a water puppeteer.

He recalls the difficult days of 1985, when not only Thang Long Water Puppet Theatre but the entire country was on the brink of financial collapse and starvation. The Hanoi Cultural Service agreed to sponsor the troupe, providing capital and facilities and most importantly, guaranteeing to pay minimal wages to the artists. Success was not sudden, but built gradually by hard work through many ups and downs. Since 1993 the theatre has run without sponsorship, except that the city still pays a small portion of the puppeteers' salaries. Le Van Ngo is immensely proud that the Thang Long troupe is the only theatre in Vietnam that performs three hundred sixty-five days a year and the only cultural activity that earns a profit – in excess of three billion dong ($250,000) annually (1996). He is also immensely pleased that his artists can afford to live on their earnings, about two million dong ($166) per month. To join the Thang Long troupe, puppeteers go through a four-year course at the College of Arts, then serve an apprenticeship with a troupe in one of three villages (Chua Thai, Nam Chan, Nguyen Xa).

To recruit puppeteers, commercials are placed on television, but only high school graduates, residents of Hanoi may apply. First, candidates must pass an examination in the theatre to test their ear for music and their ability to perform. Then they must pass a second examination at the college. These days there are twenty-four puppeteers, two full troupes that alternate performances, sometimes one touring. A troupe is made up of ten puppeteers plus two assistants, six musicians plus a music assistant, a lighting person and a director.

'The troupe is no longer made up of family members, 'but members must be from the village of Hanoi.' The artists range in age from twenty to fifty, two or three generations. The puppets are replaced every three years and are made by the artisans. We have two or three troupes of puppets in store. They change only a little.'

Nowadays, about half the three hundred seats are filled by Vietnamese, a sign that foreign approbation can rekindle enthusiasm for indigenous culture. As my Swedish friend who attended a performance with me, put it, 'Who could resist the water puppets? They are irresistible.'

It isn't until I ask Le Van Ngo about the character of Teu that his face really lights up.

'Teu acts as a master of ceremonies, he always opens the performance. What he says changes, he makes social commentary. Even if it is a tragedy, Teu makes it endurable by making it funny.'

I can see that you love Teu. 'And my puppeteers.'

As a journalist, often through the years I have been given small mementos of trips abroad. When I open the cardboard box that Le Van Ngo hands me and find a miniature carved and painted water puppet, a peasant girl with her fishing basket, complete with a string to pull to lift the basket, I am delighted. I shall long treasure the miniature water puppet given to me by the water puppet man.

A few days later I am invited to a gathering of retired puppeteers.

I have never seen a cricket dancing – nor playing a flute for that matter. This is quite a large cricket wearing a smart, cut-away tailcoat with a mischievous gleam in his painted eye. He has leapt from the pages of a Vietnamese children's fable onto the stage of the recently formed *Union Internationale de la Marionette Vietnam,* a club for retired puppeteers.

Its guiding spirit and founder, Nguyen Huy Hong, in whose suburban home and garden the club meets, is a lively, retired puppeteer in his seventies with flowing grey hair, who feels it a personal mission to alert Vietnam's veteran puppeteers to the urgency of passing on their skills to younger puppeteers before they shuffle off to the heavenly stage.

A water puppet theatre has been built in Hong's garden on the bank of the To Lich river in Hanoi's suburbs, beside which a small museum contains a multitude of ageing puppets and two thousand books on puppetry.

As the cricket dances his jig, a boy behind me with a cast on his leg, taps his crutch to the rhythm. The tiniest toddlers sit in the front rows, their almond eyes wide with pleasure. Larger children, ranging from eight to eighty, sit in plastic chairs surrounded by overflow spectators, standing. Still more people peer down from windows, stairs and balconies.

Naturally, being a Vietnamese gathering, it begins with much hand-shaking, exchange of cards and tiny cups of tea served around low tables under fruit trees. But it isn't long before we get down to serious puppeteering, half the audience enraptured, the unsmiling professionals watching critically.

First off are the water puppets, buffalo boys, iridescent gilt fish, a fox that runs up a tree with a duck in his mouth and boatmen rocking gently in their boats as they row, a boy and girl singing *quan ha* ditties back and forth to one another, boat to boat. In the front row a tiny tot gets so excited that he tips forward out of his plastic chair and almost falls into the pond. I am told that many a child has slid down a slippery bank into the village pond while watching water puppets. A woman with long grey hair sitting beside me, sings along with the singers and she whispers that she used to sing professionally.

The next performer is a scantily clad Cham temple dancer, a wooden marionette, who thanks to the numerous strings attached to the puppeteer's hat, shoulders, belt, hands, each finger and even his feet, executes a beguilingly graceful, finger-rippling dance, the black shadow of the puppeteer mirroring her actions in full view behind her.

Had I not seen the next act assembled, I would never have believed it. Two female puppeteers place ruffled ballet *tutus* on their heads covering their faces and bend forward over a table, their bare arms becoming legs. Two more puppeteers don a long white satin glove on one arm to form a curved neck. Red beaks and eyes at their fingertips become the heads of swans – dancing *Swan Lake* – what else? And a convincing performance it is, too, learned from friendly Eastern Bloc puppeteers.

Turning our chairs front to back the audience now faces a high purple-curtained opening like a *Punch and Judy* stage, where a fuzzy rabbit, his friend the bumble bee and a whingeing wolf appear – Russian hand puppets.

'I'm so tired and hungry', whines the wolf. 'I have such a hunger for a little rabbit!'

The wolf catches the rabbit in a wolf-hug and the poor rabbit squeals, bringing the bee to his rescue. The bee, attached to a springy wire, sets about stinging the wolf until the wolf lets go of the rabbit and keels over. Then comes the stealthy approach of the bee and the rabbit to the carcass of the wolf.

'Is he dead? Is he really dead? Is he really, really dead?'

The Vietnamese children respond with *'da, da, da'* (yes, yes, yes). Imagine my surprise after the applause to discover that the puppeteer is none other than the grey-haired woman who was singing along beside me.

After the jigging cricket and three sequined dancers from the Central Highlands, string puppets, we settle to sipping tiny cups of extremely strong rice wine – at 10 a.m.! The cinnamon-flavoured peanuts just about keep my words coherent, maybe.

The rest of the day is spent feet up.

HAPPY BIRTHDAY, MR QUANG

Press the seeds for oil
Don't press the hearts for marriage
— Vietnamese proverb

One morning I am introduced to Mr Quang by The Gioi's chief English editor, who after a round of hand shaking, invites both of us for coffee in a nearby pavement cafe. Mr Quang is of a vintage to have been educated during the French colonial period. He is a translator from Vietnamese and English to French. His Spanish isn't bad either. During the coffee conversation, Mr Quang says that his birthday is coming up in a couple of weeks time and he would like to invite me to his birthday celebration. Assuming that our mutual friend will be coming, and imagining a large Vietnamese family gathering, I am delighted to accept. I hear no more from Mr Quang for some days. Then one day in the middle of the day, there is a knock at my fifth floor, bedroom-cum-office door and to my surprise, there is Mr Quang, telling me that his birthday celebration will take place the coming Thursday. When I ask for his address, he explains that as it is difficult to find, he will pick me up on his motorbike at 5 p.m. on the day. I very much look forward to meeting his family.

On the morning of his birthday, he telephones to confirm the appointment and arrives punctually at five, muttering something about his daughter and a taxi. I take this to be the daughter he proudly told us about over coffee, who works as a petroleum engineer. To my surprise, a sparky little girl of ten appears, coming from school, another daughter, presumably from a second marriage.

We wait and wait and the taxi does not come. Mr Quang goes to telephone and finally, a taxi appears. His own house, he explains, is being renovated, so he is staying with his niece and nephew. The taxi drives through the embassy quarter of broad, tree-shaded boulevards lined by French colonial villas, then through the narrow streets of the old town, the Thirty-Six Streets.

When the taxi stops, we hop out and walk single file through a maze of narrow lanes between high walls, constantly approached from both directions by bicycles and motorbikes, past a small pavement market. Finally, Mr Quang announces at a gate that this is the house where his niece and nephew live. Beyond the courtyard, we enter a tiled living room where polished wooden chairs and a settee stand along one wall beside a single wooden bed with a straw mat. Popular Western music issues from an elaborate cassette player. Mr Quang's niece and nephew, a couple in their thirties, are all smiles and handshakes. The nephew disappears, returning immediately with a tea tray. How very sensible the Vietnamese custom, never to ask a visitor if he would like tea, but simply to serve it.

While waiting for the taxi, Mr Quang had said that he was divorced. Divorce in Vietnam is not only frowned upon, it is considered downright unlucky, if not shameful and many people, rather than admit it, prefer to say that their former spouse is dead. With such a young daughter and one so much older, I have assumed that this younger daughter is from a second marriage. So over tea I stick my big fat Western foot in it by asking when his wife will appear. He replies that his former wife does indeed still live in Hanoi, but as they are divorced, she will not be coming. Ouch.

The nephew switches on the television news, a welcome distraction from my embarrassment. Normally I watch CCN News on VN-TV with a Vietnamese voice-over a day late. Now with a simultaneous translator, I get a running commentary. Mercifully, in a few minutes the niece appears carrying a huge fish curled round a platter under a dressing of sliced mushrooms and carrots. The big black fish, *ca bo,* brushed with vinegar and herbs and broiled over charcoal, is a delicious freshwater fish. Next come small rounds of fried pork and 'new rice' cakes, *cha com.* The children finish – for the niece and nephew have a son of ten – and set up a fast-moving game of chess on the patterned tile floor. The table is cleared and to my chagrin – supper thus far has been ample – another course begins to appear: a plate piled high with bits of pork, another of chicken, another of omelette and tiny shrimps. These are added to a bowl of soup containing fresh herbs, mint and noodles, *cun thang.* The combination of different tastes and textures is so good that I eat every last morsel. Then, in come plates of fresh papaya and persimmons, prettily sliced in a zigzag pattern.

Silently I wonder how soon I will be able to rise, if ever, when my hostess suddenly remembers the pineapple upside-down cake I brought from the French bakery. She races out and serves it. What to do? If I refuse to eat cake, they will not eat cake. Perhaps they, too, are too full to eat cake, but are too polite to say so. So, like a drunk facing yet another brandy, I face the cake and decide that tomorrow will be an abstemious day. Quang smiles somewhat ruefully and says, 'It is a very special occasion.' We all proceed to make gluttons of ourselves.

Going home, I feel so sorry for the cyclo driver that I give him a bit more than he and Mr Quang have agreed.

HALONG BAY – HERE THERE BE DRAGONS

Divination makes spirits appear,
the brush drives away filth
— Vietnamese proverb

No photographs of Halong Bay quite prepare you for the first glimpse of this surreal landscape. A huge vastness of layer upon layer of steep, slate blue limestone karsts thrust abruptly from the emerald water of the bay, stretching, beckoning, beyond and beyond. How easy, faced with this spectacular, monstrous landscape, to empathise with the early Viets who created myths to explain the existence of this mysterious, unnatural seeming world in which they found themselves.

Halong means 'where the dragon descends into the sea.' According to the legend, the three thousand islands in this vast area of five hundred fifty square miles (1,424 sq kms) stretching from Halong Bay to the Chinese border were formed by a mighty dragon who lived in the mountains, making a dash for the sea. En route, his huge flailing tail gouged out deep holes that filled with water, leaving only the sharp points of the disturbed land showing above the surface.

Getting to Halong Bay from Hanoi over the splendid new road takes just over four hours by bus for the ninety-six mile (154 km) trip because of the heavy traffic.

Halong is a town divided by a narrow strip of water leading to a huge inland lagoon. Most of the hotels are in Bai Chay on the west bank. The city proper, known as Hon Gai, lies on the east bank.

In Bai Chay I arrange a boat trip for the following morning with Hong Ngoc, the proud owner of a fleet of excursion boats. He insists that I hop on the back of his motorbike to zoom a little way down the coast to see his new boat under construction. This is no mere dragon boat, this $100,000-yacht designed by a French architect in the style of Halong wooden houseboats, has a highly polished hardwood superstructure housing eight double cabins, each with a luxurious bathroom. To cruise Halong Bay aboard Ngoc's boat would be travelling in romantic, grand style.

Boat inspection over, I return to Bai Chay and cross by ferry to Hon Gai to find the market and a floating fishing village moored below a rocky cliff face. I wander along the narrow catwalk braced against the stone cliff, passing within a few feet of the tightly packed fishing boats, moored side by side. Three hundred years ago, the Emperor Ly Thanh Tong (he who founded the Temple of Literature) walked this way and composed a poem, which has been carved into the cliff face of what is now known as Poem Mountain. But as people can no longer read the old *chu nom* ideograms, I can find no one to translate the poem. How easily a body of literature and the cultural past can slip away when a nation discards an old form of writing.

The floating village creeps onto the shore. Narrow muddy lanes weave through wood and thatch shacks. The smiles of adults and children dispel any misgivings as to whether a foreign she-devil should wander here alone. Along the seashore, fish have been spread out on long strips of netting. The two girls, rolling up the edges of a net to 'pour' the dried fish into wicker trays, say that it takes two weeks for the fish to dry. They then carefully empty the trays into deep baskets, which the two of them heave, one by one into a round basket boat in the North called *thuyen thung,* in the South, *thung chai,* four heavy baskets to each boat.

Near the market, a white-robed Buddha statue looms over the courtyard of a modern, yellow pagoda, Long Tien. Painted grapevines trail over the walls beside a wildly flamboyant dragon. More colourful figures decorate the cornice beneath the eaves. As charming as a painted gingerbread house, it could almost be the terrace of a restaurant in Tuscany. Where has the artist seen grapevines, I wonder, until I remember that grapes grow in the South near Dalat.

At dinner I learn that the tourist season in Halong Bay for Europeans runs from October to April, from April to October for the Vietnamese, when Halong Bay is cooler than most of the rest of the country. Unhappily in recent years, Halong has become known as the Thai massage capital of North Vietnam, attracting sex-tourists from as far as China.

Another titbit picked up at dinner – ironically, the local authorities refused permission for the producers of the film *Indochine* to film here, so the Halong Bay scene was filmed at Krabi, north of Phuket in Thailand.

Next morning, two grinning boatmen, one on shore and one aboard the excursion boat, hand-hold a bamboo pole for the three nervous foreigners to cling onto as we precariously teeter, step by step, up the bendy gangplank from shore to deck.

'If you fall in, I am sorry,' says the grinning captain in what turns out to be one of his few, no doubt well practised phrases in English. Our yellow-headed dragon boat noses out into the calm, violet tinged bay enveloped in mist.

The floating village of fishing boats nuzzles the far side of Hong Gai. A rusty coaster lies at anchor in the harbour. Stony karsts several storeys high erupt abruptly from the sea and gradually, turn from slate blue to green as we draw nearer. On the horizon, monstrous blue boulder rises and glides beyond boulder, sometimes humpbacked like a herd of elephants, sometimes heaving up in jagged, sharply pointed peaks, fantastical shapes, mysterious and compelling, beckoning into an infinite, floating labyrinth. As our boat moves, the mountains seem to move, too, strange new shapes emerging. It feels like floating under the feet of a herd of restless elephants. We pass beneath a natural rock formation and a little farther on, the captain mutters and points to Teapot Island. Soon a small boat carrying two tiny children – neither can be more than two – draws alongside our boat to offer small silvery fish for sale. Another boat approaches selling crabs.

Throughout the morning small boats pull alongside our moving boat selling shells, huge prawns and fish. They seem to lurk in wait for excursion boats. A woman in the far distance, fishing from a round basket boat, looks like a tiny black figure in an ink drawing, dwarfed by the monstrous peak above her. A fast moving boat passes ours, near enough to glimpse a mother rocking her baby in a hammock slung under the thatched canopy. Another boat stops alongside, hoping to sell corals. On principle we buy nothing, but I am sure that unless illegal coral picking is enforced, these poor people will go on plundering their ocean beds.

As our boat approaches to within a few feet of a steep boulder, we can see tenacious shell life clinging to the craggy sandstone. Shrubbery softens the mountain tops; the stone cliff faces, split apart by the elements, often drop sheer to the sea. As the sun burns through the mist, the water turns from violet to milky chartreuse, then melts into clear jade. A large excursion boat that has been leading us in its wake suddenly disappears and I realise just how easily pirates could operate in these waters, pouncing from behind, then simply disappearing round a boulder into a grotto, or behind an island. Dragon Island does, indeed, resemble the humped back and head of a dragon. We pass Tortoise Stone and Head Man Stone, resembling the chiselled profile of a man's face. As we approach a low, natural stone archway rising from the sea, our boatman motions for us to transfer to a smaller boat. Is this where they consign us to the pirates? Once in the small boat, we pass through a low, natural stone tunnel under a heavy boulder. No great lover of caves, I am relieved to see light at the end of the tunnel. We emerge into a perfectly round lagoon of green water surrounded by steep jungle-covered cliffs. The boatman cuts the engine and for a few minutes, time stops; we hear nothing but birdsong. It is like being reborn in a completely natural green world on the first day of the earth's existence. Very reluctantly, we return to the world of engines.

According to a sign at the bottom of some stairs on one of the islands, Me Cung cave has been declared an official UNESCO site, as early remains have been discovered here. The cave opens at the top of the hill. I later learn that in a survey of March 1997, Me Cung cave yielded a thick layer of fresh water snail shells, *melanina,* and mountain snails, *cyclophorus* – but no remains of sea mollusc or fish – supporting the archaeological theory that the ocean here gradually rose a hundred-fifty to three hundred feet (50-100m) – and reached its highest level in the mid-Honocene era five thousand years ago. Before that, the area covered by Halong Bay would have been a coastal plain crossed by streams and ponds. Rather more interestingly to me, a long twisted piece of ceramic found in Me Cung cave, dating from between ten and twenty thousand years old, proved how long ago prehistoric people have lived all along this coastline.

We anchor for lunch at Love Island 'where young people come.' A green and white tablecloth is spread on a low table on the boat and an astonishing lunch of fresh sea food is served: crabs, crayfish, tuna fish steaks, squid, a spinach type vegetable and steamed rice, followed by mandarin oranges. The cutlery is stamped Vietnamese Airlines. As we head back through open water in the afternoon haze, the huge, brooding shapes of the dark, jagged mountains surround us, floating on the horizon, giving the eerie impression of following the boat. Amidst this haunting natural grandeur, the carefree crew of three falls asleep, leaving the wheel to a youngster of about twelve who steers erratically with one foot.

It is at times like this that I feel a stab of loneliness – such an overwhelming scene and no soul mate with whom to share it.

A NIGHT AT THE OPERA

Very ugly my husband,
very handsome, another's husband
– Vietnamese proverb

As a fairly indiscriminate lover of opera, I am thrilled when the scholar, Huu Ngoc, invites me to accompany him to a performance of Vietnamese classical opera, *tuong.*

As a preliminary, he introduces me to the director of the Northern Tuong Theatre in Hanoi, Mrs Nguyen Thi Nhung, a chic woman of a certain age. How had she trained in *tuong,* I ask?

'I competed nationally to obtain a place at the Stage School. The year I applied, only thirty students were chosen from 1,300 applicants. Training for the classical theatre – singing, dancing, learning the repertoire – required four years. I entered Stage School at fourteen, just after the outbreak of war and attended from 1964 to 1968' – during the Vietnam War, not a propitious time to be involved in the arts or much else in Vietnam.

'Having completed my studies, I was appointed to the Northern Tuong Theatre, the national opera company, which had been evacuated to a country site eleven miles (18 km) from Hanoi. The troupe was divided into small groups of seven or eight and larger groups of fifteen to twenty and sent touring round the countryside, sleeping in village houses, giving performances for peasants in village halls and in army hospitals.'

I knew that popular folk opera, *cheo,* which originated in villages of the north, is farcical. 'Reformed' theatre, *cai luong,* which originated more recently around Ho Chi Minh City, adds spoken dialogue. Not wanting to ask if Vietnamese opera derived from China, I ask how long *tuong* has been performed in Vietnam.

'There are two schools of classical opera in Vietnam, that of the North, *gua ming,* and that of the South around Hue, *hat boi. Tuong* is based on mythical, epic, heroic and tragic themes.'

Then Mrs Nguyen volunteers, 'It is difficult to explain with any precision the differences between Chinese and Vietnamese classical opera. Obviously, Vietnamese *tuong* owes much to the tradition of classical Chinese opera. It is known for certain that in the fourteenth century following the Vietnamese victory over the Chinese, that an excellent Chinese opera singer, dancer and actor, Ly Nguyen Cat, was captured by the Vietnamese Tran dynasty and that he taught classical opera in the royal harem.'

I wonder if he had to become a eunuch, but cannot quite bring myself to ask Mrs Nguyen through Huu Ngoc as interpreter.

It must be said of any borrowed art form or craft in Vietnam, be it lacquer, sericulture, painting, porcelain, whatever, once the Vietnamese have inculcated the skills, the craft becomes 'Vietnamised', Vietnam being a nation of irrepressible creators. Classical *tuong,* therefore, would have evolved into something quite Vietnamese.

'No serious research has yet been done into the earliest origins of classical opera in Vietnam. According to some historians, small plays and sketches began to appear in the tenth century, long before the capture of Ly Nguyen Cat. But it is generally acknowledged that the real flowering of the form occurred under the Nguyen dynasty in Hue in the nineteenth century and the best known *tuong* composer of that period was Dao Tan.'

Although formerly every village had its troupe of amateur *tuong* players who performed at village festivals, *tuong* has suffered in recent years from the onslaught of Western pop music and these days, there are few performances of *tuong,* even in Hanoi.

Having no theatre, the troupe is obliged to rent halls, which Mrs Nhung says in Hanoi has become prohibitively expensive. As a result, nearly all of her Northern Tuong Theatre performances are given as a touring company in provincial towns or in village halls.

I am astonished to learn that a two-hour performance in Hanoi might cost as little by Western standards as $175 to $450 (£120-300) in a room to seat a hundred people.

Thinking of how popular Beijing Opera is with foreign visitors – no tourist to Beijing can miss an evening at the opera – I wonder that the Vietnamese authorities do not develop *tuong* as a tourist attraction. If the water puppet performances pack in the foreigners, why not *tuong?* Even the young Vietnamese – more than two-thirds of the population is under thirty – who are so eager to adopt Western music and styles, seeing that Westerners are keen on *tuong,* might be won back to their own traditional theatre.

Having a penchant for being on time, I am pleased when Huu Ngoc suggests that we meet forty-five minutes before the start of the performance, only a fifteen-minute walk away. We dawdle along Tran Hung Dao Street in the twilight and reaching the street where the performance is to be given, he kindly suggests that we make a detour to visit the Ambassadors' pagoda, especially built to serve the early Buddhist ambassadors whose residences were in this neighbourhood.

We step over the threshold and wander around the main sanctuary just as the pagoda keepers are beginning to close. Although disappointing to lose Huu Ngoc as a guide, perhaps just as well, remembering that in Hanoi, seats are rarely numbered or reserved.

As the performance is to be given by members of the newly formed Stage Club of Vietnam, sponsored by Press and Radio of Vietnam, it is taking place in the auditorium of Radio Vietnam. We arrive fifteen minutes early to a full house, but I have not reckoned on the esteem enjoyed by Huu Ngoc. We are led smartly to the front row where five empty seats remain, reserved for dignitaries.

Very sensibly, in summer Vietnamese men rarely wear jackets and most are in white, open necked, short-sleeved shirts, trousers and sandals, the women, elegant in flowing *ao dai*. Directly across from us, a bald headed man with a straggly beard is a dead ringer for Ho Chi Minh. No one takes the least notice of him. I am the only foreigner in the room.

The performance begins with drum rolls and a gong, the orchestra made up of a two-string fiddle, long-necked and moon-shaped guitars, a bamboo flute, a bowl-shaped gong and my favourite instrument, the *dan bau*.

A man and a woman sing in unison to the accompaniment of a flute and wood knockers. An aria, perhaps? Certainly, this is not an opera performance as I know it.

Then a female singer, flashing red and silver sequins, places a brass tray holding red cellophane-wrapped parcels and candles on a low table. Huu Ngoc whispers that she is a medium, part of the cult of holy mothers: the skies, the sea and the mountains.

Four pretty girls enter wearing glittering red headbands, green sashes over pink tunics and black trousers, singing and dancing, waving their lacy fans. They hand the medium two wooden sticks and her movements look like rowing. Then the medium removes the silvery tunic and earrings – is this to be a striptease? – to reveal a long-sleeved white satin blouse and trousers. She slips into a yellow jacket, a yellow hat and a turquoise sash – a costume change on stage.

'The cult of the spirits,' whispers Huu Ngoc.

76

The girls dance, bowing and kneeling. Having finished with the oars, the medium is handed two wooden swords and the dance begins to look like riding on horseback. The attendants bring out teacups and dance tipsily from side to side in a graceful rendition of drunkenness. Then the medium takes up a cane basket full of flower blossoms and scatters them into the laps of the musicians. Off come the hat and the yellow jacket, to be replaced by two enormous silver rings around her neck, an embroidered orange headdress, a gold shirt and a glittering green brocade jacket.

She places the tray of red parcels on her head and dances, kneeling and rising. The four attendants reappear carrying candles and lotus blossoms and the medium hands out the red cellophane-wrapped triangular parcels to those of us in the front row, like at the evening of the Traditional Folk Music Club.

'Dried sugar rice flour cake for the cult. You can eat it,' whispers Huu Ngoc.

A dazzling lady from the Voice of Vietnam Radio, obviously a personality, wearing a shocking pink *au dai* with clouds on the sleeves and a glittering procession of peasants under parasols marching diagonally from hip to hem, explains that the club has been founded at a moment when the theatre is in decline, in an attempt to revive it. Her *ao dai* alone should do the trick. There are fewer and fewer performances, she explains, because few people understand the performances. Surely a few talks on Vietnam Radio would help. Or a few documentaries with commentary on VN-TV?

The next performer is a female singer wearing a dazzling splash of colours. Her song is anguished, almost unbearably poignant.

'She has been betrayed by her lover,' whispers Huu Ngoc.

She is followed by a beautiful girl with wild eyes who hops onto the stage in a sitting position, 'riding a horse.' She turns cartwheels and walks on her knees, then kneels as though she were looking at her reflection in a pond.

This one I am prepared for, a famous *tuong* story in which the heroine is a fox, who it has taken a thousand years 'to attain the essence of becoming human. But she has been betrayed by her lover and is fearful that as punishment, she will lose her human essence.' As she peers at her reflection, I swear, her nostrils start to twitch. Her eyes narrow and she becomes fox-like, her fingers curl into claws, her wrists bend outward and she seems to discover fur growing on her forearms. Meanwhile, her face contorts and seems quite transformed.

She keeps trying to pry her fingers straight, to remove the fur. The dance ends in a wailing lament, the mournful cry of a fox on a hilltop. A brilliant performance.

'There are Confucian implications,' whispers Huu Ngoc, but he leaves it at that. Simplistic moral of story: choose your lover very carefully. As a complete change of pace, we have a romantic ballad, sung by a singer in an *ao dai* to challenge *Joseph's Technicolour Dream Coat*. 'She is a well-known singer.'

But is it *tuong?* I am ill prepared for what comes next.

Onto the stage strides a muscular young man wearing – a boa constrictor! It becomes instantly clear that we have had our dose of *tuong* for the evening.

The new club organisers are taking no chances that the audience will go away bored. Despite the billing of classical opera, we are to be treated to a right royal Vietnamese variety show. So taking the view that everyone loves the circus, they have brought on the circus. I don't mind watching the strong man wrap his enormous snake around his neck, over his shoulders and around his thighs. I become a little uneasy when a female assistant with a somewhat smaller boa constrictor joins him and climbs up onto his bent knee to do a high kick. Then another boa constrictor appears and the young man becomes a snake-stand for two, plus the girl and her snake, of course. I begin to wonder how heavy boa constrictors are, the big ones. Eventually, the girl piles her snake onto the gallant young man and oops – he is heading for the audience. My rapid exit is physically and diplomatically blocked by the directrice of the circus to whom I have just been introduced, sitting beside me. Perhaps she doesn't like boa constrictors either, for to my relief, the snake man heads towards two young boys who look as if they would just love to say hello to a big snake. She whispers to me that this act will soon tour the U.S.

Next come two men twirling paper torches, wearing green and yellow bandannas, peasant costumes and the rouged cheeks of clowns everywhere. You only have to look at them to laugh, classic fools, no dialogue necessary.

'*Cheo,*' whispers Huu Ngoc.

A glittering, huge wooden temple dancer appears next, the puppeteer in black in full view, followed by three dancing puppets, manipulated from a single pole.

The puppets are followed by two radio actors, their scripts on music stands. The male actor is a reporter interviewing a modern

Vietnamese mother. Her parrot-like replies to his questions are jingles from television commercials for products such as soap, mineral water, yoghurt, cleansing cream, anti-dandruff shampoo, tooth paste and mosquito spray – oh yes, TV commercials have invaded even this Communist country.

The punch line is the answer to the question: 'And where is your child now?'

'Oh, he's in hospital having psychiatric treatment.' Then comes a Vietnamese version of British TV's *Two Ronnies,* two men on the street yakking about why one's wife insists on going out to sing karaoke.

Everyone, it seems, wants to do a turn. A poet wearing jeans, who reads his poem, *The Stage,* turns out to be the man who painted the Voice of Vietnam symbols on the stage backdrop.

The guitarist, who earlier accompanied the famous singer, plays *Love is Coming.* Then on comes a seven-year-old girl in peasant costume singing, *I Am a Rebel from Binh Minh* – interminably. Even I have learned the chorus by the time someone gently drags her off-stage. When she is followed by a couple of chaps crooning a sentimental ballad, I begin to wonder if someone has turned on a karaoke machine.

At last comes a farewell folk song entitled *Don't Leave.* We, and the rest of the relieved clowd, leave. Huu Ngoc's first words are, 'What time is it?' Half past ten is a very late performance in Hanoi. As we walk back towards Tran Hung Dao Street, a ding-donging vehicle approaches and liberally sprays the street – and both of us from the knees down – with water.

It feels like three in the morning.

A few days later, the monsoon arrives. Within two days, the streets are flooded, ankle-deep, and have to be waded across – or take a cyclo – the old French drainage system inadequate.

Enticing Hue calls.

(The National *Tuong* Company now has its own theatre at 51 Duong Thanh and gives one-hour 'taster' performances of grand court music as well as Vietnamese classical opera. Check which days at Vietnam Tuong Theatre's website.)

PART II

AUTUMN IN HUE

HUE – A FEW QUIRKS OF HISTORY

It's by the trial of misfortune
that one recognises a faithful subject
– Vietnamese proverb

Eight miles inland from the coast, Hue is divided by the meandering Perfume river (Song Huong). The former imperial city and the royal palaces, the Citadel, lie on the north-west bank. The newer town, some of it more than a century old, spreads over the south-east bank. Most of the royal tombs of the Nguyen emperors, their dream palaces for the afterlife, lie scattered up river, to the south.

The site for the royal Citadel was partly chosen for its position between two 'guardian' islands: upriver White Tiger Island (Con Da Vien), down river Blue Dragon Island. But local people know the latter as Mussel island (Con Hen) because mussels for a much loved Hue mussel dish, *com hen,* come from its shores.

Overlooking the river and Con Hen Island, the Huong Giang Hotel is to become my home for several pleasant months. Built in the sixties, a bullet hole retained as a souvenir in one of the glass tiles in the stairwell between the second and third floors, testifies to its age – damage during the Tet Offensive of 1968.

Decorated in what can only be described as royal Hue style, the ornate red lacquer pillars and beams and the gilt chairs of the vast royal dining room, were doubtless copied from the royal palaces. In an artistic tour de force, bamboo and woven cane decorate nearly every surface of the corridors and top floor restaurant overlooking the Perfume river. Right here let me confess to a secret longing to live in (Britain's) Brighton Pavilion. Either one of the royal suites at the Huong Giang Hotel would run it close second, if not surpassing it in oriental frivolity, the more appealing for being nearly attainable (alas, they have now been modernized). Yet for the price of a coffee or a Huda beer on the terrace of the Huong Giang, anyone can enjoy the enchanting view of the Perfume river and the boat people who moor around the tip of Hen Island, nearly the same view as that from Thien Mu pagoda, which first drew me to Hue.

Slightly upstream to be south, a sturdy steel bridge built by George Eiffel spans the river. Despite its arches, it is anything but picturesque. Nevertheless, it has achieved the status of a Hue icon, appearing in silk paintings of the city and every night on VN-TV's Hue weather forecast. And so, my premonition that gazing out over the Perfume river would figure in my future becomes reality and during the four months I spend in Hue, I never tire of watching life along the river. Sometimes, the mornings start with sparkling sunshine; more often the sun has to burn its way through a gauzy mist. As the sun ignites, the fishing stops and sampans and larger motor junks under arched, thatch roofs move upstream. From the far end of the causeway beside the hotel, two flat-roofed, open-sided ferries splutter back and forth across the river to the market. Not since my childhood can I remember such blue skies and tumbling clouds. On windless days, tiny yellow birds flit amongst the fuchsia and salmon-coloured blossoms of the bougainvillea.

Every morning, the chores of the boat people are different. Sometimes, two young boys harvest wild green convolvulus – river spinach. The younger brother squats in a slim sampan with what looks like a minnow net, scoops up the green weed and flips it into the boat after his elder brother, standing in the river, plucks it from the riverbed. Sometimes, a single fisherman, balancing on one foot on the curved end of his sampan, guides the rudder with the other foot as he drifts down river, dragging a long net. Once I see a fisherman lift quite a large fish. Usually it is only a silvery minnow. Some mornings, a large, square, yellow net attached to four poles is lowered into the river from a rickety, temporary bamboo tower. Then the woman atop the tower winds a pulley to raise it, as her husband in a sampan paddles beneath the net, pushing any fish to one side where he can retrieve and drop them into his boat. Then the net is lowered and the whole procedure is repeated.

At evening, the sunsets last no more than five minutes, a brilliant light-show of billowing clouds of every shade from mauve to violet, peach to shimmering gold, moving quickly, chased by the sun playing hide and seek above the river below, shimmering lavender and pink. A dark, narrow strip of town floats on the far shore, backed by the indigo of what Hueians call 'the screen' of the Truong Son mountains. It is mesmerising, even on a dull night when the palette of the sky is limited to subtle shades of indigo. No two evenings are the same. A sliver of a boat glides past, a woman returning from the market, a father rowing his toddler homeward, silhouetted against the silvery water.

Dragonflies zoom above the terrace, their iridescent wings gleaming in the last sunlight. Geckos chirp from the warm, white wall of the hotel. One balmy evening, inspired by a particularly pearlescent sunset, two geckos playfully chase one another up a lamppost and clutch one another.

As the sun fades and the shadows darken, tiny orange cooking fires take spark on the boats, and lights along the shore of the island begin to twinkle – a captivating sight, as twilight ebbs to darkness. The chunter of the ferry from the causeway to the far shore continues long after it is possible to make out its silhouette. Add a Huda beer at the end of a hot, heavy, humid, day and the spell is utterly beguiling. Apropos of nothing, I later learn that Huda beer is Hue's top revenue earner; entrance fees to tourist sites come second.

With the breathtaking simplicity of hindsight, but for a few quirks of history, Hue might never have been, or conversely, might still be the capital of Vietnam. It is not the *ancient* capital as stated in certain guidebooks. Very likely, 'ancient' is a corruption of the French word *ancien,* which means former.

To give it its proper distinction, Hue was the last imperial capital of Vietnam, ruled by the Nguyen dynasty (1802 to 1945), though the French very forcefully took control of Hue – and of Vietnam – in 1884.

Thereafter, the Nguyen court acted as little more than a puppet regime until the last emperor abdicated in 1945 to the Communists. Following the Geneva talks of 1954, the country was partitioned – Hue in the South – until the fall of Saigon and Reunification in 1975 (see appendix for Nguyen dynasty).

What I found most fascinating about Hue was that Vietnam's imperial feudal court continued into modern times, so recent that there were bound to be people around who still remember it.

A few Machiavellian intrigues of Vietnam's history run like this. In the sixteenth century capital, Thang Long, several generations of the Nguyen clan were active in royal court and military affairs under the Le dynasty, always in competition with another family, the

Trinh. The story goes that during the reign of Le Tang Tong (1533-1548), Nguyen Hoang (1525-1613) heard a rumour that his brother-in-law, Trinh Kiem, was plotting to have him assassinated. Hard on the deaths of both his father and brother in battle – rumoured to have been stabbed in the back – the assassination rumour seemed all too credible. To escape court intrigues, Nguyen Hoang managed to get himself appointed governor of the expanding frontier Southern Region and in 1558, moved south with his extended family and a good many artisans.

Nguyen Hoang quietly worked away, ostensibly to develop the Southern Region, while gradually building up his own military strength and establishing an administrative structure mirroring the royal court in Thang Long. In 1570, he was appointed governor of an additional southern area, Quang Nam. This gave him even more land and he busily settled more emigrants, who either volunteered or as often as not, were forced to move to the new territories.

Had the rumour of the assassination plot not reached Nguyen Hoang in the first place, he would never have moved south and most probably, the Nguyen clan would never have developed a sufficient power base from which to challenge Trinh power in Thang Long. Nor would there be a city called Hue.

A few generations later, the Nguyen lords had become quite powerful in their southern fiefdom, not even bothering to pay tribute after 1627. For more than two centuries they were almost constantly at war with the Trinh. The animosity between the North and South goes back a long time.

What has become Hue was first established in 1687 at the village of Phu Xuan, but the capital of the Southern Region moved several times in the area nearby, before finally settling back in Phu Xuan in 1744. By the late eighteenth century, Nguyen mandarin were incurring the wrath of the people by levying too heavy taxes. From a family of merchants in the South, three brothers from Tay Son mounted a rebellion (1774-1779), first against the Nguyen lords, who they defeated; then the Trinh in the North, who supported the powerless Le dynasty. The leader of the Tay Son brothers, Nguyen Hue, then did battle against Qing dynasty invaders from China, who opportunistically thought they had detected a moment of weakness in their southern neighbour. The Chinese were defeated in 1788 and Nguyen Hue crowned himself Emperor Quang Trung of a country unified from Qui Nhon northward. But the energy of the Tay Son brothers was spent.

When speaking in English, incidentally, the Vietnamese usually refer to their former rulers as kings, explaining quite reasonably that the Vietnamese empire only extended over the Chams to the South, so it was more of a kingdom than an empire. However, as they wore elaborate silk robes and their courts seem extremely imperial to the Western mind, the word emperor feels far more fitting to reflect the absolute power exercised by a Vietnamese ruler, who might crook his little finger and order that a mandarin lose his head. As Emperor Quang Trung – the Vietnamese always changed their names when they became emperor – Nguyen Hue married Princess Ngoc Han, a girl of sixteen and the favourite daughter of the weak, former Le king, Hien Tong. As emperor, Quang Trung ruled for only four years before his death in 1792 at only forty. Despite the age gap and the obvious political advantage of marrying the daughter of the deposed ruler, the marriage must have been a happy one, for the young queen, a widow at twenty, expressed her grief at his death in a now famous poem.

Wind pours its cold into the room
Orchids wither on the veranda
Smoke covers the crypt of the deceased,
The shadow of the royal coach is gone.
Alone, I weep over my fate.
Heaven, why did you shatter our union?
How to tell my misery, my pain
Deep as the ocean, boundless as the sky,
I look to the East, sails glide in all directions,
I see only immensity of sky and water.
I look to the West,
Mountains and trees spread as far as the eye can see.
To the South, wild geese wander,
To the North, mist covers forests with a white shroud.
Though I search, the more this separation weighs upon me,
Will my affliction awaken echoes in that far beyond?
I see the moon through sorrow, its brilliance tarnished,
A fine dust veils its silvered glow.
I am ashamed to look at myself in the mirror,
My love shattered, alone, I wander on the deserted shore.

The flowers I look at return my grief.
Camellias cry tears of dew.
Watching the flitting bird, my heart is torn,
A turtle-dove flies solitary, seeking its companion.
Each landscape wears its own desolation,
Where are the joys of former days?
One moment only and the world collapsed,
So life goes, to whom can I complain,
Love and fidelity, as immense as heaven and earth,
My grief grows as my days endure.
To whom may I confide my torment and pain?
Let sun and moon bear witness!

(tr Huu Ngoc)

By the time of Quang Trung's death, his brother, Nguyen Lu, had grown feeble and the third brother, Nguyen Nhac, was too busy enjoying himself to care much about state affairs. The succession was left in the hands of Nguyen Hue's young son, Quang Toan, who nominally ruled from 1792 until 1801, power vested at first in the hands of mandarin acting as regents.

It is thought by some that if the liberal Emperor Quang Trung had lived to rule, say for twenty years, the country might have remained united with the capital – perhaps not in Hue – but at his family seat in Qui Nhon, two hundred fifteen miles (346 km) south of Hue. Not surprisingly, a huge statue has been erected in Hanoi to commemorate the hero, Quang Trung, who first unified the country from Qui Nhon northward and who sought to liberate the people from the worst repression of feudalism.

Meanwhile in the far south, the defiant fifteen-year-old son of the defeated Nguyen family of Hue, Nguyen Phuoc Anh, had escaped assassination in the Mekong delta and reappeared under the self-appointed title, Great Marshal. He went about inflaming the people with the pioneering spirit of the Nguyen lords and by 1790, had rallied sufficient support to dominate the entire Mekong delta, eventually attracting the allegiance of the former generals of the Tay Son armies, who by then had become disenchanted with the rule of Quang Trung's successors.

Then the wheel of fate went spinning. From the Mekong delta, Nguyen Phuoc Anh travelled to Bangkok, seeking military support from the Thais. He found it, but also through the French

Bishop of Adran, Pigneau de Behaine (1741-1799), who as an act of faith took Nguyen Phuoc Anh's four-year-old son with him to Paris and arranged an audience for him with Louis XVI. Imagine the stir the tiny oriental prince must have created in the glittering French court. He was painted by Mauperin and allowed to play with Louis-Joseph, the dauphin. To this day, it is because of this early collaboration with the French that many Vietnamese in the North blame the Nguyen dynasty for handing over the country to France.

By 1802, Nguyen Phuoc Anh had sufficient military strength to wreak vengence on his father's enemies, the Trinh, and having unified the country for the first time from the Mekong delta to the Chinese border after three hundred years of internecine war, proclaimed himself the first Nguyen emperor, Gia Long. Naturally, he moved the capital to his family's traditional stronghold, Hue – and destroyed the Citadel in Thang Long, the old northern capital.

At last, the long struggle between the Trinh and the Nguyen was over. However, the bitterness between North and South remained and remains still. Looking back to original sins, if there had been no rumour in the sixteenth century that a Trinh was about to assassinate his Nguyen brother-in-law, the South would never have become such a power base. If Nguyen Hue as Emperor Quang Trung had survived a longer reign, the northern part of the country might have remained unified. And if Nguyen Phuoc Anh, alias Emperor Gia Long, had not invited the military support of the French, but received more aid from the Thais or even the Dutch, how different the history of Vietnam might have been. But for another quirk of history, it might even have been the Americans who came to the aid of the Nguyen!

In 1858, Napoleon decided upon armed intervention in Vietnam, under the pretext of defending the Catholic population. French gunboats shelled Danang, (then variously called Tourane, Turon by the French), and in 1859 the French took Saigon. By 1867 they had seized all of the Mekong delta, Cochin China. In 1873, while Frenchmen Jean Depuis and Francis Garnier were attacking the Citadel in Hanoi, the Emperor Tu Duc in Hue commissioned one of his mandarin, Bui Vien, to seek military aid from other Western powers to thwart the advance of the French. Bui Vien sailed immediately for Hong Kong, a voyage of two months in those days, and did the diplomatic rounds. With a letter of introduction from an American diplomat in Hong Kong, he set out by ship for Yokohama, then on to San Francisco, hoping to enlist the military assistance of

President Ulysses S. Grant. Consider the arduousness and length of such a journey in the mid-nineteenth century: by ship from Vietnam to Hong Kong, by ship from Hong Kong to Yokohama, then the long voyage across the Pacific to San Francisco and from there, cross-country to Washington. Astonishingly, in Washington Bui Vien did manage to arrange a meeting with the President, but as he carried no proper credentials, it was impossible for him to conclude any formal agreement between the two countries – that's the story. I wonder how they communicated, or if President Grant even knew where Vietnam was? Bui Vien dutifully retraced his journey to Vietnam to obtain the proper credentials. Unfortunately, by the time he had once again reached Washington, the Emperor Tu Duc had died (1883) and the French had established complete control over Vietnam in 1884.

What might have happened if Bui Vien had carried proper credentials on that first journey to Washington? Would the US have turned on France, her former ally, who had helped to defeat the British in the War of Independence a century earlier? In the unlikely event that America had responded favourably to the call for help from the Vietnamese to defend their independence – a newish democracy aiding a feudal ruler to retain power – and if the French had been defeated, Vietnam would have remained unified under self-rule, the capital in Hue. There would have been no need for a French Indo-China War, possibly no cause for a Communist revolution and no second Indo-China War against the Americans. The tantalising 'what ifs' of history become mere footnotes, dramatic political actions taken because of a rumour, complications caused by lack of an official document, by death and history overtaking time lost in a long journey. By what arbitrary details, history is sometimes determined.

The Perfume river came by its name, not because it boasted any special fragrance, but because historically, the ingredients for perfume were traded along its shores. Naturally, many girls in Hue, reputedly the most beautiful in Vietnam or so the locals claim, are named Huong. The first Huong I met was my first guide to the Citadel and I never think of the Citadel without remembering the elegance of her purple *ao dai* and her mischievous wink.

'From England? I was the guide for Mr Michael Palin of the BBC when he was in Hue. He was a very funny man' – wink, wink.

'The Buddha is not fat because he drinks too much beer' – wink, wink. A Palin-esque pleasantry, perhaps.

MADAME TON NU HA

Affairs of State take precedence
over those of the family
— Vietnamese proverb

Almost on arrival in Hue, I hear of Madame Ton Nu Ha's Garden of Tranquillity restaurant (Tinh Gia Vien), and that reservations must be made a day in advance.

Apart from being Vietnam's last imperial capital, Hue is famous for its food. Even Hanoi gourmets grudgingly concede that Hue cuisine is special and that Hue places great emphasis on presentation. In fact, the people of Hue attach great importance generally to style, not unlike their former French colonial masters, particularly in their refinement of the decorative arts, in gardening, in poetry games and competitions, in dress, even in manners. Yet this is distinctly Hue style.

At twilight when the riverboats have become silhouettes, another guest of the hotel and I take cyclos over the bridge, through a gate in the walls guarding the Citadel and into the leafy lanes of the old imperial city, now in parts practically rural, thanks to bombing. One of the pleasures of Vietnam is to take a cyclo on a still evening. Westerners sometimes voice objections to taking cyclos, having tender, humane scruples about being pushed around by the muscle power of another human being. Long ago, I came to a conclusion that it is far better to leave one's Western values at home and to abide by local customs. In Vietnam, one of the ways poor men earn a living is by peddling cyclos. To refuse is therefore to deprive them of much needed earnings. So until cyclos are replaced by taxis, I take cyclos.

Tinh Gia Vien restaurant is in Madame Ton Nu Ha's villa in a narrow lane. The cyclos drop us inside the gates. This is intimate dining, only half a dozen lantern-lit tables on the terrace with balustrade railings. Flowering orchids hang from the arches, potted bonsai and cacti crowd the railings. One of Madame Ton Nu Ha's pretty daughters, Ton Gian Hien – Gian Hien means Tender – wearing a purple *ao dai,* seats us and presents a handwritten menu. On the table, the bouquet of orange and white flowers has been artfully sculpted – from carrots and green papaya, standing on slender stalks of spring onions! The first platter to appear is a ravishing Dancing Phoenix, one of the four sacred animals, its feathers, thin swirls of paté and ham. The phoenix cocks an imperious peppercorn eye from its carved carrot head before disappearing as an *hors d'oeuvre*. The delicious soup that follows is thick with vegetables, mostly unknown. Next, two huge grilled shrimps under chopped garlic appear, rapidly followed by half a plump river fish smothered under a mildly spicy tomato sauce on a bed of 'seaweed' – shredded green papaya.

The Fantasy Chicken has the rounded rice-paper body of a sitting hen with feathered carrot wings, a sprightly onion tail, a round white turnip head and a pert, red pepper beak. The next creature to appear is a Swimming Turtle, its head and feet of carved carrots, the Cantonese rice of its body under a latticework of omelette to resemble a turtle shell. The creative presentation of the food reveals a playful, innocent whimsy. Moreover, it tastes very good. Having given up more than pecking, we are looking forward to *Fruit Tropique Déguisé,* only to bite into – something like marzipan! By the end of the meal I am determined to meet Madame Ton Nu Ha, the *chef extraordinaire* behind these creations.

'Please come tomorrow at half past seven,' she says, smiling, explaining that Vietnam-TV will be there making a film, and that there will be beautiful food to photograph. She means half past seven in the morning.

Next morning, my cyclo rolls through the gates into the sun-drenched garden just before half past seven, a busy, charming, garden unlike any I have ever seen. A bronze sculpture of two young lovers, lost in one another, the young man tenderly touching the arm of his beloved, stands beside the entrance. White china elephants bearing pot plants guard the steps to the terrace. More than two hundred bonsai line the paths past a two-storey tea house cage holding gerbils in the penthouse, a squirrel on the ground floor. Low trees blend in a leafy tapestry: grapefruit, apple, palm, cedar and a tropical weeping tree with needle-like red blossoms at the tips of the branches. In every direction, the eye falls upon a different contrived scene: artfully arranged standing stones, a miniature fig tree – with figs, the white statue of a young Vietnamese girl holding a candle-shaped lamp.

Madame Ton Nu Ha has been preparing food since five and I am just in time to see the last two platters being completed.

She works on a folding table on the terrace beside a goldfish bowl from the top of which sprout the tiny leaves of a bonsai. A huge plastic basket acts as the palette for her edible collages: red peppers and tomatoes, orange carrots, yellow bamboo, pale green *chou chou,* green and white cucumbers. A meat platter offers more shades: salamis in tones of pink, red and beige; white and brown cooked chicken meat. Bright green gherkins and mayonnaise await the call for a flourish of green or cream.

A sinuously undulating dragon is taking shape on one platter, his scales individually cut from tiny round slices of paté and salami. Two girls cut, chop and notch vegetables. A thin man like a Giacometti statue himself, is sculpting a head from a potato. Two months ago Madame Ton Nu Ha fell in a climbing accident and broke four bones in her left elbow – and she is left-handed. A month later, her elbow was still swollen and the doctor operated. Two months after the accident, it is still giving her pain and slowing her work.

I feel like a sorcerer's apprentice, watching as she lines the edges of an oval serving bowl with thin slices of ham and paté, then fills the centre with thinly sliced omelette and fried rice. She places a platter on top of the bowl and tips it upside down – the bowl has acted as a mould. Soon, four scored reptilian carrot feet, a curled tail and a head join the oval body, its carrot head held upright in the same position of curiosity as the heads of the stone turtles that support the stelae in the Temple of Literature in Hanoi. At a jaunty angle in his mouth he brandishes a spring onion, a reference to the legend of the sacred turtle in Hanoi's lake of the Restored Sword.

Cutting carefully around carrot templates, the girls are making the turtle shell from lean brown meat. The thin man introduces himself as Phan The Binh, a sculptor and professor of sculpture at Hue College of Art. It is he who created the statues of the young lovers in the garden. Despite very little English he manages to convey the plight of creative artists throughout the world: 'With this money', he motions to the food platters, 'I can sculpt.'

The television crew arrives. Two pretty girls in red and purple *ao dais* arrange a vase of red gladiolas and stroll through the garden for the benefit of the TV cameraman. From upstairs come the sounds of pounding and the cries of a baby. The little white dog, Lucky, settles down for a snooze beneath the stairs. It has already been a long day by nine. Madame Ton Nu Ha disappears and reappears wearing a purple velvet *ao dai,* splashed with silver bead-work, a sparkling necklace round the high-necked collar. The effect is – imperial. Four platters about to be filmed are placed on a purple tablecloth, the four sacred animals: phoenix, turtle, kylin or unicorn, and the dragon.

Madame Ton Nhu Ha explains that the TV producer would like for *me* to wear an *ao dai* so that she can teach me on camera how to carve a flower. Oh, dear. Reluctantly, but to show willing, I slip into one of hers and the girls tactfully try to arrange a round crown of purple velvet over my fluffy fringe and loose hair. Vietnamese women traditionally wore their hair severely parted in the middle and sleeked back in a bun beneath these crowns.

The young daughter of one of the kitchen staff explodes in a fit of giggles and I search out a mirror. Always trust the honesty of a child. It looks positively witch-like. I refuse to wear the crown and we are all happier. The TV cameraman politely shoots a few minutes of Madame Ton Nu Ha demonstrating how she works and then to my relief, one of her pretty daughters takes my place and the chef teaches her how to sculpt a flower from a green papaya. It makes a pretty scene. I have yet to see a Westerner who looks anything but ridiculous in an *ao dai.*

Madame Ton Nu Ha's husband, a slim man in shirt sleeves, returns carrying a briefcase like a businessman returning from the office and the TV crew insist upon his saying a few words to camera.

Next morning I have Madame Ton Nu Ha to myself. The Ton in her name indicates royalty. Seven generations of her family served at court as mandarin in the days when to become a mandarin meant passing stiff examinations.

'My great-grandfather acted as an emissary to China and received many gifts from the last empress dowager of China – but they were all burned, destroyed during the bombings of Hue (1968). When (Emperor) Bao Dai abdicated in 1945, life became very hard for my family. We were very poor.'

Out of necessity, Madame Ton Nu Ha developed her numerous talents. At the beginning, she trained as a nurse and her first job in 1963 was in Quang Tri, a neighbouring province where already in her youth there was war and much poverty.

She became head nurse in emergency, then after another examination, a teacher of nursing. In 1965 she went to Saigon to study nutrition under the Americans and cooking at a French school, then returned to Quang Tri. In 1967 she moved back to Hue and married. In 1968 she received the highest medal attainable for nursing, one of only three to be awarded in the entire country. She met her husband-to-be while studying at nursing college. He was already teaching traditional Vietnamese music at Hue College of Art. 'He plays five instruments,' she tells me with pride.

Madame Ton Nu Ha has passed the age for coy modesty.

'Many persons loved me, but I was afraid,' by which I think she means that she had many suitors. When she first caught sight of the man who was to become her husband, she wanted to meet him, but felt too shy.

'The first time I met him I could see that he was a very kind person, his eyes, he had very kind eyes. With him I knew my heart would be safe. He makes me feel very tiny before him, he is very serious. I always feel he is higher, he always supports me. It is because of him that I am successful. It is for him I always try to do things a little bit better. I always say, it is because of you.'

I empathize with Madame Ton Nu Ha's attraction to her husband's gentle, idealistic spirit. They were in love for three years before they married in 1967, she at twenty-three, he at twenty-eight.

'We had only been married for five months when he went off to the mountains to fight for liberation' (Vietnam War 1965-1975).

Neither knew that she was pregnant. For seven years they were separated without a word of communication. She had no idea if he were dead or alive; he had no idea of her whereabouts or welfare, nor that he had a son.

'Those times were terrible. My house was bombed, my mother's house was bombed. But we were both spared.'

Madame Ton Nu Ha is immensely proud of her husband.

'There are only three things: party, government and motherland. Politics come first, higher than family. He is very important in the party.'

Her husband is a member of the Central Committee of Hue.

After her husband's return from the war, Madame Ton Nu Ha continued nursing and nutrition management at the University Hospital. Three daughters were born, now in their twenties. The name of the youngest, Tinh Hai, means Sea of Tranquillity and one might have thought that at last with the French and American wars past, the family could settle down to a quiet life. But 1989 brought change.

'My government wanted oil from Iraq. So I helped my government.' Vietnam sent two hundred Vietnamese nurses to Iraq in exchange for oil. Madame Ton Nu Ha was one of them. Once again, she was separated from her husband and this time her children. For two years she lived and worked in a war zone; her husband looked after the children. The nurses were paid very little, only just enough to eat. Arriving towards the end of the Iran-Iraq War, there was peace for less than a year before war broke out again, this time with Kuwait. Madame Ton Nu Ha remembers watching for several days from her fourth-storey hospital window as a constant thread of cars carrying whole families poured into Baghdad from Kuwait.

'The post office was bombed and we lost our electricity. In a hospital, that meant death to those patients who were on life-support machines. There were dead patients in the refrigerators and after five days, the odour was so overpowering that we had to bury the bodies without waiting for the families to collect them.' For six months food was scarce. While they were working in the hospital they were given sugar and a bit of meat, which in turn the nurses shared with their ambassador, who had no food at all. 'The Iraqi police were very' – she searches for a word – 'uncharitable. They were very strange. When we worked, our salary was petrol, we had very little money, we did not have enough money to eat. So in our spare time, we made hats. It would take one day for two people to make one hundred hats and we earned about 15,000 dongs ($1.50) for the lot. I had to go to the market to sell them.

'If the police caught me, because foreigners were not allowed to sell, they would put me in prison. In Iraq we were afraid. In the market, the political police would come and stamp on the merchandise and put people in a car and take them to prison. Sometimes they had sticks. Sometimes we didn't know why we had lost a friend. Then the ambassador would go round to find the person was in prison. Then that person would be sent home in disgrace. For the sake of only $1.50, maybe prison.' The market was so dangerous that Madame Ton Nu Ha struck upon another moneymaking idea, making portraits of Saddam Hussain. 'Every officer's room had to have his picture. Because I am a woman, my paintings were soft. That's how I had the money to open the restaurant.

'There were many bombs in Baghdad, like Hue in 1968. My ambassador was afraid. Everybody was leaving Baghdad. Only soldiers, security and government stayed. Others deserted the city. But I was not afraid. God gives us life or death' – this, from a staunch Communist. Eventually, to get out of Iraq they drove nine hours to the border, the highway littered 'with burnt-out cars, still smoking, and 'lots of bodies. On the way at night, it was very cold.'

At the border they were not allowed to cross, so they had to turn back and return along the same road to Baghdad. Finally, the Vietnamese government asked the UN to assist in their release, and nine days later, once again they attempted the journey to the border.

This time they were allowed to cross into Jordan to a refugee camp. Madame Ton Nu Ha had brought her pastels and pens for drawing portraits, thinking, 'If we are suffering, I can use my pens to get enough food for many friends.'

While they were waiting in the camp, Madame Ton Nu Ha wanted to go out and see something of the country, but the officials refused. It was only after she had painted a portrait of King Hussein that they lent her a car for a bit of sightseeing. 'I was so glad to return to my country. I love my land, I cannot explain how we love our country. It is in the blood.' The returning Vietnamese nurses managed to reach Hanoi on 16 January 1991 – not quite in time to get home to Hue for *Tet,* the important annual New Year holiday. Madame Ton Nu Ha pauses, remembering those times.

'We have to be very strong. Many friends say a big knife can cut tiny or big pieces. A small knife can only cut small pieces. Many things I can do.'

And indeed, apart from making hats and portraits, at various times she has made and sold concrete flower pots and administered injections to earn money. In 1973, she received a certificate for proficiency in English from the Vietnam-American Association and in 1975, she obtained a bachelor's degree in law, earned during the last years of the Vietnam War.

'Four years of study, as well as working at the hospital. After the revolution, it was of no use for work, but it has been very useful in life. People of high rank didn't work with their hands, didn't sell in the market. But after the revolution, labour was considered to be good, so I sold things to make money.' She planted flowers and bonsai and sold them in the market. 'Anyone will tell you, I am a trader,' she says, seemingly oblivious to the contradiction of a born marketeer being married to a high-ranking Communist official. But then, times in Vietnam are changing, towards a market economy. The 1943-vintage villa in which she lives once belonged to a former princess. 'During the war it was broken in half.' Madame Ton Nu Ha bought it from a descendant, added the terraces and the garden.

A few years ago, she opened the restaurant.

'I love my cooking. I have always cooked, my cooking is from my childhood. In the hospital every day I cooked for 1,200 patients, three times a day. I have cooked for the president of Thailand, the prime minister of Vietnam, for many ministers and officials.' One year, all of the government party officials met in Hue and she cooked for three hundred. Once she did a wedding for five hundred. She has even been televised cooking for four hundred people in the Throne Room of the Citadel. She gave up her job at the hospital only a few years ago. Until then, it was the hospital early in the morning, the restaurant at night. I loved my patients, I could not leave my patients. But the restaurant became very busy and I had worked for the patients for a long time, thirty-two years.'

Rarely for a Vietnamese, she has ticked off travelling to both extremities of her country although she seldom travels with her husband. He is too busy. The North she managed when she was given five days off from the hospital for an appendectomy. She rested for two days after the operation, then set off on a day-and-a-half train journey to Lang Son bordering China, where she hoped to add a purple blooming variety of the *hoa dong tien* flower to her collection of twenty-one. On arrival she collapsed and never succeeded in finding the plant. Recently, she has visited the southern extremity of the Mekong Delta. It appears that whatever Madame Ton Nu Ha does, she does with passionate energy. 'I cook with my heart, I am an artist, I like to please my clients.'

Asked how she sees the future, for a moment Madame Ton Nu Ha looks nonplussed, as if she has never looked beyond today. Then after a moment, she says vehemently: 'I like to learn. Every day if I have the time, I go to a big bookshop. I am always reading. If I I want to do something, I learn to do it and always try to do it well.'

Apart from her obvious, extraordinary talents as a chef and a restaurateur, Madame Ton Nu Ha is a truly inspiring, phoenix-like survivor, a resilient and elegant Hue woman for all seasons and political climes. What she has lived through in triumph made me feel quite humble. What soft lives we lead in the West.

A DESCENDANT OF THE ROYAL NGUYEN FAMILY

A single drop of blood is worth a pond of clear water
– Vietnamese proverb

In Hue I am thrilled to meet a man – amongst a few others he assures me – who might have become emperor. His name is Nguyen Phuoc Bao Hien, he is in his seventies and lives in the tomb of his grandfather, the Emperor Thanh Thai.

Nguyen Phuoc Bao Hien is neither a recluse nor an eccentric living amongst tombstones. A royal tomb in Hue is not a bad place to live, if you happen to have one handy, a complex of buildings and courtyards including temples dedicated to the dearly departed. In the case of Bao Hien, he is joined in the tomb complex by some thirty members of his family: his two wives, ten children, a son-in-law, a daughter-in-law and his grandchildren. He has ten children, six sons and four daughters ranging from thirty-nine to fifty-three years old. Each wife had five children.

I tried to keep things balanced,' he says with a twinkle. How very Confucian of him.

There were thirteen emperors of the Nguyen dynasty. Bao Hien's home serves as the burial place for three: the fifth emperor, Duc Duc; the tenth emperor, Thanh Thai (Duc Duc's son and Bao Hien's grandfather); and the eleventh emperor, Duy Tan, (Bao Hien's uncle). Bao Hien's father was Duy Tan's younger brother, the thirteenth son of Emperor Thanh Thai.

So much for primogeniture in Vietnam. An emperor's choice of successor, quite apart from his first-born, court intrigue and later, the intervention of the French, played havoc with anything like a simple, direct line of succession.

The period encompassed by the rule of Bao Hien's ancestors between 1883 and 1916 was a turbulent epoch in the history of Vietnam, as the country struggled against and finally succumbed to French domination in 1884. Bao Hien receives me in the temple dedicated to his grandfather. He is a lean man with taut skin and gives a dignified impression of strength as he sits bolt upright, wearing

96

khaki trousers and an open-necked white shirt with a biro in the pocket. Despite the gold-framed glasses, he looks anything but meek, which is the meaning of his name, Hien. We sit in straight-backed, red and gold painted chairs that might have been lifted from a royal palace and he pours tea from a tray on a glass-topped table, beneath which are numerous colour photographs of smiling faces. Beside the tea tray lies the brown, leather-bound volume with gilt lettering of the Nguyen family tree (see appendix).

The temple has an interior of dark wood and pillars. Around the corner I glimpse a low wooden bed with a straw mat, presumably Bao Hien's. Two red ceremonial parasols stand propped in one corner. A revolving fan perches on a wooden box. Beyond the open door, a rooster struts under a green brocade court robe, flapping on the clothesline beside the temple building.

Bao Hien starts at the beginning of his family's history.

'Nguyen ancestors descended from the Dinh dynasty of the tenth century. Vietnam won freedom from the Chinese in 938 in the time of the Ngo dynasty. The Dinh reigned towards the end of the tenth century, having defeated twelve feudal lords. Later Nguyen descendants served under the Ly, Tran and Le dynasties.'

I knew that a Nguyen lord had moved from Hanoi as governor of the Southern Region in 1558 and that after nine generations as governors and a long civil war, another Nguyen lord had ascended the throne in Hue in 1802 as the first Nguyen emperor, Gia Long. There were only four Nguyen emperors before the French forcibly occupied Hue in 1884 after which, like it or not, the Nguyen emperors were little more than puppets.

'As Tu Duc had no children – it is thought he became sterile through having had smallpox as a child – he adopted three nephews. One was the son of his younger brother (Thoai Thai Vuong Hong Y), the fourth son of the third emperor, Thieu Tri. The other two were sons of Kien Thai Vuong Hong Cai, the twenty-sixth son of the emperor, Thieu Tri.' At the request of Bao Hien, a young relative – his 'uncle', he insisted – such are the convolutions of Vietnamese families where there are many wives – heaves a huge trunk onto a nearby table and rummages through a pile of photographs, eventually unearthing a faded photo of three little boys encased in stiff court robes. These were Tu Duc's three adopted sons.

'The eldest of his adopted sons, Duc Duc, ruled for only three days in 1883 before two senior mandarin dethroned him and threw him into prison where he died of starvation. The second and third adopted sons, Dong Khanh and Kien Phuoc, were passed over and the Emperor Tu Duc's younger brother, Hiep Hoa, aged thirty-eight, was crowned emperor. He was only allowed to rule for four months before two senior mandarin forced him to drink poison.

'The second adopted son, Dong Khanh, was again passed over in favour of the third, Kien Phuoc, aged fifteen, who ruled for seven months before dying of smallpox.

Once again, the second adopted son was passed over and yet a younger brother of Kien Phuoc, Ham Nghi, ascended the throne, aged fourteen. He ruled from 1884 to 1885 when the French stormed the Citadel.

'Young Ham Nghi resisted as best he could, but was overwhelmed and fled to the mountains with the royal golden seal where he tried to raise support to resist. In October 1888, he was arrested by the French and exiled to Algiers where he was held in the village of Elbiar a few miles from the city.

'At first the emperor refused to learn French, but on reflection, decided that if he were to understand his captors, he would have to learn the language. To pass the time, he painted. He continued to wear the traditional Vietnamese court robes and was known as the Prince of Annam. In Algeria, he was well liked and eventually married the daughter of the French judge, Laloe. They had one son and two daughters.

'One daughter, Nhu Mai, distinguished herself by becoming the first Vietnamese woman to graduate from a European university, *l'Institute d'Agronomie* in 1927. Known as Mademoiselle d'Annam, when asked why she continued to wear the traditional Vietnamese *ao dai,* she replied, "To please my father, the Emperor Ham Nghi."

'At last, after Ham Nghi, it was the turn of the second adopted son, Dong Khanh, to become emperor. His rule lasted less than four years from 1885 to 1889 when he died at the age of twenty-three of a brain disease.

'The story goes that before he became emperor, Dong Khanh asked his mother to go to Hon Chen Temple to ask the goddess when he would become king. She dutifully went to the temple, spent the night there and the goddess appeared, telling her that in six months her son would be crowned. The prophesy came true. Six months later, the French placed Dong Khanh on the throne. In gratitude, the new emperor repaired Hon Chen Temple and thereafter considered himself to be the younger brother and student of the goddess. Previously, there had been pictures of seven students of the goddess in the temple. Dong Khanh added his own.'

Bao Hien then tells me the story of how his own branch of the family came to power.

'When Dong Khanh died in 1889, Thanh Thai, the son of Duc Duc – he who had been dethroned, imprisoned and starved to death by the mandarins – was placed on the throne. How it came to be he rather than the son of Dong Khanh, who was ten years old when his father died, is a curious tale – not recorded by historians.

'By that time the succession was virtually controlled by the French. The royal family decided that Dong Khanh's son should become emperor, but they had to seek permission from the French resident superieur. The royal family duly sent a representative to meet the French resident. Because the French resident spoke no Vietnamese, he had an interpreter.

'As it happened, this interpreter's wife was the elder sister of Thanh Thai. So the interpreter explained to the French governor that the royal family would like for the next emperor to be – not Dong Khanh's son – but his wife's brother, Thanh Thai, the son of Duc Duc (who the mandarin had starved to death). The royal representative duly returned to the royal family, saying that the resident would prefer for Thanh Thai to become emperor.'

So, quite treacherous, these interpreters. Such were the machinations of the succession during the Nguyen dynasty. Thanh Thai, Bao Hien's grandfather, was only eleven years old at the time he was crowned. He ruled for seventeen years from 1889 to 1906. Bao Hien hands me another photograph sealed in plastic of his grandfather as a wide-eyed boy in an enormous court robe. Despite his relatively long rule, the boy grew up to resist the French. He in turn was dethroned and imprisoned in South Vietnam in Cap St Jacques, now known as Vung Tau, sixty miles (96 km) east of Saigon.

Bao Hien tells the story of how, during one lunar New Year season, his grandfather, the emperor, 'dressed in ordinary clothes and went to Kim Long, a village known for its beautiful women, in search of a concubine. Finding no one he fancied, he took a sampan to return to the Imperial City.

'Getting into the boat he noticed that the boat girl was around twenty, quite timid and blushing. He called out to the girl, "Say, Miss, how would you like to marry the emperor?"

The girl regarded him with alarm. "Please don't joke. They will cut off our heads."

'Touched by her sweet voice and sincere manner, the emperor took another tone. "I tell you sincerely, if you would like to marry the emperor, I will be your go-between."

'The young girl blushed even more and looked away. An old man passing who had heard the exchange, called out to the girl, "Say yes, miss, and see what happens."

'With all her courage, the girl said yes. The emperor, enchanted, stood up and took the hand of the young girl, leading her to the bow of the boat saying, "Now, my dear lady, sit down and I will row in your place," and with these words, he began to row to the astonishment of everyone who recognised the emperor. Onlookers were delighted but also apprehensive. The boat continued along the Perfume river to the Phu Van Lau Pavilion (still there) in front of the Citadel where the emperor announced in front of everyone, "Now leave the sampan and come with me, my dear lady, to the Court."'

The poor girl must have been terrified. But she accompanied him to the palace and remained a favourite wife of the Emperor Thanh Thai, Bao Hien's grandfather.

'Thanh Thai's son and successor, Duy Tan, who ruled from 1908 to 1916, also tried to raise a rebellion. It was unsuccessful and in 1916, both he and his father were exiled to the island of Reunion.

It was at that time, that the families of Bao Hien's grandfather and uncle, Emperors Thanh Thai and Duy Tan, more than a hundred people, were moved by the French into this tomb complex, held under guard and restricted from speaking to the common people. Even the servants, who worked for the royal family were guarded by the Vietnamese secret police, controlled by the French. Bao Hien fills me in on these turbulent and terrible years for his family after the death of the fourth emperor, Tu Duc.

'The later emperors are labelled as collaborators with the French, but in my opinion, the tenth and eleventh emperors were patriots. They didn't want the French to dominate, they wanted to resist, but lacked the power.

The two emperors who followed Duy Tan were from another branch of the Nguyen family. The son of Dong Khanh, Khai Dinh, ruled from 1916 to 1925 when he died a natural death at forty-one. His son, the last emperor, Bao Dai, reigned from 1925 until 1945 when he abdicated in favour of Ho Chi Minh's Communist

Government, saying that he would far rather be a citizen of an independent country than the emperor of a country in slavery.

'Bao Dai was invited to act as advisor to the new Communist Government, but following a mission to China, fled to Hong Kong and waited to return to Vietnam until it was once again occupied by the French in 1947. The French invited him back as Chief of State, which he remained nominally from 1947 to 1954, passing his time travelling, hunting around Dalat and relaxing in his villa overlooking the sea at Nha Trang. Following the French defeat at Dien Bien Phu, he went to live in France.' He died there in 1997.

Bao Hien was born in 1927, started school at seven under the French system 'and was taught to work for France until 1945.

Due to the war with the Japanese, Bao Hien was unable to continue his education, his one regret.

'Vietnam suffered greatly during World War II. The Japanese requisitioned so much rice in Vietnam that two million people, one out of five, died of starvation.'

Throughout the war Bao Hien remained in the tomb looking after his grandmother, the empress widow of Thanh Thai. In 1945 his uncle, the eleventh emperor, Duy Tan, was killed in a plane crash flying from Africa to France. Some people say he was assassinated. His grandfather, Thanh Thai, was only allowed to return to Vietnam in 1947 when the French freed him, but was not allowed to return to Hue. He had to stay in Cap St Jacques (Vung Tau), south-east of Ho Chi Minh City.

The last emperor, Bao Dai, was Thanh Thai's nephew and although they had very different views, the two met to discuss the protection of the royal family tombs and how to preserve the royal palaces. Bao Hien hands me a murky black-and-white photograph sealed in plastic of his lean-faced, high-browed austere-looking grandfather wearing a dark suit, seated beside a round-faced Bao Dai, wearing a light sports jacket and black-and-white spectator shoes. The two men look as different as two men can. The man who hands me the photograph looks remarkably like his grandfather, Thanh Thai.

'Up to 1945, although their movements were restricted, the French had supported the royal family financially. Members of the family were allowed to take part in court ceremonies, but the French always noted which princes took part. After the revolution in 1945, the royal family was very afraid that the Communists would turn against the monarchy.

To their enormous relief, the temporary government continued to pay an allowance to the old people in the family who could no longer work. The family felt moved by this generosity and had second thoughts about the new government. When the French returned to Hue after 1945, the French once again supported the royal family financially.'

Bao Hien remained in Hue, under the French, under the Japanese during World War II, under the French again, and during the war with the Americans.

'I have lived under many regimes, but I have always helped the people. I am very happy that I could be useful, especially during the French War. There were very bloody battles in this city between the French and the Vietnamese.

At that time I worked for a Buddhist charity organisation. Many soldiers were killed and I and some other people, after the battles were finished, we would take the bodies of both sides and organise burial of the dead soldiers. I knew it was very dangerous but I was not frightened. At the time, I and some others carried a white flag so that both sides would know that we were working for charity. And I always thought, because what I was doing was a good thing, if I were killed, my spirit would go to heaven. During the wartime, I was very lucky because nobody shot me. At that time I thought, if a person didn't help, if he had just stayed idle at home, surely he would go to hell. That thought gave me comfort.

'Before Liberation in 1975, I worked for a state organisation concerned with relics management of the old regime and after Liberation, I continued to work for the new organisation set up by the new government – until now. According to new government regulations, officers have to retire at sixty. Now I am in my seventies, but our office, the Conservation of Monuments Center of Hue, still agrees for me to work in the Center. I feel that it is a privilege to continue to work for the government. Many members of the royal family followed the Communists and many became leaders in the government. After the Liberation, those who took part in the resistance of the country, the government still appreciates them.'

And the royal family now, how many members of the royal family continue to live in Hue? I ask. Musing for a moment, Bao Hien estimates that perhaps around sixty thousand people with royal blood over the age of eighteen live in or around Hue, out of a population of a million in the province. The second emperor, Minh

Mang had so many children – one hundred forty-two – he explains, that he actually set down a system for naming and labelling each succesive generation.

Bao Hien's guess is that there are perhaps two million members of the royal Nguyen family alive and dispersed throughout the world. world. So not a very exclusive club.

Apart from his job in the Center, Bao Hien serves as the master of ceremonies, the chief mandarin or Minister of Rites at the royal banquets staged for tourists, who don the golden robes of emperors for an evening of Vietnamese food and music at the Huong Giang Hotel. Many an evening I have seen him clomping regally around the hotel grounds in his scroll-toed platform boots, wearing a brocade court robe and a winged mandarin hat. All of his immediate family now works for the Monuments Conservation Center, the Huong Giang Hotel or in the royal feasts business.

The colour photographs beneath the glass table top, it transpires, are pictures taken at the many royal feasts over which he has presided. He is pleased to tell me that he is also well known because he likes bonsai.

Our interview at an end, he gallantly invites me to lunch at a nearby restaurant. He claps on a felt hat, hops on the back of his young uncle's motorbike – a might-have-been emperor, a prince on a motorbike – and off we go, me in a cyclo.

At the Blue Sky Restaurant (Thien Thanh), the tannoy is playing *Besame mucho*. As we sip Heineken beers, Bao Hien insists that I choose one dish. I skim the menu and finally point to grilled shrimp with garlic, salt and pepper. Imagine my chagrin when one shrimp arrives in the centre of a plate, prettily garnished with slices of tomato and cucumber.

Clearly, I have ordered – the wrong thing.

In a moment, another plate arrives bearing four well-browned sparrows, complete with their little round heads, beaks and fragile, stick-like legs. As though I were presented with a plateful of tiny brown birds every day of the week, nonchalantly I grasp one with my chopsticks and drop it into my rice bowl. Taking another long draught of beer, I pick up the tiny bird with my chopsticks, close my eyes, think of England and take a bite out of one side. Very crunchy. After another large gulp of Heineken, I take a second bite. That's it. I simply cannot bring myself to eat the pathetic looking little legs and the head and leave them lying forlornly in the bowl. Politely, nobody says anything. By then a huge plate of delicious spring rolls, *nem,* stuffed with pork, bean sprouts, herbs and mushrooms, have arrived and I do my best to forget the tiny birds. Later, I ask the owner of the restaurant how they remove the feathers.

'By dropping them in boiling water,' she replies. 'They are sparrows and had to be ordered especially from the market.' I refrain from asking if they arrived at the restaurant alive.

During the course of the meal, Bao Hien tells me that he has never been abroad and has no desire to leave his country. I ask if he is worried, as the country opens its doors to the world and rushes towards a market economy, that Vietnam might lose many of its long held cultural values.

For a man whose family has uniquely flourished in the past, then suffered and survived terrifying and distressing times, one might have expected him to take a conservative view. Instead, lifting his arms wide, he replies with just three words: *'Ouvrez les portes!'* – 'Open the doors!'

THE CITADEL – VIETNAM'S LAST IMPERIAL CAPITAL

The mandarin passes by,
the people remain
– Vietnamese proverb

Reflected in the moat by day or floodlit by night, Ngo Mon, the main gate to the walled city within the Citadel, is one of the most majestic structures remaining of the former Imperial City of the Nguyen dynasty. Its massive, squared U-shaped, stone base looms like a fortress, 'signifying the open arms of welcome.'

You could hardly imagine a more forbidding gate. Green and yellow glazed tiles gleam from the roofs of the open Five Phoenix Pavilion floating above it, the corners of its roofs turned up like any self-respecting oriental building. I am surprised to learn that Ngo Mon (Noon Gate) was built as recently as 1833 (restored in 1992 with Japanese aid).

Accompanying me this time is Tao, a knowledgeable young music student, daughter of a distinguished historian, Phan Thuan An, who I met at the Conservation of Monuments Center. We are ambushed by little girls selling strings of miniature straw hats and note cards, each with a hand-painted landscape on silk.

'The central entrance beneath the imperial, yellow-tiled roof was formerly reserved exclusively for the emperor,' Tao explains – and presumably, his palanquin bearers. Civil mandarin filed through the left archway, military mandarin through the right' – under ordinary green-tiled roofs, I note. 'The two wing entrances were reserved for horses, elephants and soldiers.'

It must have been quite a spectacle. Paris may have its Arc de Triomphe, Hue has Ngo Mon, Hanoi has – well, Ho Chi Minh's Mausoleum. Naturally, dragons exult heraldically on the roofs of the Five Phoenix Pavilion.

'Dragons, simultaneously represent the symbol of power and the power of the emperor,' says Tao. So it is little wonder that stone and mosaic dragons ripple and hiss over nearly every ridge-line of every palace, pagoda and temple in Vietnam and that inside, they curl and wind themselves around every carved, painted, gilt and lacquered pillar as well.

'No women were allowed to enter Ngo Mon,' says Tao. 'During royal ceremonies, only female members of the royal household – the queen mother, the queen and perhaps a few privileged wives – were permitted to watch discreetly from behind the wooden screens of the Five Phoenix Pavilion, where they could not be seen. Common people had to watch from beyond the lotus ponds of the moat.'

Up in the pavilion, we find ourselves among a hundred thick, glowing, red lacquered pillars, crawling with golden dragons. Suddenly, in the glowing, reflected red light, though not at all the same colour, oddly, I am reminded of a jewellery box I was given as a child by a sailor in the family – a lacquered box with a few brush strokes to evoke a branch of bamboo and inside the hinged lid, tiny thin-walled compartments, cushioned and lined with shocking pink silk. Could this precious, long forgotten childhood treasure be the source of my fascination with Asia? Memory and the subconscious are strange countries.

'Until 1945, in feudal times a yellow flag emblazoned with the imperial dragon flapped from the flag pole,' Tao explains, pointing to the monumental, pyramid flag tower opposite.

Tao then leads me to the exact spot in the centre of the pavilion where the last emperor, Bao Dai, stood to abdicate in 1945, saying that he would far rather be a common man than emperor of an enslaved nation. I look out over the empty court and lotus ponds towards the flag tower. By the time he abdicated, thanks first to French colonisation, then to Japanese occupation, followed again by the French, Bao Dai might well have felt himself more a common man than an emperor.

'The huge drum was struck whenever the emperor arrived or departed, and its boom signalled to the flag tower sentries to fire the cannons, marking the closing of the gates to the Imperial City at the end of every day.'

The drumhead has been slashed, perhaps to symbolise that the drum of feudalism has been silenced, hardly surprising in a city that has survived three major military conflicts. Looking out from the Five Phoenix Pavilion, it is hardly discernible, but the walled Citadel, built roughly square to accommodate the curve of the river bank, measures nearly six miles (10 km) in circumference. The original walls, raised in 1805 by the first Nguyen emperor, Gia Long, were of earth. The second emperor, Minh Mang, covered them with brick between 1818 and 1821. Ten entrances pierce these walls, eighteen feet high and sixty feet thick.

Below, in the lily-choked moat protecting the city walls, fishermen in boats are trying their luck. The scene is breathtakingly, orientally exotic.

From Ngo Mon, paved walkways and bridges lead from one official palace to another – Ngo Mon was clearly the ceremonial gate. However, throughout the Nguyen dynasties, the majority of the population actually lived within the walls of the Citadel – a royal walled city. Inside were two more walled enclosures: the Imperial City, also known as the Great Enclosure, where court ceremonies were held and mandarin went about their business and the innermost sanctum, the Forbidden Purple City. When Tao explained that only emperors were permitted to wear yellow and that yellow tiles could only be used for the emperor's palace. It raised a question, why the Forbidden *Purple* City? One plausible explanation is that the Chinese character for forbidden or hidden is phonetically pronounced *chia*. In Vietnamese, *chia* means purple. Also, the walls of the innermost sanctum were originally painted purple. Like most things Vietnamese, the innermost Forbidden Purple City was also known by several other names: the Everlasting Longevity Palace and the Great Within.

'Into this inner sanctum, only the emperor and the royal family, his wives and concubines, servants and eunuchs were allowed' – albeit a crowd of several hundred. Even mandarin were excluded and there came a time in the life of every young royal prince, at sixteen for princes, at thirteen for princesses, when they were thrust out of the Forbidden Purple City to be educated in the (middle) Imperial City. I suppose it would have been unwise not to separate royal princes from the numerous idle and bored, young 'wives' of the royal household. Having been built of wood, few of the original buildings of the Forbidden Purple City remain. Those that do or have been restored, are a glory to behold.

'A masterpiece of urban poetry' is how Amadou-Mahtar-M'Bow, director general of UNESCO described Hue in 1983. Yet it took another ten years before UNESCO declared Hue a Site of World Cultural Heritage. According to the director of the Hue Monuments Conservation Center, Nguyen Thai Cong, restoration of Hue's monuments is only limited by the funds available. The Center has a ten-year master plan, a middle-term plan for the next five or six years and a detailed plan for each year.

A jade and marble collage mounted on one wall of the Five Phoenix Pavilion depicts a ceremony that doubtless took place here many times, the Proclaiming of the List, announcing the candidates who had successfully passed the triennial doctoral examinations. In the tableau, four rows of candidates kneel in the courtyard of Ngo Mon, the select, destined to become mandarin.

Elaborately caparisoned elephants mark the four corners of the courtyard, flanked by orderly lines of musicians, soldiers and mandarin, placed to exactly balanced, Confucian perfection. The last such ceremony took place here in 1919 under the penultimate emperor, Khai Dinh.

From Ngo Mon, we stroll over the Central Path Bridge, crossing square Lake of Great Waters, bordered by white flowering frangipani trees. Bright pink lotus blossoms spike the green lily pads like stepping stones on the surfaces of the lake, dew glistening like mercury on the dry lily pads. No need to be a Confucian to appreciate the beauty of the scene. Four slim bronze columns, trailing dragons and clouds, form an open gateway at the end of the bridge, each column topped by a colourful enamel lotus bud.

The Nguyens left no surface, no pillar nor post undecorated, and decorated finely with elaborately carved, cast, gilt, painted, enamelled or mosaic designs. Yet the plethora of embellishment culminates in a harmonious whole, each element, following the Confucian ideal, symmetrically balanced by another. Beyond the bridge lies the paved Great Rites Court, also known as the Esplanade of Great Salutation, where ceremonies were held. Tao points to the rows of stone stelae along the sides.

'Each stelae marks the row where mandarin once took their positions, according to rank, grades one to three on the upper level nearest the emperor, grades four to nine in the lower court, the colours of their robes and headgear indicating rank.' It must have been an impressive sight.

At the far corners of the courtyard stand two bronze 'kylins', which Tao translates as 'unicorns', English lacking a wide selection of mythical beasts; they have not the slightest resemblance to single-horned unicorns.

'The role of these mythical beasts, despite their ferociousness – part lion, part crocodile, part dragon – is to act as harbingers of peace and as reminders of ritual solemnity.' To the uninitiated, they look like rather savage temple dogs.

108

Overlooking the Great Rites Court is the Palace of Supreme Harmony (Thai Hoa), also known as the Throne Palace. Inside, the focal point, dwarfed between an elaborately carved, three-tiered gilt canopy above and a three-tiered dais below, is the smallish gilt chair that served as the throne for thirteen Nguyen emperors. Tao tells me that from this throne, one could distinctly hear sounds made anywhere within the palace, a phenomenon so far no acoustics expert has been able to explain. No one is allowed to pose for photographs sitting on the royal throne.

A workman perches up a ladder, re-gilding the canopy. Feudalism may have passed, but craftsmen continue to do the same work. Each of the eighty, thick, ironwood pillars carries more than ten gleaming layers of red lacquer and splendid, prancing, golden dragons. (UNESCO provided the money to replace the pillars, eaten up through the centre by termites.)

A cornice of decorative panels, alternating poems and flowers, rings the upper walls.

'The poems were composed by emperors and their mandarin, praising either an emperor or a landscape.' The lower walls gleam with lacquer and gilt panelling. It was here in the Palace of Supreme Harmony that certain solemn ceremonies took place: the emperor's coronation, the crown prince's coronation, the emperor's birthday, the ambassador-receiving ceremony. Large meetings of the emperor and the mandarin were held here twice a month.

In 1910 a Frenchman, Robert de la Susse, described a court ceremony held in the Palace of Supreme Harmony under Emperor Duy Tan (Bao Hien's uncle).

'The Emperor sat on the throne, frozen in a formulated posture. He wore a golden crown, a yellow silk robe and was separated as a sacred man from the court by a wisp of smoke which arose from the incense-burner in the dim light below the canopy . . .

'Outside, in a brick-paved court, about two hundred high-ranking mandarin, all in court robes, lined in strict order according to their ranks and titles. On both sides of the court were several persons holding parasols, musicians, singers and soldiers. Farther, stood richly adorned elephants, then the imperial sentinels and finally the massive background of the Noon Gate, magnificent with the Royal Screen Mount looming on the horizon in the hilly area beyond Hue.

'Suddenly in the lingering silence, arose a singsong tune wafted by a melody with a strange rising and falling rhythm. Then in a unanimous movement, all princes and mandarin bowed, knelt down, prostrated themselves on the ground and resumed their position. These prostrations were repeated several times during the ceremony. What an imposing and significant scene! High-ranking mandarin, most of them were white-haired elders, attired in court robes of precious silk, blazing in the sun, prostrated themselves in respect to an existent and remote monarchy.'

Nine imperial dragons graced the Emperor's crown. With his yellow-gold robe, he wore a jade belt, brocade platform boots and held in his hands a thin jade tablet, a *tran que,* which had a mirror on one side 'to emphasise the solemnity of the ceremonies or perhaps to ascertain that everything about his person was in place' – or that no one was lurking behind him.

Only four high-ranking mandarin and princes were allowed to stand inside the Palace of Supreme Harmony, the others, outside in the sunny courtyard. Fortunately for the mandarin, most such meetings were held very early in the morning and ended at sunrise. Otherwise, in summer they would have baked in their court finery.

To left and right behind the Palace of Supreme Harmony stand buildings once used as offices for the mandarin. How ironic that their ceramic window screens form the Chinese character for longevity. In the building on the left, commoners can now don court robes to have their photographs taken, seated on a replica throne. Surprisingly, a good many Vietnamese do. In the grassy field behind the Palace of Supreme Harmony, a forlorn potted palm marks the former position of the Great Golden Gate (Dai Cung Mon), the gate to the Forbidden Purple City. Within stood the Palace of Audiences (Can Chanh), 'the emperor's working palace.'

Two huge bronze cauldrons rest in the grass where Can Chanh Palace once stood, only the foundations discernible. According to Tao, ten or more of these victory cauldrons are strewn around Hue, cast from Dutch cannons to celebrate the defeat in the mid-eighteenth century of the Dutch Navy.

One story goes that the origin of large urns as a symbol of an emperor's power derived from one of the first rulers of the newly independent Vietnam, Dinh Bo Linh (923-979), after the Chinese were ousted in 938. In the courtyard of his palace at Hoa Lu, then the capital, south-west of Hanoi, he displayed a huge cauldron and a caged tiger, having decreed that: 'Those who violate the laws will be boiled and gnawed.'

Historians adamantly remain unable to verify this account from written records.

Behind the working palace stood the emperor's private residential palace (Dien Can Thanh) and conveniently near, off to the left, the palaces of his wives. The working palace and the residential palaces of the emperor and empress were demolished by bombs during World War II. The quarters of the royal wives were destroyed during the Tet Offensive of 1968.

In the far reaches of the grassy field, two tiny tea-houses have been reconstructed, thanks to a $10,000 grant from the Canadian government, their mosaic dragons rollicking along the ridge lines of their roofs. How little it takes to accomplish restoration work here.

Beyond the tea houses, two stone lions guard a desolate stairway to nowhere that once led to the European style villa of the last but one emperor, Khai Dinh.

Off to the right is one of the most exquisite buildings of the entire complex, the completely rebuilt theatre within the Imperial City, its gilt and lacquer gleaming. This is how it must have looked when it was first built.

Standing with our backs to the Throne Palace, Tao then says that it is very easy to miss the important temples off to the left, down a leafy walled lane, past a lady in a post office kiosk, who greets everyone with a cheerful *bonjour*. Off to the right lie ruins of the queen's former palace (Dien Tho), and her tea house. A few steps further on the left, a narrow doorway leads to three historically significant royal temples. The first is Hung To Mieu, built in 1804 by the first Nguyen emperor, Gia Long, to honour his parents, particularly his father, Nguyen Phuc Luan, who had been assassinated by a jealous mandarin (restored 1997). Next door to Hung To Mieu temple is the almost identical The To Mieu temple, constructed during the reign of the second emperor, Minh Mang (1820-40) and now, dedicated to all of the Nguyen emperors (1802-1945). Under French domination (1884-1954), only seven emperors were honoured: Gia Long, Minh Mang, Thieu Tri, Tu Duc, Kien Phuc, Dong Khanh and Khai Dinh. The anti-French emperors – Thanh Thai, Duy Tan and Ham Nghi – were excluded until 1959.

The much-photographed rank of nine imperial bronze urns – one of the first photographs I ever saw of Vietnam – stand in a line in the courtyard between Thieu Tri Mieu and the Hien Lam Pavilion.

The height of the restored second-storey tower of Hien Lam Pavilion, at forty-two feet (13 m) high, marks the upper limit for any building within the Citadel.

The casting of each urn, each dedicated to an emperor of the Nguyen dynasty, required two tons of bronze at a time when melting pots held just over half a kilo (one pound). Casting an urn therefore needed an enormous number of melting pots to produce the necessary quantity of molten metal. To get all of the pots to the melting point simultaneously must have been a delicate task. Modern moulders think it likely that the urn mould was turned upside down and the molten bronze poured through the openings for the three slender legs of the urn. Casting of the urns (1835-1837) was ordered by the second emperor, Minh Mang, who is recorded to have said: 'I see that the urns are being prepared with great dexterity, quite worth praising. Therefore, among the goldsmiths working, those who are the original members of the handicraft unit who came from the region of Thua Thien and the province of Binh Dinh, are to be rewarded one *quan*. The remainder called up by the provinces as supplementary personnel for the unit are to be rewarded two *quan* in the case of those who came from Ha Tinh or Nghe An, and three *quan* in the case of those who came from Ha Noi.'

Today no one knows the value then represented by a *quan*.

The decoration on the sides of the urns – bats, turtles, dragons, cranes, carriages, trees and flowers – were cast separately and riveted to the surface. The idea of casting nine commemorative urns derives from China. Minh Mang named each of the nine urns in advance, so the posthumous name of each future Nguyen emperor had to incorporate the name of the waiting urn in turn. For instance, Minh Mang's urn was called Nhan; therefore his posthumous name became Thai To Nhan Hoang De. Tu Duc's urn was named Anh; his posthumous name became Duc Tong Anh Hoang De. These days the urns have adapted to political correctness and honour the reunification of Vietnam.

Might it be that because the Vietnamese were ruled by a feudal court for two thousand years, first by the Chinese from a distance, then by their own, that I feel much closer to Vietnam's history standing in Hue's Citadel than say, standing in the much older Temple of Literature in Hanoi?

SERVANT TO THE QUEEN

To a frog at the bottom of a well,
the sky is as big as a lid
– Vietnamese proverb

Pham Van Thiet is a very old man. His eyes in his hollow-cheeked, bony face, have a far-away look. He welcomes me with a sinewy, outstretched arm in the garden of the large French-style villa where he lives, wearing a short-sleeved khaki shirt with a Ho Chi Minh collar and incongruously, Prince of Wales checked trousers. The villa was the home of the former queen mum, Tu Cung, mother of the last emperor, Bao Dai. She died in 1980 at the age of ninety-one.

A photograph of the queen mother as a young woman takes pride of place on the carved, red and gilt altar that fills the entrance hall. Pham Van Thiet leads me into a long, formal salon where two rows of threadbare, silk upholstered, gilt dining chairs stand rigidly to attention like mandarin, facing one another across a court of low tea tables. Elaborately carved, black and gold Vietnamese style, glass-front display cabinets line the walls, holding the family photographs that would have been dear to a granny. Pham Van Thiet identifies the subjects in the photographs. In the place of honour in the first cupboard are two tinted photographs of her son, Bao Dai, and his young wife, Nam Phuong, taken at the time of their wedding in 1933.

'He would have been twenty, she nineteen – and a Catholic. They met on board ship en route back from France where Bao Dai had been a student. On the death of his father, Khai Dinh, Bao Dai was crowned emperor at the age of twelve, then returned to France to continue his studies. During his years in France, four senior mandarin looked after the affairs of court – those not looked after by the French.' The photographs of the young couple show not the slightest hint of what transpired before they were allowed to marry.

'When Bao Dai told his mother that he wished to marry a Catholic, she was distraught. This would mean that the heir would be Catholic and therefore, unable to celebrate the ceremony of the ancestors to the gods. The court had the same concern. But Bao Dai was steadfastly determined to marry Nam Phuong.

'The wedding took place the 20th of March 1934 before the court and the representative of France within the Imperial City and Bao Dai immediately declared his new wife queen.'

In earlier times, the noble title often would not have been bestowed upon the favourite wife of an emperor until after his death.

'Bao Dai also created a new title for her: 'Perfume of the South' and proclaimed a new law permitting her to wear yellow, the colour previously reserved exclusively for the emperor.'

Even more of a heresy, the marriage was celebrated in Can Chanh, the work palace, where two high ranks of mandarin stood to attention facing one another before the emperor. This was the first time in the history of the Nguyen dynasty – or in Vietnam for that matter – that a woman had been presented to the mandarin at court. The bride wore a huge royal robe with turned-up toed silk shoes and a royal hat decorated with jewels and pearls. She came before the emperor and prostrated herself three times, then as instructed, seated herself on his right.

'The ceremony, lacking ritual precedent, was fairly quick.'

In one corner of the drawing room, a glazed porcelain head of Bao Dai rests on a pedestal. Nearby is a family photograph of Bao Dai, his wife and their first two children, a boy and a girl, taken with granny around 1937.

'Bao Dai converted to Catholicism in 1980 – realising his mother's worst fears – and thereafter, theoretically, was allowed only one wife. But he had several' . . . Pham Van Thiet trails off, leaving me to find an appropriate word. A large painting of Khai Dinh, husband of Tu Cong, the queen mother, shares the wall above the cupboards with a matching portrait of the young queen (mum) – wearing a yellow court robe and a crown – in retrospect – she would never have been allowed to wear yellow during her husband's reign.

'The portraits were painted from photographs by a Japanese artist in 1944, Khai Dinh having died much earlier in 1925 at the age of forty-one.' Then I hear the most amazing story . . . 'Bao Dai was not the son of emperor Khai Dinh,' Pham Van Thiet confides – a fact not recorded by historians.

'He was the son of another member of the royal family. According to much evidence, Khai Dinh was a homosexual, but that hardly relieved him of the requirement for nine wives. 'His "escort", a euphemism for lover, was well known in court circles and even attained the fifth rank. The story of Khai Dinh's first wife, De Nhat

114

Giai Phi Truong, was rather tragic. The daughter of a mandarin, she married him before he attained the throne. As a crown prince, he had little money and like many a crown prince, was probably bored, took to gambling at cards and invariably turned to his wife to ask her father to pay his gambling debts.

'The father, although he was a mandarin, was not particularly rich. What he had, he had saved judiciously through the years. Finally, in a true test of luck, the prince wanted to go for broke, but his gambling friends refused unless he produced the wager in cash.

'He told his wife to ask her father for the money to save his face. His wife, despite her sadness at her husband's physical "incapacity", recognised equally his cowardliness and refused. He was furious, insulted and threatened her.

Desperate and angry – she could not approach her father for money yet again – she felt obliged to leave everything, the palace, her life as a royal wife. She retired to a pagoda that she had built for herself on a hill in the village of Thanh Thuy in the district of Huong Thuy, two miles (3 km) from Hue. Later, after he became emperor, Khai Dinh sent a mandarin to the pagoda to bring her back to the Forbidden Purple City, intending to give her the noble title of Wife of the First Rank, but she refused.

'Khai Dinh's second wife, Ho Thi Chi, was the daughter of an ambitious father who accepted the lonely, loveless life of a royal wife with the intention of gaining power and riches, and ultimately, the title of queen mother. It was to no avail. She died childless, alienated and old in a Catholic monastery.

'Bao Dai's natural mother, Tu Cong, was not of a noble family. She was Khai Dinh's third wife, became queen and ultimately was honoured as queen mother, only because she had a child.'

Of course, my romantic curiosity is stirred. Had the last emperor, Bao Dai, been the love child of some secret alliance, was he the product of a political ploy by another faction of the family, or a child born out of grim duty contrary to the strict Buddhist beliefs held by his mother?

Naturally, I was intrigued to know who Bao Dai's real father was, but oriental discretion ruled, even so many years after the old lady's death.

Later, in a little book written by one Nguyen Dac Xuan, I found an astonishing story. Khai Dinh, recognising the need for a successor, consulted a relative of his own age, concerning his difficult

115

situation 'with whom in the past he had had an intimate relationship and unforgettable good memories.' Together they concocted the story that 'one day, after taking a perfumed medicinal concoction laced with ginseng, Khai Dinh felt so strong and passionate that he desired a woman and took his third wife, who became pregnant.'

Then we have a most appalling trial of a woman, perpetrated by women. Not believing her story, Tu Cung's mothers-in-law, Khai Dinh's two 'mothers', the two wives of Dong Khanh, his natural mother, Thanh Cung, and his wet-nurse, Tien Cung, and others in the family, had a hole dug eight inches deep and made Hoang Tu Cung lie stomach down in the hole, beating her in turn to find out if she was truly pregnant by Khai Dinh. No matter how much they beat her, Tu Cung insisted that Khai Dinh had made love to her and made her pregnant. Finally satisfied, the grandmothers were delighted and proclaimed that their son was to become a father. Everyone had to accept the story, whether they believed it or not.

Much later, a mandarin of the fifth rank, Phan Van Dat, declared the concocted story untrue, saying that the pregnancy was by Huong D, the relative to whom Khai Dinh had turned for advice. He stated as evidence that when he became emperor, Khai Dinh bestowed power and wealth on Huong D.

The mandarin took further evidence from the family history written by the son of Huong D, Ung Dong, who recorded that at royal family gatherings at the palace, his father was often referred to by the title, 'the professor brother of the former king', thus proving that he, Ung Dong and Bao Dai were cousins, or half-brothers, of whom the father was Huong D.

The son, Ung Dong, often said, 'In 1912 my father and the prince (Khai Dinh) were two dear friends, eating and sleeping together on the same mat. In October 1913, the prince Bao Dai was born. A month and a half later, Ung Linh, the official son of Huong D was also born. These two children as adults resembled one another a great deal.'

Ung Dong also recorded that his maternal grandmother often went to visit the queen mother, Tu Cung, the mother of Bao Dai, who always called her Di, grandmother, although his grandmother had no family tie with her whatsoever. This, he maintained, further proved that the mother of Bao Dai considered Huong D to be her husband. The queen mother would often say to the mother of Huong D, 'When his majesty returns, will you bring Linh, (the son of Huong D) here,

116

so that he can help him.' The two boys grew up together like brothers. The following anecdote reinforces the story.

In 1934 when Huong D attempted to visit Bao Dai in the Imperial City, the French guards refused to let him enter. Returning home, Huong D went into a rage and reportedly shouted, 'Dogs, they have no respect for me – although I am the father of the king.'

As might be expected, there are many photographs of the eldest granddaughter and grandson, Bao Long. In one photograph the handsome grandson stands erect in the white uniform of a French soldier, taken while he was a cadet at St Cyr. Opposite is a photograph of him as a small boy of seven, almost choked by heavy brocade court robes, taken at the ceremony when he was named crown prince. Bao Dai had five children and there are group photographs taken of them in Paris as well as individually, wearing royal robes when they were younger.

In open-handed fairness, the old servant points to the next cupboard, devoted to Bao Dai's second family, which holds the photograph of his (simultaneous) second wife or mistress, Mong Diep, by whom he had two more children.

Then he proudly hands me a black-and-white snapshot taken in October 1945, developed from a negative he had only recently found. It is a photograph of Bao Dai, Ho Chi Minh, an American officer, General Garogret and several famous Vietnamese scholars.

Exactly how Pham Van Thiet came to live in the Forbidden Purple City to become the only manservant of the queen is a very Vietnamese sequence of events.

'While the prince, Bao Dai, was still a child, his forward thinking mother had gone to a pagoda and asked a Buddhist monk to look for a suitable little girl that she might adopt. The monk introduced her to one of his own nieces and the queen mother adopted the child, bringing her into the palace as a royal princess.'

The little girl missed her little brother so much that the queen mother asked her to introduce her younger brother. Obviously, a boy could not be adopted by the queen mother, so at the age of twelve, Pham Van Thiet joined the queen mother's royal household as her one close manservant, a neat Vietnamese solution. It had been the queen mother's fond desire that her son should marry her adopted daughter, Pham Van Thiet's sister. But the plan was thwarted when Bao Dai fell in love with Nam Phuong on board ship.

117

'There was even talk that Nam Phuong had been intentionally planted on the ship by the French who wanted Bao Dai to marry a Catholic.' Pham Van Thiet's disappointed intended sister later married a younger brother of the queen mother, thereby still making a royal alliance, albeit not quite of the same grandeur.

It was in 1937 that Pham Van Thiet first came to the royal palace in the Forbidden Purple City to serve the queen mother in the French style villa in the Citadel where now the steps lead to nowhere.

'In the mornings I attended school, in the afternoons I returned to the palace and learned to play classical musical instruments. In the evenings I studied the royal rites of the palace and at night, slept in the servants' quarters of the Imperial City.'

At that time the queen mother would have been about forty-eight. Once Pham Van Thiet had finished his education, he took up his full time duties. He finds it rather difficult to describe exactly what they were, 'Something like a bellboy.'

He was allowed to get up whenever he pleased, because mostly his duties involved going to houses to invite friends to come to play cards or *mat chuoc,* a Vietnamese form of *mah-jong.* It was his duty to be there for the queen mother, to do whatever needed doing, particularly whenever a pair of male hands were needed. Apart from Thiet, there were ten female servants: a cook, an ironer, a shopper, a driver. 'There were too many servants, so sometimes they were idle, but whenever the queen mother called, someone had to rush to her. Sometimes when the queen mother went out, a servant went with her to carry her box of betel leaves and areca nuts. Every night when the queen mother slept, there were usually four female servants on hand to massage and fan her, because she didn't like mosquito nets. She was rather strict.'

While serving the queen mother, young Thiet wore a long black gown and a black headband. Even when he went to bed, he always kept the headband nearby because sometimes she would call for him in the night. 'There were female mandarin, who wore ivory tablets to indicate their rank. Whenever the emperor wanted to see his mother, a female mandarin would bring the order from the emperor. A female mandarin was also charged with discipline of the female servants, having the authority to punish or sack them. There was an equivalent male mandarin in charge of male servants.'

Pham Van Thiet remembers very few instances when he was punished, rarely more than a reproach, when the queen mother had wanted him to do something and he had done something else, having misunderstood. At exactly eighteen, he married a girl to whom he had been introduced by the queen mother. His wife was not allowed to enter the Imperial City, so in the daytime from time to time, he was allowed to leave the palace to spend time with her. At night he had to sleep with the royal servants, although 'sometimes with special permission, he was permitted to stay outside.' Usually he 'had to stay at home to await orders from the queen mother.'

Until the August Revolution of 1945, he lived inside the Imperial City with the servants and contact with other people was restricted. 'It was only after 1945 that the royal servants became freer to go out and began to learn about society.'

Pham Van Thiet's first wife left him after the August Revolution. He later married another woman and had five children. She died in 1996. He has six children, three sons and three daughters, some in Hue, some in Ho Chi Minh City.

'After the revolution, the queen mother had to move out of the palace and into an enormous villa outside the Citadel.' In her changed circumstances, only Pham Van Thiet and one close female servant remained to serve her.

'She was given an allowance, as were all nine of Khai Dinh's former wives, most of whom were only seventeen to nineteen years old when he died. Unlike in times past, they were even allowed to remarry, although they had to give up the allowance if they did. Six found new husbands. Of the three who never remarried, one was the queen mother. One went to live with relatives and the third went to a pagoda as a nun.'

Pham Van Thiet's own salary was not very much, so in addition to working for the queen mother, he worked as a building contractor – got estimates and supervised the work – to earn money.

'After Bao Dai's abdication and move to France, the former emperor tried many times to get his mother to join him. But she always refused, saying, "I was born in Vietnam and I will die in my birth place." She loved her country very much. She had come from a peasant family, she treated the servants well and tried to help the people. She was a very devout Buddhist '

In 1956 the queen mother was forced to move once again when President Ngo Dien Diem of South Vietnam allocated her villa to his brother. She then bought this villa and had it repaired.'

Pham Van Thiet has lived here ever since, serving her until she died. Only a few things have been changed. After her death he moved the inlaid mother-of-pearl sofas and tables from the central hallway to the dining room where we now sit and installed the altar in the entrance hall. Musical instruments hang from the walls: a moon-shaped lute, a couple of fiddles, and at the far end of the room, a monochord lies on a low marble-topped divan bed *(sap)*, beneath a wall calendar.

Yes, he used to play music for the queen mother and she passed the time by visiting friends, playing cards.

'But every first, fourteenth, fifteenth, sixteenth and thirtieth of the lunar month, she would be upstairs at an altar praying to Buddha and her ancestors.' Pham Van Thiet retains warm sentiments for the queen mother. He had lived with her since he was a child and loved her almost as a mother. When she died, he wrote a poem expressing his grief, which is part of a carefully handwritten manuscript describing his life that one day he hopes his nephew in California will be able to have published.

Has he any regrets? The old man thinks for a few moments before replying. 'I have not followed any regime, not French, not Japanese, not American, nor the present. I have always felt comfort that I did not have to follow any government.'

He goes on to explain that he feels fortunate that his position has been respected by the many regimes. Now he raises birds – sparrows, blue birds and parrots – because the queen mother as a devout Buddhist would not allow him to keep caged birds while she was alive. He takes up the moon-shaped guitar and haltingly plays a piece, *Flowing Water (Luu Thuy)*, once much loved by the queen mother. Then we move to the far end of the room and he settles with one leg folded under the other, a toe resting on the instrument's soundboard as he plays the monochord. Several pairs of sandals line up beneath the divan bed on which he sits.

'Southern melodies are melancholy.'

A TRADITIONAL MUSIC LESSON

Girls look for talent, boys for beauty
– Vietnamese proverb

'Rhythm is a very big problem,' says Thao emphatically, regarding me with serious eyes from behind her glasses.

Thao means 'grass', an odd name for a charming young girl, I think, until I consider the poetic connotations. In Vietnam, grass is forever green, as soft as velvet, cooling and restful to the eye.

Rarely does a writer find the perfect source, someone who knows everything you want to know about a subject, who has a tidy mind and can explain things in an orderly way, who doesn't swamp you with more information than you can possibly assimilate, and in this instance, most important of all, whose command of English is not only idiomatic, but who knows the correct musical terminology to explain exactly what she means.

Thao is just such a source, an English graduate from Hue University, who first qualified as a tour guide – it was she who took me through the Citadel the second time – and who has subsequently completed a master's degree in traditional Vietnamese music.

'Rhythm isn't written down, exactly,' she explains. This is an understatement. But let's hold off notation for the moment. As I started university as a music student, I am particularly interested in Vietnamese traditional music. Thao begins by saying that traditional music is different in the North (Hanoi), that the instruments are different, and even the instruments in common are tuned differently.

'The speaking voices and the singing of people in the North are higher than those of people in the centre of the country and further south.' One assumes then, that they never try to sing together.

'The five basic instruments are the same North and South.' Tao lists them:

horizontal sixteen-string zither that is plucked, *dan tranh*
long-necked round, moon-shaped guitar, *nguyet*
two-string fiddle, its sound box shaped like a pipe bowl, *dan nhi*
pear-shaped lute, *dan ty ba*
monochord, *dan bau,* my favourite

I secretly think of it as the 'vibrator', because of its thin upright wooden cane curled at the tip, which the player vibrates with the left hand while one horizontal string drawn over the sound box is plucked with the right hand. The *dan bau* produces a sorrowful, lingering melodic line. Other instruments include a kind of oboe used in religious music, bamboo flutes, various drums and percussion instruments such as wooden knockers, coin clappers and china teacups, two held in each hand and rung together a bit like maracas.

Vietnam has long been a very musical nation and traditional Vietnamese music includes a wide variety of genres.

'There are various types of court music, *nhac cung dinh.*'

Thao explains that court music might be 'small music', performed by an ensemble of eight to ten instruments; 'great music', performed by a chamber orchestra of forty-two instruments; or 'elegant music', performed at important ceremonies by an 'eight material' orchestra made up of thirty to forty instruments, the instruments constructed from the eight natural materials: bamboo, gourd, wood, earth, stone, metal, silk and skin.

'Vietnamese classical opera, *tuong,* originated in the North,' but as Mrs Nguyen Thi Nhung had told me in Hanoi, it reached its highest development in Hue under the Nguyen dynasty.

'Of course, there are folk songs of many kinds – *Ho, Ly* and *Ve.* One of the characteristics of folk music in and around Hue is that as it was taken up by the Nguyen court, it became refined, more sophisticated and eventually, transmogrified, and joined the body of traditional classical music. The famous Hue singing *(ca Hue),* is a repertoire of melancholy love songs performed as chamber music or on the river boats. The music played in the water puppet theatre is yet another kind of folk music. So is the music of comic folk opera *(cheo),*that is sung and danced, both of which originated in peasant villages of the North. Another type of theatre music, *cai luong,* which evolved from *cheo,* originated in the South around Saigon as a part of twentieth century musical drama.'

Then Tao unravels the mystery of the elegant woman seated on a mat at the Folk Music Club in Hanoi, singing a long narrative, during which the audience tittered throughout. 'In the North there are long epic poems, formerly performed by a solo singer in a public house for a paying patron, who beats a tiny drum to register his response. These are called *ha't A Dao* after a famous eleventh century singer. *H'at* means singing, *A* means Miss and *Dao* was the singer's family name.'

So *ha't A Dao* means, rather touchingly, 'Miss Dao's singing.'

'Then there is a whole body of religious music, again, several different types.' I would never have guessed that the page Thao hands me is musical notation. 'Not much music has been written down in Vietnam', she explains, 'and there is no standard notation for what has been written down. Young musicians must learn the repertoire for their instrument by rote, by ear, from a master musician.'

The page of notation she shows me has been specifically written for the moon-shaped guitar, which she is learning to play. She impresses upon me that it is important to know that it has been annotated by a musician named Hoang Yen around 1915, according to his own style and system of notation. Each musician uses his own individual style of notation!

The only similarity between this Vietnamese musical score and say, a piece of Western instrumental part music, is that there is a five-line staff spread across the page and a few vertical lines. Each note of Vietnamese music is written as a *chu nom* ideogram beneath the staff – in calligraphy. Early music was meant to be read from top to bottom, right to left like a Chinese scroll. This score conforms to the custom of reading Roman script, from left to right. The notes of one of the five-tone scales translate approximately as: do, re, (no mi), fa, so, la, (no ti). The five-tone scale, Thao impresses upon me, dates from before Christ.

'Two or more additional modes or scales may be added and played simultaneously in order to obtain – more notes.'

When I try to find out what pitches are represented in these additional scales, things get very complicated. As there have been books written by musicologists discussing the differences between the scales in the North and the South, we decide to leave it to the experts. Suffice it to say that a Vietnamese can tell instantly whether an ensemble is from the North, Central, or South of the country, hearing the differences in the scale.

'There are no key signatures. Everything is played in one key. Nor is there a standard pitch. Musicians try to tune to the flute, but each bamboo flute is slightly different.'

Returning to notation, the music staff marks the end of similarity to Western notation. A tiny round circle breaking a horizontal line indicates – not a note – but a bar, or a measure.

A vertical line marks the beat. Then the interpretation begins. 'There is no indication of tempo, nor dynamics. The length of any note is indicated by the space between the printed *chu nom* characters for say, do and la. If one note is very close to the next, it is a very short note. If there is a wide space, a long note.' And we worry about printers' errors in the West!

'Students have to learn from another musician to get the rhythm right,' says Thao. That must take some time.

There are a few more markings on the score.

'A hump-shaped curve over two notes means that they are "tied" as they would be in the West. An 'x' beneath a *chu nom* ideogram (a note) translates as an accent. A 'comma' beneath an ideogram indicates a different kind of accent.'

But these signs pertain only to music for Thao's instrument, the moon-shaped lute – as annotated by Hoang Yen.

It is therefore no surprise that performers may add any notes they like to improvise, to ornament or embellish. Thao assures me that Vietnamese audiences never tire of hearing the same piece of music played over and over again, because no two performers ever play it the same way and even the same performer never plays it the same way twice.

To my delight, Thao asks if I would like to accompany her to her Hue singing lesson the following Sunday afternoon.

Thao picks me up on her motorbike and to my amusement, we only zip round the corner. Her teacher is a wizened old lady in her seventies named Nguyen Thi Man, who sits with one black silk trouser leg crosswise on the wooden armchair, her blackened hair pulled back severely in a bun. At first I think her red mouth is stained by betel chewing, but no, it is cherry-red lipstick. Nguyen Thi Man is a self-taught professional Hue singer, who became famous fifty years ago, singing on the radio.

Our hostess, Nguyen Thi Loi, wearing a smart, striped pyjama suit, introduces herself as the mother of two children, who she had rather late. The Vietnamese are very open, or perhaps it's because I am a foreigner. She welcomes us into her large sitting room where we perch on plastic stools round a table with a cheerful, tulip patterned tablecloth, a single rose impaled on a steel pincushion in a low dish in the centre. Nguyen Thi Loi pours very strong, tepid green tea into tiny china teacups.

Pink curtains are tied to one side of the metal grilled window that opens to the veranda and courtyard across the front of the house. Wood-slatted armchairs line one wall. A ceiling fan turns slowly; a fluorescent bar close to the ceiling lights the room. A large wall clock hangs where the ancestral altar might have been, above an interior grilled window. A formica-topped table, holding a vase of bright pink, artificial tulips and a family-sized bottle of Coca-Cola stands beneath the interior window.

Propped against this interior window grill is an oil painting of an old man wearing a light blue court robe and what I take to be a mandarin's hat. Following my gaze, the hostess identifies the subject as a royal prince, Tuy Ly, eleventh of Emperor Minh Mang's seventy-eight sons and a well-known poet from whom her husband's family is descended. The portrait, she explains, has been painted by a famous artist, now living in Paris, for the occasion of the one hundredth anniversary of the prince's death and will be presented by the family to a temple.

Down the central hallway, shoes and slippers have been pushed casually to one side beside the stairs. Beyond are the kitchen and outside, a walled, paved courtyard. From time to time, the children peep at the proceedings in the sitting room through the grilled interior window. A lute hangs on one wall. A couple of sixteen-string zithers and surprisingly, a wooden Western style guitar, are propped in one corner. Straw hats on a cane hat stand occupy another corner and beside the front door, an enormous red ghetto blaster distributes its width across two plastic stools.

With three rooms downstairs and probably as many upstairs, this is an affluent household. Thi Loi's husband, Buu Y, taught French before retiring as well as having been a writer and a journalist.

At the table is a young man, who Tao introduces as her friend and teacher of the moon-shaped guitar. The young man's beautiful instrument is fashioned of black lacquer and intricately inlaid mother-of-pearl. Around the table sit the old singer, our hostess balancing a *dan tranh* across her lap and Yoshimi Hirata, a Japanese teacher who plays the *koto,* a Japanese stringed instrument. Like me, she has come along to listen.

Sitting in the oriental manner with one leg across the chair under the knee of the other dangling leg, is a toothpick of a red-haired girl from California who taught English for two years in Vietnam, now on holiday for a week from teaching in Laos.

125

I am surprised that a music lesson is such a gregarious occasion. Perhaps this is one way to avoid stage fright altogether, if a novice singer performs before an audience from her first lesson. There is much chatting and tea sipping while strings are tuned. Thao gets out her music, numerous notebooks in which she has written the words of songs and others in which she has handwritten annotated clefs and notes.

The young man plays a wandering melody and the old lady idly taps the coin clappers and wooden knockers. Thao starts to sing in the alto range, reading the words from her notebook. As she sings, she knocks two wooden sticks together that make a pleasantly resonant sound. The beat of the wooden knockers seems to mark the beginning of a bar, though in some songs it comes more frequently and seems to mark the beat. The moon-shaped guitar player also taps his sound box with a plucker occasionally to produce a knock of a different quality.

Thao has a much sweeter voice than the professional singers I have heard and I hope that training won't alter its quality. Every Sunday afternoon she has a lesson and several times during the week, goes to the old singer's house to learn new songs. The old singer says something to her from time to time.

With great animation, they discuss what Thao should sing next. Thao starts and the old lady belts out a few notes in unison in a well-projected, harsh nasal tone that starts somewhere at the back of the throat and escapes through nearly clinched teeth. To the Western ear, Thao's teacher sounds not unlike an anguished, amplified cat, but no doubt a Wagnerian soprano would make an equally disturbing impression on the Vietnamese musical ear. She sings in the middle register, the tonic based somewhere around the E-flat above middle C, ranging barely an octave higher.

Our hostess takes up her *dan tranh* and checks the tuning. In English she says, 'I am very absent-minded.' Is this a modest apology in advance? The old lady then sings alone, accompanied by the moon-shaped lute and the sixteen-string zither, so that Thao can listen and learn. Thao passes me a note, saying I have just heard the northern mode and now I am about to hear the southern mode. Just as well she told me. Somewhere in the middle of the song, our hostess stops playing and everyone laughs.

Has she dropped a clanger or forgotten the music? I am none the wiser. Perhaps the not too distant drums are the neighbour

126

children warming up for the Mid-Autumn Tet holiday, the equivalent of Christmas for Vietnamese children (full moon of the eighth lunar month, usually around mid-September by the Western calendar). The more important Vietnamese New Year, *Tet,* falls at the end of the lunar year, towards the end of January or into February.

'This is a *Ly* folk song,' Thao whispers.

The old singer has a piercing projection bordering on a low howl. Perhaps it is the strong green tea through the years that galvanises the vocal chords and turns their voices to copper, I muse silently as the old lady joins Thao from time to time.

Our hostess carries in plates of mandarin oranges and green bananas, tiny fruit forks and small saucers of candied pineapple.

'I made it myself.' More tepid tea is poured round.

With the roar of a motorbike and a little flurry, a young Vietnamese woman with long, flowing black hair arrives. Thao introduces her as Le Thi Anh Thao, the best *dan tranh* player in Hue, who has performed in many countries abroad. She teaches at the College of Art where Thao studied traditional Vietnamese music.

Anh Thao is an attractive woman with a wide, open face and full mouth. She smiles broadly, but her face immediately turns serious as she sits down to tune one of the *dan tranh* instruments belonging to the house, laid across her lap. She has brought only her three pointed plastic pluckers in a small leather coin purse, which are pushed onto the thumb and first two fingers of her right hand. The fingers of her left hand 'bounce' along the strings to mark the pitch, occasionally trembling to produce vibrato. As she plays, she sits in rigid, straight-backed attention, her features set in tense concentration.

When they finish, Thao explains that this was court music, one of ten royal pieces. The young man sings a folk song, Thao accompanying him on the *nguyet.*

The Japanese girl is persuaded to have a go on the *dan tranh* with sixteen strings. Her own instrument, the Japanese *koto* has thirteen, so the tuning and repertoire are entirely different. Thao sings to the accompaniment of the *nguyet.*

'That was a *Ho* folk song, the sort sung on the Perfume river by the boat people.' Next comes a sad folk song about the fourteenth century Vietnamese princess from Hanoi, who was forced to marry a Cham king in exchange for ceding northern Cham territory around Hue to the Viet king of the North.

To the Western ear, Vietnamese songs end quite suddenly, even abruptly. As there is a return to the tonic after every phrase, there is no musical anticipation as to when a song is nearing the end. It can be at any moment.

Through Thao, I ask the old singer how many *ca Hue* songs she knows. Her answer is simple: 'All of them.'

AN EMPEROR'S DELIGHT

Ten girls are not equal to one testicle of a boy
– Vietnamese proverb

At Thao's singing lesson, she had asked excitedly if I knew that a famous musicologist, probably the world's leading expert not only on Vietnamese music, but on all Asian music, was staying at my hotel? She described him and immediately I recalled seeing an elderly gentleman with a cane at breakfast, rather large for a Vietnamese, with the broad face and mellow features of a Cham statue. This was Professor Doctor Tran Van Khe, who now lives in France and taught at the Sorbonne.

The following morning I introduce myself and he kindly agrees to find a few minutes for me in his busy schedule of official lunches, newspaper, radio and television interviews and lectures at Hue's College of Art and Music.

When I ask him about the difference in scales, North and South, he launches into a technical discussion that leaves me standing at middle C. Seeing my baffled expression, without skipping a beat, he shifts down and explains that the main difference between Western music and the music of Vietnam – of Asia – is that Western music is like a building.

'In the West we look at the whole in a vertical sense, at harmony and polyphony, whereas Vietnamese, Indian – Asian music in general – is horizontal. We look at music as though we are looking at a painting or embroidery. To the melodic line, we can add the leaves and flowers.'

What a pleasant analogy, illustrating visually what Thao had earlier explained about embellishment and ornamentation in individual performances. The professor, now over eighty, has lived in France for more than fifty years.

'I was born into the fourth generation of a family of musicians in Saigon. In those days, there were only two university degrees, medicine and law, so I chose medicine, at a time when there were fewer than a thousand university students in the entire country.

'When I finished university during the Japanese occupation in the forties, millions of people were dying from starvation. So I and my family went out performing and gave our earnings to the poor.'

I tell him of my up to now thwarted desire to attend performances of classical opera, *tuong,* and traditional court dancing.

'But there are regular performances of *tuong* in Danang', he assures me, 'and performances of court dancing here in Hue.'

I explain that this may be true, but that it is not easy for a foreigner to find them. The genies of culture must have been listening. No sooner have I spoken than the good professor's phone rings. It is the directrice of the traditional court ballet company in Hue, inviting him to a performance that very evening. Unfortunately, he is committed to a formal dinner, so on the spot, he suggests that I go in his place.

The cyclo driver drops me at the address written down, a dark government building, and I am wondering if this can possibly be the right place when a motorbike zooms past me round the side of the building and disappears. I follow it and find a few people grouped outside a side entrance. Among them is the lady whose name I have been given, who arranges official tours for French-speaking tourists in Hue, Truong Thi Cuc.

The auditorium might be in a small secondary school, a not so large stage, half a dozen high ceiling fans. A fringed canopy of red velvet, heavily encrusted with embroidered gold dragons, matching 'pillars' at each side and a red velvet backdrop, give the illusion of a royal palace interior.

Eight musicians wearing blue satin court gowns, file in at the back of the stage: a monochord, a sixteen-string zither, a small and a large guitar, a fiddle, an oboe, drums and a gong. The music starts with lots of boom-boom, the oboe and a female singer. Eight dancers wearing a kaleidoscope of bright colours make their entrance, twirling wooden swords. Strict Confucian balance is maintained in this traditional court dance choreography. Four dancers left, four dancers right, move in patterns of exact symmetry. Two splendid male spear bearers, brandishing fringed shields, leap in for the finale.

Two young men and two young women place a tray laden with offerings and candles on a small table centre stage. Clearly a religious ceremony, the young women kneel on each side of the table, pink scarves draped over their heads like madonnas, here more likely to be goddesses or shamans. Graceful arm waving and hand movements are accompanied by drums, wooden knockers and a singer, but the performance, it must be said, owes more to symbolism and colourful spectacle than to virtuoso dancing.

The next number over-compensates for any previous lack of energy. Three young men, two dressed as mandarin, one as an emperor – I know, because of his turned-up-toed boots – flourish what look like drum sticks and leap about like demented Cossacks.

In what looks like a dance of the dolls, two lines of girls carrying handfuls of mini-candles in their outstretched palms, seem almost to float as they mince in tiny steps on tiptoe in concentric circles. How do they keep their palms from being burnt?

The lights come up on a dragon – no, a unicorn. Often I have been perplexed by a statue, not knowing the difference between a dragon and a unicorn. I now hold the key: two unbranched antler-like horns and you know you have a unicorn, in this case two unicorns, one green and one yellow.

Their cavorting antics are very comical, about as scary as a giant soft toy. Huge, gaping, smiling mouths reveal pink plush tongues, their reflector eyes rolling as they toss their heads and one seems to be – licking the back of the other? Could there possibly be amorous unicorns? Amorous mythical beasts?

As I am considering this notion, suddenly I think I am seeing things – a baby yellow unicorn appears from nowhere. The baby rolls about, shakes its head and crawls about appealingly on all fours. But which is the mother unicorn? How do you sex a cloth unicorn? Answer: watch the baby unicorn, which very soon nuzzles up under the tummy of the green unicorn – mummy! – before climbing up on the haunches of daddy unicorn to ride 'uni-back'. During the applause and bows, the baby unicorn removes her cloth head to reveal a very pretty little girl.

In the innocently flirtatious fan dance, two lines of girls glide on to the stage, each hiding her face behind two fans for charming fan fluttering and coquettish peekaboo. In the pretty finale, the girls form a circle, standing tall at the back, kneeling in front, and as the circle moves, fans fluttering, a skilful display of synchronisation. The costumes for the lantern dance are dazzling: glittering red and yellow headdresses like those of Cham gods and goddesses, tunics of multi-coloured satin streamers. Sixteen dancers appear in rows of four, each bearing a lighted lotus bud lantern in each palm. Pattern weaving symmetry plays a major role in the choreography, the final scene, a four-tier pyramid of dancers forming a lotus bud. All sixteen of the French tourists and I think it a bewitching performance. The logical question is, why doesn't this troupe perform on a regular basis with well-advertised programmes so that all tourists to Hue, and the Vietnamese themselves, can enjoy the dancing?

It seems that fifty people, dancers plus wardrobe and lighting people, are required to mount a performance at a cost of around $200. Dear me, so they do not perform unless they have a firm booking to cover their costs.

A few days later, I ask the Deputy Director of Culture for Hue Province the same question. Apart from the musicians and singers who perform at the royal banquets in the Huong Giang Hotel and on the riverboat trips in the evening, performing groups seem almost clandestine in Hue. He replies by giving me a brief introduction to musical forms.

'There are six genres of music: court music, court dance (the ballet), classical opera *(tuong),* Hue singing *(ca Hue),* a kind of folk opera based on Hue singing and folk songs called *ca kich,* and folk songs. None of these groups perform regularly for the public. They give more performances abroad – in Japan, Korea, Thailand, or France – than in Vietnam.'

I protest, gently, that foreign visitors would love to see performances by these groups. The smiling, enigmatic response is, 'We know our shortcomings.'

The director of the classical opera *(tuong)* company, who is at the meeting, smilingly agrees that I might be allowed to watch his company rehearse sometime during the next week or two – if they are sufficiently ready in their preparations for a trip to France in a few months time (it never came to pass.) They have already performed in Hong Kong, Japan, France and America, many times. Pity about the home market. The *tuong* opera troupe also performs the singing drama of central Vietnam, *ca kich,* except that they only seem to perform abroad – in Vietnam only at *Tet.*

But plans are afoot, according to the Deputy Director of Culture, for a music museum to open in Ty Ba Trang Street near the Citadel in memory of Hue musician, Nguyen Huu Ba, who for many years was director of the Hue College of Art and Music. The museum will display three hundred musical instruments, musical documents and recordings of folk songs from many parts of the country. Bravo!

I mention that I have seen a VN-TV programme about a Hue sculptress, whose work reminded me of Henry Moore and the Deputy Director of Culture looks much happier.

'Dien Phung Thi is a famous sculptress from Hue, who spent many years in France, a member of the Artists Institute of France, so well known that her name appears in the Larousse dictionary. Her husband died a few years ago and she has returned to Vietnam with more than two hundred of her works, which she plans to bequeath to the people of Hue. We have given her a building. Her studio in Phan Bai Chau Street is open every day and she is devoting her last years to teaching disabled children.'

He goes on to tell me that at the College of Art and Music, a new three-year course in 'elegant music', a form of court music *(nha nhac),* has been introduced. This type of music originated in China, Korea, Japan and Vietnam and of the four countries, the music has been preserved best in Japan because of its long uninterrupted royal dynasty. Most of this music has been lost in China, but South Korea and Vietnam preserve some parts of it. So naturally, a four-country club has been formed for more performances in each of the four countries – abroad.

'The College is doing its best to encourage young musicians to continue in their musical traditions. There are degrees in *tuong* opera and court dance, in Hue singing and the central Vietnamese singing drama, *ca kich,* in the traditional music of Hue and in musicology. We have made some programmes of this music to perform for tourists, so we can organise a performance of one hour or more for tourists.' Such a pity that tourists have not the slightest inkling that such a possibility exists.

The Deputy Director of Culture tells me that there is a Hue singing *(ca Hue)* and court music club, to which membership is by invitation only, the invitation extended to the performer considered to be the best on his or her instrument or in her genre of singing. I might attend their weekly rehearsal if I like, a special concession I suspect, to a persistent culture-vulture, writing a book. Suddenly, I think that the translator has lost his way when he says that in Hue there is a kite club. Questions as to when and where it meets are greeted with charming smiles. Usually, the members enter competitions abroad, or sometimes they fly their kites for festivals. Which festivals? When?

The inevitable response is *Tet* and sometimes the mid-autumn *Tet* festival, which this year fell in mid-September, only a week ago

133

while I was in Hue. How could I and every other tourist visiting Hue in September have missed it? Well, we did see the kids dancing under huge dragon-heads in the streets as they 'tricked and treated'. I might visit the most noted kite maker in Hue, if I like, whose name I then hear for the first time, Nguyen Van Be.

At the Deputy Director of Culture's suggestion, come Sunday morning I take myself to what I have always thought of as a cinema. It is a cinema, but round the back is a room, barren but for a white bust of Ho Chi Minh in one corner, two long tables covered with oilcloth and numerous folding chairs. Ah yes, and there are framed photographs of the kite club and the court music club, performing, of course, abroad.

The painter, Dang Mau Tutu, who was at the meeting with the Deputy Director of Culture, has kindly come along to explain to the musicians and a singer who the round-eyed, big-nose is and why she is has come here.

'Normally, they have a serious practice,' I am told by a high school student of fifteen, the daughter of one of the female musicians, whose English is excellent. Her name, Ynhi (pronounced Knee), translates as 'swallow'. Six of the fifteen performers in attendance teach their instruments – many play several – at the College of Art and Music. All are professional musicians paid by the government, three over eighty, who come to rehearse and where appropriate, to pass on their technique to a younger musician.

As they sit around waiting for the latecomers, they chat and pass a cigarette from one to another, the men ranging upwards from about thirty. There are four women, one of whom is Le Thi Anh Thao, who I met at Thao's singing lesson. One is a zither player, another a Hue singer and the fourth, the mother of my young interpreter, who teaches at the college and who seems to have come along as understudy, just to listen to her elderly colleague playing her instrument, the lute.

There are the usual instruments: a sixteen-string zither, the moon-shaped guitar; a two-string fiddle, but this one has a large sound box and therefore a lower tone; plus a smaller three-string guitar *(tam);* a bamboo flute *(sao);* wooden sticks for knocking; coin clappers and a wooden bowl that is struck as a percussion instrument by a young blind man. The flute player doubles as a teacup-trembler.

Two tiny teacups held in each hand are 'rung' together, producing a pleasant tinkling sound.

The painter acts as spokesman, explaining that these instruments – wind, string and percussion – are made of the five materials, the same as the five elements: metal, wood, fire, water, and earth. I ask which is made of fire and which of water? He replies with a twinkle that it is symbolic. I later learn that he has confused the eight materials for the five elements.

The first selection is one of the Ten Royal Pieces that requires all of the instruments. This is indeed beautiful music. Unfortunately, there are no recordings of this group for sale. The young translator points out that the old boy at the far end of the table, gently tapping a wooden triangular piece of wood with a wooden stick, is the best percussionist in Hue, Nguyen Manh Cam.

After much discussion, for the second selection they choose a Hue song *(ca Hue)*, a sad lament sung by a middle-aged woman, 'the very best *ca Hue* singer in Hue,' my young translator whispers. I hardly need telling that it is a song about the loneliness of waiting for her lover.

Next comes Ancient Music *(nam binh)*, a song describing the beauty spots of Hue, followed by a folk song in the northern mode. The flute player, a true virtuoso, comes into his own, making his instrument purr, tickling the nape of the neck with its warmth, twittering like a bird with his vibrato. Had they not told me afterwards, I would never have believed that the snappy rhythm of the next piece was religious music *(chau van)*, during which the spirit of god enters the body to dance.

'Shamanizing,' says Ynhi. The flute player makes loud finger-snapping, percussive sound and the singer belts out a song that would have carried across the river.

Following the rehearsal, Ynhi and I load into one cyclo – Ynhi is quite tiny – to go in search of the kite maker. Nguyen Van Be (Mac Dinh Chi Street) is a genial man perhaps in his fifties, who we find preparing his kites for a competition on the island of Reunion. His father and grandfather, his sons and grandsons, are all kite makers and huge kites stand stacked like colourful gossamer around the walls of his modest workshop.

There are six enormous butterflies and a dragon, its feathery body in flight stretching 130 feet (40 m)! Were he to sell it, the price would be around $260. Two phoenix hang on one wall and there is a splendidly realistic peacock. Nguyen Van Be gets out his portfolio: a scrapbook of photographs of butterfly kites, whose bodies are ladies wearing *ao dais;* a singing kite which has a large bamboo flute attached; a pair of loving doves; a bat; an orange and white polka dot fish; an elephant – so elephants really can fly; an eagle carrying away a maiden in distress. There is a Vietnamese legend in which a woodsman rescues a princess from an eagle that has imprisoned her in his cave. Alas, his wicked brother claims the glory. But in the end, the hero gets the credit and wins the princess, and the wicked brother gets his just deserts.

Heart-wrenchingly, perhaps inevitably, there is also a kite in the shape of – a silver plane.

(Note: The Royal Ballet Company now gives two, one-hour performances daily in the Duyet Thi Duong Theatre in the Citadel.)

CORRUPTING THE YOUNG

Poverty fetters wisdom
– Vietnamese proverb

One day in a camera shop, the young girl in front of me finishes her transaction and sits down to look at her photos. As I present my receipt, asking if the pictures are ready, hearing English, the girl leaps to her feet, says hello and asks where I am from. When I say London, she claps her palms to the sides of her face, lets out a little shriek and practically jumps for joy.

Are you studying English?

'Yes, I study English at Hue University,' and she is off. How long have I been in Hue? How long will I stay in Hue? How long have I been in Vietnam? Do I like her country? So excited is she that she even forgets the standard question, how old are you?

These formalities dispensed with, she comes straight to the point. Can she come to my hotel to practise her English as long as I am in Hue?

'Yes? When?' The following day at five, Huy Anh turns up with two of her friends. I lead them through the foyer and out to the hotel terrace where we chat, sitting round a table as the sun dips, throwing silver shadows across the river. Both parents of my new friend, Huy Anh, are teachers. Her father is principal of the primary school where her mother teaches. She has two younger sisters and a brother. The father of one of her classmates makes coconut candy; her mother sells it in the market. The parents of the third 'stay at home,' her mother a former nurse, her father a barber. All three are twenty – I would have taken them for about fifteen – in their second year at university studying English as a major subject. Huy Anh's ambition is to become a tour guide, the second girl wants to be a teacher, the third is undecided. We talk about brothers and sisters, their ages and where they live.

The following evening Huy Anh comes on her own. Again, we sit watching the sunset as she tells me how much she would like to learn English, really well. She admits that she has never visited the Citadel – this from a girl who hopes to become a tour guide.

137

I ask how much it costs for a Vietnamese, as there is a two-tier entrance fee. It costs five dollars for foreigners.

'Five thousand dong' (US$0.35).

It is difficult for a foreigner to get a real grip on how poor is poor, of what the ordinary Vietnamese on the street considers to be necessities and what luxuries, in short, how the average-income Vietnamese lives. Huy Anh is nicely dressed in the jeans that are the status symbol of every young Vietnamese girl, her family has a telephone and a television set and she loves to watch films, cartoons and animal programmes, but is only allowed to watch on Sunday afternoons. Her parents are strict; the children have to study. She says that she tries to persuade her parents to have cable TV so that she can watch English-speaking channels, but they refuse. Almost in the same breath, she expresses anxiety that her mother will be cross with her for having lost a biro, leaving her with only one.

'I want to learn so much, I want to learn everything.'

Her ingenuousness is touching. When she says that she longs to travel – 'to Danang, to Ho Chi Minh City' – I am brought up short by the limits of her life up to now. Danang is only three and a half hours away, a three or four-dollar fare in a tourist minibus, much less in the bigger, crowded buses used by the Vietnamese. Huy Anh's yearning for knowledge, for experience, for adventure, for life, is touching. It reminds me a little of myself at her age, yearning to escape a smallish city to discover the world beyond. But hers is such a naked, almost anguished hunger that I silently agree to do what I can while I am in Hue to ease her yearnings, by speaking English to her and by gently, gradually trying to help her span the enormous gap in experience between that of a young girl living in Hue and the life of a teenager in Europe. But is that wise? As a parent it seems to me that the life of a teenager growing up in Hue is far more innocent and wholesome than that of a teenager in the West. With this thought in mind, I set about finding out a bit more about life as a student in Hue. Apart from English, what other subjects does she study?

'Computers, economics, philosophy.' Philosophy means the philosophies of Ho Chi Minh, Marx and Lenin. So in Moscow where students now concentrate on studying how to build an international capital market and in Hanoi where the open door policy of *doi moi* led to galloping private enterprise, in Hue, at least academically, they still hold to the old ways. What do students do in their spare time?

Huy Anh's eyes open wide at the question.

'I have no spare time. I go to school and I study.'

'Boys', she explains, 'if they have spare time and get up early, play football. After school they drink coffee with their friends. Girls have to stay at home. Sitting in cafes drinking coffee is bad. Some girls from wealthy families, they are bad. They drink coffee every day and go dancing with their boyfriends. Parents in Hue are very strict with girls. They have to come straight home after classes.'

Huy Anh herself spends what spare time she has at the college library studying, or sometimes when a friend has a birthday, they have a party. It was from such a party that she had been collecting two prints of photographs when we met.

Do I have English-speaking television in my room? she asks. Please, could she watch, in order to practice English? Having visited several of what I assume to be middle-class Vietnamese homes, I wonder if it is wise to flaunt a Western style hotel room before the eyes of a young girl accustomed to the spartan furnishings of probably an ordinary Vietnamese household. It would seem niggardly to refuse and to her, no doubt incomprehensible, so I took a deep breath, wondering if I am corrupting the innocent with Western materialism, 'Come on, then.'

My room at the Huong Giang, a three-star hotel (then), it must be said, though very pleasant and comfortable, is amongst the smallest and least expensive and measures approximately fifteen feet square (20 sq m). It is carpeted, has wide windows hung with peach-coloured nylon drapes and swags. There is a double bed with a cane headboard, an air-conditioner, a mini-fridge and a television. Woven and narrow strips of cane decorate the desk and bedside tables, the ceiling and the door frames. A mirror in a carved wooden frame hangs above the desk. The dark varnished doors have been carved with peach blossoms. I know that this room will represent another very distant world, about as remote to Huy Anh as Mars. It's one thing to see a Western style interior on television, quite another to find it on your doorstep and to realise just how unlikely it is that you will ever possess such luxury. When we arrive on the first-floor, open veranda that leads to my room, Huy Anh is already agog, twirling on her sandalled heels to look out over the egrets on the lawn and the drive in front of the hotel.

'You can see everything from here!'

At the sight of the carved door, her face lights up with the kind of joy that one might express at a work of art. I open the door

139

and she steps in, again twirling around, trying to take it all in at once. She touches the black china lamp, inlaid with mother-of-pearl and the pleated cloth lampshade – a florescent strip high on a wall is the usual lighting in a Vietnamese room. Huy Anh rushes to the window to look out at the distant view of the river and the nearer view of the pool, surrounded by newer blocks of hotel rooms with balconies.

'It's so beautiful,' she gasps, astonishment in her wide eyes. The depth of her amazement leaves me feeling exceedingly uncomfortable. I explain the wooden suit valet and the dangling shoehorn. She picks up a couple of empty photograph print folders lying on the bedside table, which I immediately give to her. She takes in the bed and the headboard, then moves over to pick up and thumb through a pile of postcards lying beside the television set. She is transparently unaccustomed to having anything unnecessary just lying around. Obviously, every hundred *dong* counts in Huy Anh's household. There is a little squeak as she spies the photographs stuck in the frame of the mirror. I introduce her to my big son, six-feet-two-inches tall, the photographs taken when he was seventeen and of my daughter at nineteen, explaining that the other photograph of them was taken when they were younger, twelve and fourteen.

She tells me that she is studying Word Windows on computers at university, so I open my laptop and switch on Windows. Yes, it is the same as hers. She is amazed at how small the Canon printer is. I explain that it has to be small in order to travel.

Huy Anh is far too excited to concentrate on CNN television news. She has pounced on the portable CD player and I push the play button – Brahms. With awe she touches both speakers, not so tiny as I would have liked. Then there is another squeak as she discovers the short wave radio. I explain that the button for switching bands is broken, so I can only hear London on one band, at 6 a.m. or 10 p.m. The radio seems to her a miracle. Certainly, there are radios in Vietnam, ghetto blasters aplenty, but perhaps her family does not have a short wave radio. I decide that the bathroom (tub, shower, telephone and hair-dryer, liberally strung with underwear) can wait for another day. Modern bathrooms in Vietnamese apartment buildings, often shared, if they have a shower, spray the entire room.

Huy Anh touches each book in the shelf and I explain that these are my reference books on Vietnam that I use for my work.

'Did you *buy* them?' she asks incredulously.

'And you live here, all alone?' Clearly she is astounded,

coming from a large family, that any one person could occupy such a huge space without sharing it. Finally, I have to nudge her gently homeward with a copy of *Vietnam Economic News,* so that I can have some supper, promising that she can watch television again, so long as it is after five o'clock when I stop work.

The experience troubles me greatly. Of course, I am happy to help her as much as possible with English, though I am anything but a natural teacher. Yet to have exposed this eager, ambitious and impressionable girl to what to her must seem like envy-provoking wealth, is that wise? Or would seeing how the West lives act as a further spur to study hard in order to qualify for a good job that might yield her some of the things she saw for the first time in my bedroom at the Huong Giang Hotel?

Would this experience sour Huy Anh with envy? Would she grow to hate the haves, because she is a have-not? Already she is as ambitious as one can be. Never having worked, never having earned, it is all too easy when one is young, I remember, to forget that those who have, at least in the West, usually have worked hard to earn it. In Vietnam, it must be said that it is often those who work least, who have most and those who work hardest, who have least.

In my assumed role as *loco parentis,* I resolve to try to inspire Huy Anh in a path that will lead her towards achieving her goals, but also to impress upon her the worth of the less materialistic values of her own culture, the preciousness of close family relationships, the warmth and generosity of spirit in dealings with others and the joy of learning, not just as a tool to earning power, but for the pure pleasure of it. I am more than a little concerned at what I have taken on.

Even after a stay of several months, it is still difficult to grasp the relative values of earnings and the cost of living in Vietnam, partly because prices for foreigners are inflated sometimes ten times those charged to locals. Just how much must a head of household earn to support a family with two children – the recommended number – though many families have three or four, like Huy Anh's.

Estimated per capita figures wander over such a wide range that it is difficult to make much sense of them. Largely, income depends upon location, urban or rural. Even accepting that there is real poverty in Vietnam, that in some parts of the country people are still hungry at least part of the year, it is difficult to understand how most people exist, particularly at the lower level of society, even in a low-cost economy.

141

Then there are the rich, either those in senior government positions, who head government-run companies, private companies, joint-ventures or the *nouveau riche,* who have soared to wealth in the property boom in Ho Chi Minh City and Hanoi through renting office space and residential accommodation to foreigners. As there are regulations prohibiting foreigners from renting any but Government licensed accommodation, this eliminates the possibility of a foreigner being allowed to lease a low-rent property in exchange for doing it up. This monopoly system has acted as a get rich quick scheme for owners of land, buildings and houses – though quite who property owners are in a communist country is mystifying. Moreover, any Vietnamese, it seems, can borrow to build and rent to foreigners.

It is quite common to see houses and flats in Ho Chi Minh City and Hanoi advertised for US$2,000-3,000 (£1,300-2000) per month. The first week I was in Hanoi, I was shown a new two-bedroom flat in a prime location overlooking a lake with a rent of $3,500 (£2,300) per month. It was easily let to a foreign executive whose international company paid the rent. Anything under $1,500 (£1,000) per month is cheap. With this kind of money pouring in, the happy property owners are suddenly rich beyond their wildest fantasies. The men rush out to buy a BMW or a Mercedes, their wives pile on the gold jewellery, spend time in beauty salons and lavish imported toys on their children. They go wild buying air conditioners, cameras and camcorders, television sets, videos, ghetto blasters and electric rice makers. And of course, they build a new house or another storey on top of the one they have. They dine out in restaurants formerly catering for Westerners and finish an evening in an ice cream parlour. At the other extreme, government workers earn very low salaries $24-50 per month ($288-600, £192-400 pa) plus an extra month's bonus at *Tet,* not enough to live on. This means that they supplement their income through moonlighting in order to survive. The result is a nation of hustlers, and inevitably, corruption.

A new working class is being created by foreign companies offering factory jobs, paying higher wages than the average. This is not because foreign companies are magnanimously generous, but because the Vietnamese are still adjusting to working in factories. One might think that poverty would send them fleet-footed to new factory jobs. But this is not a mobile work force, beyond the distance a bicycle or a motorbike can commute. Many of the new factories are in economic zones, inaccessible by cheap transport.

142

Young people, out of financial necessity, have to live at home. However, wages in new factories are pushing up earnings for some, well beyond the norm. In time, the rural poor will feel poorer as the new middle class earns more. Meanwhile, the black economy flourishes. Yet earnings can be topsy-turvy. In Hue, a lower-paid area than Hanoi or Ho Chi Minh City, a cyclo driver can make $5-7 a day ($1,800-2,500 pa, £1,200-1,666 pa) – considerably more than a Government worker. His wife as a teacher earns only $20 per month ($240 pa, £160 pa). An English-speaking waiter in a hotel gave up his $20-a-month job teaching English at high school level to earn $66 per month ($792 pa, £528 pa) as a waiter. It is therefore not difficult to understand why my young English student's parents have difficulty supporting four children on their combined earnings of around $480 per year. Distributed among six people, this breaks down to $80 per person per annum! Nearly all women contribute financially to their families' income, either by having jobs or by selling something. Earnings statistics, however, hold little meaning without measuring them against the cost of living. As time passes, I try to collect a few indicators from individuals.

Most people live in an extended family house or flat, all family incomes contributing to household expenses. In Hue a new three-storey, six-room house would cost around $43,000 (£30,600). A smaller, three-room house might cost around $17,500 (£11,600). To rent a nice two-room house might cost only $34 a month!

This particular house is rented by a rare man from another town, who came to Hue to work. As the rent is more than he earns, if his wife didn't also have a job, he could not afford this nice house with a bathroom. I am told that there are flats and houses that are cheaper, but not so nice. Clothes are comparatively expensive. When I first start asking how much the Vietnamese pay for clothes, the response is – 'new?' There is a thriving market in used clothing.

A new man's shirt in the market costs $4-5, a pair of trousers $10, an *ao dai* $16-21, a pair of sandals $4. One step up the socio-economic scale, a man's suit, new, might cost $43, a pair of loafers $15, a smarter woman's *ao dai* made to measure $40, smart leather sandals $13. A pair of trendy jeans is one of the most expensive items in any girl's wardrobe, $10-15. So most ordinary Vietnamese only buy used clothes. During the autumn rains in Hue, one young girl told me that while the bridge was flooded, she had to go home by boat and that the boat owners charged a lot – 4,000 dong each way ($0.27).

That reminded me of the 5,000 dong Huy Anh never had to visit the Citadel. (I was delighted to give the potential tour guide a tour of her own heritage.)

Yet I couldn't help wondering how so many young people could afford to buy a Chinese motorbike for $750 (£500)? Banks will not lend for motorbikes. 'I borrowed from granny' is the usual answer. But where did granny get the money? Did she sell her gold jewellery?

It surprises me that young men have the money to sit around in pavement cafes drinking draught beer, iced milk coffee, or even iced green tea at four cents. Also, many young men smoke and in Saigon and Hanoi, the girls, too.

While occasionally chafing at the determined efforts of boys selling postcards, at kids trying to entice you to their mothers' soft drinks stalls, at cyclo drivers who follow you down the street when you have said that you prefer to walk, at children begging, it is understandable that the Vietnamese should try every ploy imaginable to redistribute some of the obvious to them wealth of Westerners, who walk around unwittingly flaunting it. What the Vietnamese fail to see is how carefully we have to manage our, enormous to them, incomes in a high-cost standard of living economy. They only know that to most of us, a dollar is not a lot, whereas to most of them, a dollar is enough to buy food for a day. Considering that a young backpacking tourist in his or her first job in the US might earn $45,000 (£30,000) – 69 times the average Vietnamese per capita income of $650 (£430, 2008) – and the disparity becomes all too clear.

Even against Ho Chi Minh City's higher per capita income, the multiple is still in double figures.

Given the long tradition of haggling and bargaining in Vietnam, so alien, even distasteful in our own culture, it is easy for a tourist to feel that he is being financially got at every time he hops into a cyclo or a taxi, books a flight or stays in a hotel, licensed by the government as suitable for foreigners, forgetting the enormous disparity of incomes. All too often the tourist is made to feel that he is a milch cow, simply there to be squeezed by the Vietnamese, by both the individual and the establishment, to extract as much hard currency as humanly possible. In theory, I don't mind paying a cyclo driver ten times more than what he would charge a Vietnamese, as long as it is within reason in a Western context. I don't mind overpaying for taxis, flights and hotel rooms, so long as the authorities have not set the rates ridiculously higher than international rates, which is the case

144

with postage and international telephone calls set by the postal authorities, who seem to be trying to clear the national debt at a stroke. The result is that foreigners who would normally make international calls, simply do not, thereby costing the postal authorities much-needed revenue. Western cash cows can fight back. Because so few Vietnamese have had the money or been allowed to travel, they have yet to learn that they must compete in the international tourist market, by offering good value for money, compared to their more polished and experienced South East Asian neighbours. If they demand extortionate prices, the wonderful cash-bearing tourists will simply go away and not return. One mid-career, professional American tourist was recently asked by a Vietnamese in Hue, how much he thought he would spend in Vietnam during a two-week holiday. After a bit of ready reckoning, he replied, 'Probably about $1,500,' after which the Vietnamese did a bit of reckoning.

'In Vietnam, that would feed ten people for ten years.'

Not so long ago in *Vietnam News,* on the page that carries Then and Now photographs, two photos appeared, illustrating how the ordinary Vietnamese woman lives. The first photograph showed a woman kneeling at an open fire to cook. The caption read: 'Earlier this century, country women used three bricks for a cooking fire with their pots made of baked earth. Women were usually barefoot while cooking.' The Now photograph, also showing a woman kneeling at an open fire to cook, bore the caption: 'Today, the cooking pot is usually made of cast iron with straw used as the main fuel. Women often wear (plastic) slippers and (conical straw) hats to avoid dust and ash.' Some improvement. Makes you think. It is true that most areas of Vietnam have been electrified and television has infiltrated even remote areas, along with motorbikes. But these two photographs seem a shocking indictment of progress at the rice roots of Vietnamese society.

Come October, for several days it rains steadily under sepia skies, the river floods into the hotel garden and I begin to wonder how much dragon boats cost – to buy. The warm South beckons and I head for the new town, relatively speaking, of Saigon.

(Note: Earnings and prices have gone up considerably since writing. Huong Giang Hotel has been renovated and upgraded to a 4-star establishment and the annex that held my old room has been demolished in favour of a car-park).

PART III

FURTHER SOUTH

SAIGON – CITY ON THE MOVE

One often abandons the old for the new,
one often abandons the lamp for the moon
– Vietnamese proverb

Morning, and the city streets feel like a jangling funfair, not quite real, everyone slowed by the heat, bicycles and people swimming through the viscous humidity as though the air were jellied.

I pick my way through pavements heaving with hustlers touting cigarette lighters, postcards, T-shirts and wooden Mickey Mouse wall plaques. On the traffic island of one boulevard, a vendor has set up a stand selling the national flag, gold star on a red field. Vietnam may be a Communist country, but the Vietnamese have become wildly entrepreneurial.

A kid of four, or maybe it's seven, approaches.

'You buy postcards? You number one, you buy from me.' It seldom fails with tourists, at least the first time.

The cacophony of traffic noise approaches disco level. The screeches of motorbike and car horns punctuate the stripping of gears and gunning of engines large and small. However, unlike Jakarta or Bangkok where traffic stands still, here the traffic weaves and flows, mercifully at a fairly slow pace or the pavements would be strewn with dead Vietnamese.

What the pavements are strewn with, apart from vendors, are parked motorbikes. Strings mark off parking areas and watchers make sure that mirrors and horns – and presumably motorbikes – don't just disappear. On one corner, an impromptu garage advertises itself with a bicycle tyre hanging up and a half bottle of yellow fuel displayed on the pavement to tempt thirsty motorbikes. A bicycle pump and a squatting mechanic on a low wooden stool complete the forecourt.

146

Apart from pavement cafes, there are cafes on the move, baskets bobbing at the ends of carrying poles holding fresh ingredients, utensils, china bowls, a flower pot charcoal burner and sometimes stools. Itinerant cobblers, tea ladies and fruit sellers bounce by. Whatever it might be, you can buy it from a Vietnamese, who will stop for a moment to open up shop en route to his or her pitch. Shouts of 'madame', an echo of French colonial days, rend the air as vendors approach. The raucous babble of voices is everywhere. Inscrutability is long gone. The real shops, those with doors that close at night, tend to be in narrow buildings one room wide, going back eternally and up five or six storeys. Yet having indoor premises does not prevent a family from living outside, understandable in a hot country where people wish to catch any trifling breeze going. I pass one granny, relaxing in a lawn chair on the pavement with an electric fan – outdoors – blowing a hot breeze over her.

In addition to commercial and social activities, pavements also serve as playgrounds. Children teeter on bicycles, kick footballs and shuttlecocks and chase one another with toy guns where they can. Toddlers play tag and giggly hide-and-seek around parked taxis as the traffic whizzes past inches away. Chubby babies, bare-bottomed, as soon as they can walk, wander aimlessly, clutching soft toys.

Ho Chi Minh City feels like a brighter, warmer, slower world where people still remember how to live with one another instead of locking themselves away in anonymous flats and detached houses behind hedges, dashing from box to box in sealed containers. Amongst the Vietnamese, keeping oneself to oneself is clearly anathema, reserve in the British sense, unknown. But then, so presumably, is privacy.

In the interest of self-preservation and that of the Vietnamese you might stumble over, pavements are an attention-riveting place to walk. But then, the slowly ambling Vietnamese, often arm in arm, prevent you from walking fast, ever.

When the cruise stopped at Saigon, I learned that what one calls the city depends upon the company one keeps. The man on the street still calls it Saigon, at least the central area. In politicized company, amongst government tour guides and officials, it is politely referred to as Ho Chi Minh City, especially from Hue northward. In print, it is abbreviated as HCMC.

This time in Saigon, I stroll along Ly Tuy Trong, the boulevard leading to the old twin-towered *Hotel de Ville,* built by the

147

French and now housing HCMC's People's Committee. It remains an elegant, unmistakably French colonial building with steep mansard roofs, glowing ochre in the sunlight.

Conversely, the French-built red brick church was probably never much of an architectural gem. In the open space in front of the modest, French-built opera house, now used for fashion shows and pop concerts, there is a bit of a carnival atmosphere with young boys selling balloons to the parents of children only slightly younger than themselves.

I window shop along Dong Khoi – the notorious street of bars and nightclubs during the Vietnam War – now replaced by smart shops selling 'antiques', lacquer ware, carvings and gorgeous silk. When I reach the waterfront, a woman waves and shouts from her boat, wanting to row me up river.

'One hour, two hours, very cheap.'

I chide myself, but even now, I am too wary to step into a boat alone with a stranger, even a woman. Supper that night is in a state-owned restaurant, probably seized from a Chinese owner and nationalized after reunification in 1975. A good many Vietnamese boat people were Saigon Chinese, who had their businesses confiscated. A man carrying a huge wooden, model sailboat appears outside the window, plaintively gesturing, hoping to sell me the boat. I watch as he continues down the street, stopping wherever a restaurant has diners beside a window.

Two more men stop beneath the window and squatting on the pavement, unselfconsciously, draw a board with chalk on the lined tiles and begin a game of chess. The Vietnamese may have very little, but they manage with what they have.

Next morning I head for Ben Thanh market. By the entrance, a small child sits staring dreamily at a bowl of noodles, sucking a tin of Diet Coke through a straw. A man sleeps on a sun lounger, his face to the market wall. He may have started his walk to market in the cool of night. Beside him, a young mother suckles her baby. Another squats with her three toddlers, spooning food to each like a mother bird with three chicks. Western supermarkets feel a million miles away.

Mandarin and green-skinned oranges, mangoes, guavas and unidentifiable leafy greens are piled high in baskets on the pavement. Women and children stroll past, carrying trays laden with steaming bowls and cups of tea.

A few beggars, young children and old crones, hold out their hands or upturned conical hats. Sun-bronzed, sinewy cyclo drivers sit with their legs crossed in their cyclos, jokily touting for custom, many of them ex-soldiers who fought for the South, now barred from other jobs.

In retrospect, Ben Thanh market is probably best visited very early in the morning, before the heat mingles the stench of meat and fish. Inside, limp *ao dai* tunics hang on hangers, some flourishing swirls of sequins. Elaborately embroidered T-shirts hang in rainbow layers beside the loose, two-piece 'pajamas', so admirably suited to the climate. There are heavy, raw silk jackets in deep-hued colours. A jewellery showcase displays jade and gold jewellery, the gold so pure it is orange.

Trainers and sandals dangle in aisle after aisle; many brand name trainers are manufactured in Vietnam. Customers squat on three-inch-high wooden stools to try them on. Lord knows how a Westerner gets up again. What I call the South East Asian squat, is how the Vietnamese relax or wait for hours for a customer. Whenever I try it, I topple over backwards. Leaving the market, I wander, glancing up through the trees at balconies festooned with laundry, plants, birdcages and corrugated plastic, shading drying clothes.

That night, durian-flavoured ice cream is on offer. This gut-turningly smelly fruit grows on trees throughout South East Asia: large ungainly puke-yellowish globes slightly larger than cantaloupes with nubbly skin. Once its sickly odour has assaulted your olfactory sensors, you will never forget it. I mean to try it whenever I come to South East Asia, but somehow, have never quite summoned up the courage, having read somewhere that eaten at the wrong point of ripeness, it can be very sick-making and mixed with alcohol, actually lethal. Locals have assured me that once having tasted durian, people become passionate devotees. Like glue sniffers, maybe. Forever curious and finding it presented as ice cream, this is the moment.

Well, it doesn't taste half bad. Neither is there much chance of addiction. Its tangy, turpentine after-taste stays with me for hours.

At my hotel, a very international Philippino band is trying to create a happening each night in the bar: jazz night, Italian night, Mexican night, country western night – good grief, what does one have to do to get away! It does seem odd to sit sipping a *margarita,* watching the cricket test match, while a Philippino band belts out Mexican *mariachi* music in what used to be called Saigon. The city is

149

full of that kind of incongruity, helped along by optimistic ex-pats who try to recreate a little bit of Italy or France, Indonesia or America, by opening a bar or a restaurant. Saigon is a boom town of foreign and local entrepreneurs. Restaurants and bars open and close so fast that guidebook publishers can hardly get them into print before they disappear.

In Detham Street, backpacker haven of cheap mini-hotels and open-front cafes that act as local tour operators, the congregation of young backpackers presents a bizarre, unglamorous assemblage of Western youth in frayed jeans and shorts, T-shirts, tangled dreadlocks, ponytails and unshaven chins – in bold contrast to the neat, chic youth of Vietnam. All of us look extremely pink, plump and steamy in the heat. I feel a generation past it until a pleasantly grizzled French couple turns up at Sinh Cafe. I buy a ticket for tomorrow's minibus tour to the Mekong delta – much cheaper than booking a car and driver and less fraught than trying to do it by public transport. Feeling like a bloated capitalist, I return by taxi to the Rex Hotel, a favourite journalist hangout during the Vietnam War.

Like many a Saigon establishment, the Rex has a past. It started life as a garage, was converted into a hotel, at one time served as headquarters for the US Information Service, then the military. Now, it is one of several fairly up-market hotels run by a Vietnamese Government tourist organization that has had the good sense to preserve its exotic lacquered decor. The rooftop bar is royally kitsch. A giant crown and Rex flags reign over a fish tank where enormous carp roam villainously back and forth like aquatic tigers. Garden features include multi-tiered bonsai trees, topiary deer, birdcages, a life-sized sculptured elephant rearing on its hind legs and a moose. A moose? At night, fairy lights twinkle among the bonsai. Bougainvillea-drenched pergolas form intimate, romantic nooks. It might have been designed by a drunken journo. No doubt it afforded any who might have been there in 1975 an excellent view of the oncoming tank, were they fool enough to find themselves on a fifth-floor rooftop. Relaxing in a cane chair with a cold Tiger beer in hand, to me the Rex bar represents the epitome of fading *Indochine,* redolent of Graham Green and Somerset Maugham.

(Note: Sadly, the Rex has been renovated, losing much of its atmosphere, but the view from the bar is still superb.)

TO THE MEKONG AND BACK AGAIN

Throw away the fishhook to eat the fish
– Vietnamese proverb

At half past eight in the morning, the minibus gently noses through swarms of bicycles and motorbikes. Rush hour. Cyclo drivers compete to see who can assemble the most ridiculous load: packets of towels piled higher than the driver, who tries to rubber-neck round them; the same with a stack of empty plastic bottles ten feet high; a bundle of long aluminium strips, bouncing fore and aft.

Winner of this morning's ridiculous load competition has to be a double wardrobe in the chair of a cyclo, an outrider pedalling a bicycle alongside to steady the load.

Traffic pauses as a black converted bus bearing a coffin moves slowly past, surrounded by silent mourners on foot wearing white headbands. Dying may be a release of the spirit for Buddhists, but it is still a sad affair.

Once out of urban Saigon, ribbon development edges the highway to the south-west: terrace after terrace of open-front shops; tiny neighbourhood markets, fruit and vegetables laid out in baskets under parasols; builders merchants where bamboo poles and palm fronds lay stacked beside the lumber.

Wooden houses under thatch or corrugated iron roofs stand primly behind lily ponds among banana trees, bamboo groves and haystacks, and sometimes, rice spread out on straw mats to dry in their earthen courtyards, surrounded by pots of bougainvillea. Two-plank wooden footbridges over frothy green ponds tether the houses to the roadside. Open-sided, thatched restaurants thoughtfully provide hammocks for the afternoon siesta.

From the dried-up paddy fields, the occasional flashy modern factory springs up like a giant square toadstool producing paint, ceramics, textiles or Japanese water – presumably a Japanese company selling purified water? Heat jellies the brain.

151

On the far side of the Freedom Bridge, the first bridge across the Mekong, 1,535 metres long – a $35 million dollar (£23 m) joint project between Australia and Vietnam – we enter the Mekong delta. Coconut palms stud the dried clay paddy dykes. Simultaneously, as the level of the land subsides, flooded green rice paddies begin to appear – with the first TV antenna atop a thatched roof.

Standing in the midst of Saigon's roaring traffic, one would hardly imagine that the intensely rural Mekong delta, quintessential Vietnam, is only an hour away.

We pull into a smart, modern BP station that might have been lifted from Britain, except that the forecourt features a topiary deer complete with leafy antlers. Mercifully, there is a clean stand-up, Asian style toilet with loo paper doled out by an attendant for a few *dong*. Back on the road, we pass a nursery filled with pots of pink, blooming oleanders – in a country where oleanders grow wild. Perhaps they are destined for the balconies of city dwellers.

At My Tho, a tile-roofed town on the Mekong, the minibus group files into the Vinh Trang pagoda, a century and a half old. Beyond its carved pillars sit three ranks of gilt Buddhas. Bound copies of Buddhist scriptures in a dusty glass-front bookcase look as if they have been locked away far longer than the sixty odd years of Communist rule.

I take a turn around the market. The French woman comes back with a chicken basket. I wonder what she'll use it for. I snap pictures of a beguiling cherub, snuggling in her grandpa's lap, and he scribbles an address in my notebook.

Then it's into a boat, not a very large boat, but at least a motorboat with a canopy to protect pale-faced Westerners from the broiling sun.

Our guide, Ho, tells us that here we are about thirty miles (48 km) from the sea. Except for the width of the brown river, it might be the Florida everglades. Dense vegetation with finger-like roots clutch the riverbanks. In a few minutes the tangled fingers of the mangroves melt into palm fronds emerging directly from the water as though they have been flooded: water palms.

At Unicorn Island, a winding path leads to a thatched pavilion where we have lunch. It all looks a bit primitive and I am relieved to recognize a fried egg, a few bits of identifiable pork atop a bowl of rice, a bowl of vegetable soup, spring rolls, green beans and carrots. During lunch we are entertained by chamber music: a two-string fiddle, its sound-box fashioned from a coconut; a two-string banjo and a wooden tapper that sounds like a cricket, powered by an elderly gentleman, barefoot. A promising young singer of about nine tries desperately to overcome her shyness, without really succeeding. They receive warm applause and tips for their efforts.

After lunch the boat leaves the wide brown river and floats through narrow, watery tunnels, green gothic arches above us created by the graceful fronds of water palms growing from the riverbanks. White ducks play noisily in the rushes. Young boys leap daringly off a wooden bridge just in front of the boat to show off. This tropical riverscape is so ethereal, so utterly removed from Western civilization; Rousseau or Gauguin would have felt quite at home. This complete escape is everything I dared to dream of and I shall cherish forever the image of those green waterways, framed by gently curving palm fronds.

Ho tells a guide's tale about a coconut religion on one of the islands in which the followers eat only coconuts for three years. It seems a fairly undemanding religion. But the main attraction of the religion is that monks are allowed to marry nine wives, but not to have children. During the war, quite a few American GIs discovered the cult, were 'converted' and went AWOL. Unhappily for them, the military police eventually hauled them back. According to Ho, the leader of the cult was imprisoned and died in 1990. At that time there were still six hundred monks. Naturally, everyone wants to go and visit the Coconut Cult, but Ho abruptly changes the subject.

Instead, we call in at a coconut candy 'factory', a thatched hut where the milk and pulp are cooked in a huge cauldron over an open fire, rolled out into long thin wooden moulds, then sliced and wrapped in edible rice paper. Seven girls pack from 7 a.m. to 5 p.m. and earn $1.50 a day, which I learn is a fairly decent wage for a street vendor or a local factory worker. The candy sells for 5,000 dong a packet (about $0.30). In another hut, we sample the coconut candy and sip tea flavoured with honey and the juice of small green limes in doll-sized cups – a tea party for grown-ups.

That night in Saigon I make a quick decision. I am so taken with the Mekong delta that I go straight back, this time staying over in Chao Doc and Can Tho. To my dismay, en route the guide explains that there are at least six ways to say hello in Vietnamese, depending upon the age and gender of the person being addressed, which explains why, after asking your name and where you come from, the next question a Vietnamese invariably asks is your age:

chao ba – old woman	*chao ong* – old man
chao co – young woman	*chao anh* – young man
chao em – girl or boy	*chao chau* – children
cam on – thank you	*tam biet* – goodbye

At Vinh Long we clamour into slim, wooden rowing boats, each propelled by a woman, who squats at the prow wearing black pyjamas and a conical straw hat. The stream is narrow and she pushes off the tall malucca trees of the rain forest, draped in vines, more often than rowing. This is dense jungle, no houses, only birdsong. Occasionally the rower reaches her hand into the stream bank to pluck out a snail or to pick pale purple water hyacinths, eaten dipped in *ngoc mam,* the nutritious fermented fish sauce ubiquitous throughout South East Asia.

At one point the rower turns with a wide smile and indicates a mud bunker with a loose straw roof on the bank not six feet away: 'Viet Cong headquarters, Xeo Quit.' I shudder to think how terrifying it must have been to fight in this jungle, squelching up to the knees in mud and water and leeches, never knowing whether the enemy was behind the next tree or crouching around the next bend in the stream. And it was in this area that some of the worst and most intensive fighting took place during the Vietnam War. Suddenly it brings the war down to a terribly personal level.   Soon we reach a thatched pavilion on stilts, open to the jungle, where we have lunch – sweet and sour pork.

That night I leave the tour group who are staying elsewhere, to stay at the Chau Doc Victoria Hotel, where I enjoy one of my most memorable meals in Vietnam. The menu is so tempting that for once I leave it to the French chef, Yann Chretien from Besançon. At the risk of sounding like a restaurant critic, the starter is a salad of ripe and green shredded papaya, lettuce, papaya seeds and mushrooms under a subtle sauce.

The main course is a theatrical crayfish stuffed with shrimps in a mild curry sauce on a bed of julienne vegetables, accompanied by homemade shrimp and potato crisps. Desert is a *soufflé glacé Grand-Marnier.* As a change from beer (best with most Vietnamese food), I allow myself a glass of Chardonnay, or two.

Early next morning the group sets out, five in a wooden rowing boat, up the Bassac river, past a fish farm in the river, past a floating village of more than two thousand houses built floating on boats. They are occupied by Cambodian refugees and Cham people. Women row past, tiny tots squatting in their boats.

At a Cham stilt village on the riverbank, children surround us, begging for biros. A young girl of perhaps ten is weaving colourful cotton sarongs. Showpiece of the village is the blue and white painted mosque – the Chams are Muslims – but no burqas here, only a few pillbox hats worn by young boys. Signs are in Arabic, although the boys only learn to read the Koran. They speak Cham, a Malayo-Polynesian language, and study in Vietnamese at school.

From the village we take a bus, stopping in Binh Duc, a village devoted to making joss sticks. Here a girl and a boy take slim slivers of split bamboo, roll them in sawdust and glue – the scents are a secret – and produce five thousand sticks a day. Pay: $2 a day.

From Can Tho next morning very early, we set out in a motor boat for Cai Rang floating market. Mounds of cucumbers, water melons, flowers, onions, green beans, cabbages, star fruit, turnips and coconuts are heaped on boats of all shapes and sizes: wooden canoes, big wooden-sided houseboats, small and medium-sized boats with thatched canopies, motorboats, poled boats, rowing boats. Bargaining is shouted from boat to boat. A rooster struts on the roof of one boat. Moving through this highly vocal, floating traffic jam takes much patience and skill, forward and backward in turn.

Leaving the market we head up a narrow canal between wood and straw houses, cluttered with pots, old bicycle tyres, coconut husks, all the detritus of river life without a rubbish collection service. Children line up on one roof to shout hello, dancing frantically to catch our attention.

The boat stops at a rice mill where three ageing machines press the rice to remove the husk; grinding, polishing and separating the short or broken grains from the undamaged long grains. Nothing is wasted. The husks are burnt for fertilizer; the bran left after the husks are removed is fed to animals. There are three polishings, each leaving fewer vitamins. A hundred kilos of unhusked rice makes seventy kilos of white rice. Five per cent of any bag will be broken rice, the short grains fed to the animals. The best rice sells for one dollar a kilo. It makes one appreciate what every grain of rice has gone through before it reaches our tables, not to mention the labour of planting and harvesting.

We climb into a bus and as the sun is dipping, arrive at the Thot Not Egret Sanctuary. Around a pond, white egrets flutter into the trees, already densely heavy with egrets.

Later that night in Saigon, I eat at the Brodard Restaurant surrounded by American college students, all of whom seem to know one another. One undertakes to interview me.

'What are ya-all doin' here?'

I wonder the same. They are on a two-month-long, study-cruise costing $15,000 each – all seven hundred of them – travelling halfway round the world.

Saigon is a funny kind of town. While pleasant enough, I am ready to head back north.

NHA TRANG – THE ICE MAN COMETH

New spirits fear old ones
– Vietnamese proverb

At Saigon's Tan Son Nhat Airport, five minutes before the plane is scheduled to take off, the announcement finally comes to board. We clamour into a bus and jiggle out to the aircraft where the bus disgorges us onto the tarmac in 'heat that burns your kidneys.'

A tiny ham sandwich and an orange juice later, we land at Nha Trang, known for its white sand beach stretching four miles (6 km). I remember Nha Trang from the cruise as a bustling fishing port of broad-beamed boats bobbing under red, white and blue striped sails. But my reason for coming back to Nha Trang, are the remains of the Cham temples.

En route to the Po Nagar temples just north of town, I hop out of the taxi on the bridge over the Cai river to see if the fishing boats are still there. Suddenly, far below, a huge block of ice slides precariously down a long metal track from the river bank above the water to a narrow sampan where a man with consummate skill, stops the ice from flying off the far side of his boat, no wider than a canoe. Now I know why I am not consuming ice from Vietnamese roadside carts with grinding machines that sell temptingly refreshing fruit juice over crushed ice.

The river scene is so lively that the old Cham temples have to wait. Below the bridge, people in boats are eating, washing, hanging laundry, moving fish and produce, poling sampans and manoeuvring larger, engine-powered junks. Boatmen and children wave up to me as they disappear under the bridge.

Round basket boats called *thung chai* here in the South, rather like water beetles, ferry fishermen to and from shore. *Thung* means basket, *chai* means pitch. Larger than Welsh coracles, *thung chai* can accommodate four or five slender Vietnamese. A few *thung chai* float, tethered to thatched houses on stilts, stuck somewhat askew into the riverbank.

157

Sadly, sailing junks are almost a sight of the romantic past. During the cruise I saw one in Halong Bay, used as an excursion boat. Such a pity not to have arrived in Vietnam a few years earlier. I finally turn away from the river towards the temples on the hill.

By now it is hot, very hot. Steep steps lead to a grid of freestanding pillars that formerly supported the roof of a *mandapa,* a meditation or rest house, which is amongst the oldest remains of Po Nagar. It is recorded that it was built in 817 by a certain army general, Senapati Par. The ancient Cham language used in inscriptions on stone stelae differs considerably from present day Cham. Highly influenced by the Hinduism of India, the Chams used Sanskrit as a religious language as well as their own language, which originated from Malayo-Polynesian roots. To this day the Chams around Phan Rang, sixty miles (96 km) south of Nha Trang, speak an old Malayo-Polynesian language that can be understood by a tribe in Borneo.

I had been curious about the Chams and their sculpture since as long ago as living in Cambodia. The Cham civilization appeared as early as the second century and lasted to the fifteenth, flourishing farther north around Hoi An, Danang and Hue. In its heyday, Champa extended from the Ngang Pass in the Hoanh Son mountains near the eighteenth parallel north of Hue, south to the borders of Chenla in the Mekong delta. There were several Cham rulers simultaneously, each reigning over his own clan kingdom, often warring with one another.

In central Vietnam, the Chams intermingled with the Mon-Khmer tribes, some of the latter remaining today as ethnic hill tribes. The Chams were pushed south by the northern Viets to Nha Trang, and later, still further south to Phan Rang where a concentration of Chams still lives.

On various points, historians and archaeologists disagree vehemently. The Chams are lauded by some as great traders and slated by others as the pirates of South East Asia, who lived by attacking passing trading ships. They certainly remained in conflict with the Viets to the north and the Khmers to the west during the early centuries of their development, and even with the Javanese, an ocean away to the south.

The temples of Po Nagar are mainly built of thin red bricks, held together not by mortar, but by a mysterious natural glue, which archaeologists believe may be a type of resin, *dipterocarpus alatus roxb,* that was heated and mixed with ground mollusc shells (oysters, snails or mussels) and crushed bricks, a mixture still used in central

Vietnam to coat the hulls of boats to render them waterproof. Carvings were sculpted in the brick – after the towers were built.

The first temple (south) complex of Po Nagar, its arched roofs and square sanctuaries linked by a vestibule, dates from the twelfth century. The sway-backed roof of the north-west temple is reminiscent of the matriarchal Minangkabau of (mainly) Sumatra, its walls decorated with carvings of the garuda bird, also an echo of Indonesia. On one lintel over a doorway, a carved lion and a human figure sit nonchalantly on the head of a carved elephant. One has to remember that elephants were used as transport in Vietnam, especially during wars, well into the nineteenth century. This temple was built towards the end of the tenth century.

The much-weathered north tower, seventy-four feet (23 m) high, also built in 817, is considered to be a superb example of Cham architecture and seems quite similar to the corner towers of Angkor Wat in Cambodia on a much smaller scale – in red brick rather than grey sandstone. It is one of the tallest surviving Cham towers, square-shaped with a three-tiered conical roof, curved like a fingertip.

With the pleasure of recognition, I find figures seated in the lotus position and *apsaras,* the dancers familiar to anyone who has wandered around Indian and Khmer temples. In fact, the face-framing crowns or headdresses of the Cham deities are so similar to those of Khmer statues, and so familiar the broad, placid faces with wide noses, thick lips and enigmatic smiles, that had I met them in another place, I would have taken them for Khmer. But I am an amateur temple tramp.

Astonishingly, the ironwood doors leading to the sanctuary are the originals. Inside the sanctuary, the goddess Bharagati, idolized as Yang Po Ino Nagar, the mother goddess of the Chams, sits cross-legged on a lotus throne, waving ten arms. Although statues of the goddess have been replaced many times – at each insurrection the temple statues were destroyed – the present statue was carved in 1050 during the reign of King Jaya Paramesvaravarman.

Flanking the statue of Yang Po Ino Nagar stand two carved ironwood elephants, unique in Cham art, dating from the eighth or ninth century. It is astonishing that they have survived this hot, humid climate for more than a thousand years. Having been fascinated by Asian temples since I first glimpsed the carved *bas reliefs* of Angkor Wat years ago in Cambodia, and later, the erotic carvings of Indian temples, the epics in carved stone along the terraces of Borobodur in

159

Java and the very different Hindu temples of Bali, I have longed to see these brick sanctuaries and towers built by the Chams. Today I realize an ambition – to find what looks like a strong link between the Khmer temples of Angkor, the Cham temples of Vietnam and the Hindu temples of Java, all strongly influenced by the religious carvings of India.

The Chams liberally adopted and grafted on religions as they came along, a habit still practiced in Vietnam's pagodas and temples today. In addition to the old Brahma-Hindu based religion called Cham Ba-La-Mon, in the ninth century Buddhism was added, possibly by way of Java, but there is no evidence to prove via which route it came.

One Cham kingdom further north built a new capital, Indrapura, and a Buddhist monastery called Lasmindra-Lokesvara. Some time later, Chams took up an Islamic religion known as Cham Ba-Ni. (The present-day form of Islam in the Mekong delta, known as Cham Islam, is completely distinct from the older form.)

According to their mythology, the Chams sprang from Uroja, the mother goddess of the race. In the Cham language her name means 'woman's breast', which explains the abundance of well-rounded female breasts used as borders around friezes and the pedestals of pillars in Cham sculpture, rather like Buddhists use lotus flowers in their decorative borders.

Uroja was one of a trinity of gods in the Cham Ba-La-Mon religion, but she was the only goddess and confusingly, is also known as Po Nagar, hence the name of the temples at Nha Trang.

Stone inscriptions record that the original wooden temple at Po Nagar was burnt to the ground by the Javanese in 774 and again in 784. Thereafter temples at Po Nagar were built of brick and stone over a period from the eighth to the thirteenth centuries. Of the ten original structures, only five red brick temples and towers remain.

After a stroll around the temples, I sit for a time in the shade of a banyan tree. The granite hill on which Po Nagar is perched affords a fine view of the bridge and the broad river. I watch the frilly-dressed tots brought by their parents to visit the temples, musing that families have been paying homage to the goddess Po Nagar at these temples for well over a millennium.

On the way back, I stop at Long Son pagoda. The huge white modern Buddha, high on a hill and seen from a good many vantage points around town, was erected to commemorate the monks and nuns who died by self-emulation, protesting against the Catholic regime of South Vietnam's President, Ngo Dinh Diem.

The pagoda at the bottom of the steps is presided over by a brown-robed monk and a tumble of little boys determined to sell either postcards or their services as guides. Despite the little boys, Long Son is an attractive pagoda, guarded by snarling dragons on the roof. I am touched by the translation of an admonition written by a singular idealist, presumably a monk nearing Nirvana.

'Not to do any evil,
To perform what is good,
To keep one's own heart pure,
These are the teachings of Lord Buddha.'

Followng advice, next morning I head for a small fishing cove to find a boat to visit the islands. The boat is powered by two nimble, able-bodied young men who I suspect expend more energy in starting the motor after each stop than the motor produces in the five hours. At Bamboo Island (Hon Tre), without much common language I dumbly follow the lads up a steep, rocky path over a minor mountain and down the other side to reach, wringing wet, pink and puffing, Tru beach. I would have thrown myself into the water, but was caught without a bathing suit.

We wade in up to our knees and content ourselves with kicking sand into the holes of the sand crabs that burrow on this beach. There is a long inexplicable wait in a thatched hut for a Coke. Finally, we discover that the waiter is waiting, too – for the ice man. The same ice man? We have warm Cokes.

Through a variety of signs the boat boys inform me that the Vietnamese come to this beach in the hot season to sleep. When might *that* be?

After choking the engine and pulling the cord many times, we splutter off. From an island with only one thatched hut, Swallow Island (Hon Yen) boasts a water sports concession with all manner of modern speed craft to hire. This time we have cool Cokes.

At the open-air aquarium on the next island, huge turtles swim up to investigate. They have invited quite a few of their fancy-dressed friends to the party: an orange fish with a big silly grin; a busy body, striped turquoise fish with golden fins; a brown polka dot fish with yellow fins.

161

Approaching a pebble beach at the next island, I imperiously wave the boatmen on and we proceed to Tam Island, where I step onto a floating barge-like affair off shore, built around large fish cages holding giant cuttlefish and a bright orange fish called *mu*. *Thung chai* basket boats jostle for position around the barges, each captained by a young girl and I am expected to hop into one of these to get to shore. Despite wearing rubber-soled sandals, I feel somewhat wary of stepping into a basket, considering that I probably weigh twice as much as its winsome captain. Very gingerly I step in and precariously, we bob to shore where the girl beaches the boat for my dry-footed convenience. Now, that's service.

Tam Island was best saved for last. I wander along narrow sandy lanes that have probably never felt the wheel of more than a cart, past houses built on stilts, jutting out over the water, past wooden houses with thatched roofs and earthen floors. Children play in the sandy lanes. A woman lays out her inventory of lingerie on a straw mat to sell to the squatting village matrons. Families eat under open thatched verandas. Doubtless, many strangers have visited this village, but I am made to feel welcome by the friendly hellos of the children and the broad smiles of the people, who seem not to mind in the least a stranger wandering uninvited through their domestic lives.

Back onshore, after a swim on Nha Trang's beach, that night as I sip sweet and sour fish soup followed by crab claws, I wonder if they were caught by the fishermen of Tam Island or those under the bridge of the Cai river. A half moon rests in an inky sky. As I sit on the veranda, a cool off-shore breeze soothingly rattles the thatch beach parasols. I simply cannot bring myself to tune into CNN to check on the state of the world.

DANANG AND THE CHAMS

For the bird, its nest,
For man, his ancestors
– Vietnamese proverb

It was in the port city of Danang near the centre of Cham culture that *l'Ecole Française d'Extrême Orient* established their museum of Champa sculpture. As this small, unique museum was one of the reasons why I had originally wanted to visit Vietnam, I make for it straight away.

Open to the coastal winds that blow across the courtyard and through the open windows, inside the plump Hindu baby elephant god, Ganesha, looks like he wants his tummy rubbed and a very Indian-looking Nandin bull might have dropped, petrified in an Indian road. Goddesses and nubile *apsara* temple dancers balance on one toe, sea monsters glare through bulging eyes and mythical garuda birds that served as the flying Porsches for the Hindu god, Siva, look poised for take-off.

Dancing Sivas wave a superfluity of arms and an impressive linga, the phallic symbol of Siva, stands to worshipful attention. Busy friezes from an altar depict the wedding ceremony of the Princess Sita and a game of shuttlecocks played on horseback – an eighth century forerunner of polo?

The Chams' earliest capital in the late fourth century was Simhapura, the Lion City (long before Singapore), thirty-six miles (68 km) south-west of Danang. The village is now known as Tra Kieu and many of the museum's treasures have been brought from there.

Unlike the Khmers, an agricultural people, the seafaring Chams traded from very early on with China, India and Java from their port in the Thu Bon river basin. Their old port, called Faifo by the Portuguese, is now known as Hoi An.

The original museum is remarkably small. Yet true to my expectations, its treasures bear witness in stone to the close links, well over a thousand years ago, between South India, Java, Sumatra and Cambodia and experts agree that there were particularly close ties between the Khmer of Cambodia and the Chams. A fair quantity of

163

Cham sculpture was carted off by the French to the five-storey Guimet Museum in Paris, which specialises in Asian art, and which also, incidentally, contains a fine collection of Khmer sculpture. The Champa Museum in turn, has the Guimet to thank for its very survival, as during the Vietnam War the curator of Cham art at the Guimet made a plea to spare it from bombing.

A few minutes down the road from Danang, at the foot of Marble Mountains is the village of Hoa Hai, where sculptors – perhaps the assimilated descendants of the Chams – still work in stone. Two men under a red flowering flamboyant tree, sit sawing by hand through what must be a one-ton block of marble, one man at either end of a long handsaw.

A life-sized stone lion can be bought for US$1,400 (£900), marble bracelets for two dollars. The men and boys of the village sit tapping at the stone. The women polish, finishing off with beeswax.

Marble Mountains rise abruptly from the plain, five colossal scrub-covered lumps, each named for one of the five elements: water, wood, fire, metal and earth.

The first time I visited as a cruise passenger, at the foot of the mountains I was besieged by children clamouring to lead me up the steep stone steps. Finally, I agreed to be led by a young woman with a sweet face. Up we went to cave number one, cave number two, cave number three. Some of the caves held brightly painted modern statues. One or two had old Buddhas or the goddess of mercy. Beside the entrance to one cave, the thoughts of Buddhist, Kinh Phap Cu, had been recorded:

'Hatreds never cease by hatreds in this world,
By love alone they cease. This is an ancient law.'

Ironic, considering that it was from the Marble Mountains that a good many American planes were shot down and even now, shafts of sunlight filter through the leaves that nearly cover the opening at the top of one large cave that served as a Viet Cong infirmary, its roof holed by a bomb.

Up and up the steep steps, at last we finally reached 'the gate to heaven,' presumably named by some public relations-minded monk. Once in heaven, there was a very distant view of China Beach below, where I would have much preferred to be. So down I scrambled as fast as jellied knees and childish vendors would allow. China Beach was blissfully free of parasols and ice cream carts.

As I soon came to discover in Vietnam, any seemingly unnatural geographical feature attracts myths and legends, particularly if a lump of stone juts abruptly from a plain, and most assuredly, if it is riddled with caves. Fairies and demons live in caves. So naturally, there were numerous myths and legends surrounding Marble Mountains. My favourite and one of the first stories I heard about sacred dragons, was told to me by Vietnamese scholar, Huu Ngoc in Hanoi –

Long, long ago, a poor, lonely fisherman came to live along this shore. One day, the sky suddenly darkened, a brisk wind arose and the sea turned to a foaming frenzy. Out of the roar of the gale emerged an enormous dragon. The earth trembled as the dragon writhed towards the old man's thatched hut. To the astonishment of the old fisherman cowering inside, who watched through a slit in the thatching, the dragon laid an egg on the beach and then writhed back toward the sea. A few minutes later, a huge golden turtle emerged from the surf and slowly crawled towards the old man's hut. Reaching the egg, the turtle stopped and ponderously dug a hole, carefully burying the egg. Then the turtle approached the old man.

'I am the sacred golden turtle', he announced, 'and it is my wish that you should protect this drop of blood of the sacred dragon.'

Well, the old fisherman was quite overcome and protested: 'But I am old, how can I possibly carry out such a sacred responsibility?' In response, the turtle held out one of his claws to the old man saying, 'Whenever the egg is in danger, put this claw to your ear and I will tell you what to do.'

The old man gratefully took the claw, promising to do his best and the sacred golden turtle slowly crawled back to the sea.

One day the old man looked up from his gardening to see an ox-cart full of armed men approaching. Now, as the old man had never seen another living soul along this beach, he was terrified, and doubly alarmed when he realised that the cart was heading straight for the spot where the precious egg was buried. He hurried to place himself in their path, signalling to the men to turn aside.

They shouted, 'Out of the way, old man, we change our course for no man.' Trembling, the old man put the claw of the sacred golden turtle to his ear and heard the calm voice of the turtle saying, 'Lie down in the path of the cart.'

Now this took a lot of courage, but the old man did as he was told and he was immediately transformed into a huge snarling tiger that frightened the bandits away.

After that experience, the old man decided that the egg needed better protection, so he set about dismantling his hut and rebuilt it over the egg. To his consternation the ground beneath the hut began to shift. The egg seemed to be moving, growing. No matter how hard he tried to keep it covered, it kept emerging from its hiding place. It grew bigger and bigger and the shell began to glow and sparkle, as if a giant gem filled the poor fisherman's humble hut.

Exhausted from his labours, finally the old man lay down to rest. He was awakened by the sound of crackling flames. The bandits had returned to avenge their shame. Once more, the old man called the sacred golden turtle and instantly found himself in a large, cool cave on a comfortable bed. He lay down again to rest and while he slept, the egg hatched and a tiny girl appeared.

The five pieces of the shell had turned into five mountains and it was in one of the caves in these mountains that the old man slept. Meanwhile, the daughter of the dragon was looked after by the birds, who brought her milk that flowed from the rocks and fruit from the trees. To keep her warm, they brought threads from far and wide and wove them into beautiful clothes. Much time passed before the old man finally opened his eyes, finding the claw of the sacred golden turtle still beside him and to his astonishment, a pretty young girl. She smiled at him and cried out, 'At last, you are awake. I have listened to your breathing for fifteen years. I am so happy that you are awake.'

Well, the old man was again taken by surprise when they stepped out of the cave and found five new mountains covered with bushes, trees and birds. As father and daughter, he and the girl lived together for a time and the animals who had reared the little girl became their great friends.

By then, other people had moved into the area and they had been dumbfounded when the mountains suddenly appeared. When they discovered the old man and the young girl living in one of the caves, the rumour spread that they were angels, sent to help the poor people. Many villagers visited the pair, seeking a cure for a deadly fever. The girl took a handful of stones and scattered them on the ground. As they fell, they became five-petalled flowers, which the people used as a medicine to cure the fever. Soon, word of the angel with healing powers spread throughout the land and a brave young prince came riding to the mountain, seeking her hand in marriage. Once again, the old man lifted the claw to his ear to consult the sacred golden turtle and this time, the turtle appeared before him.

'The sacred dragon accepts the prince as a husband for his daughter. So let her go with him. And now, old man, you must sit upon my back.'

The old man said a sad farewell to the girl he had loved as a daughter and the sacred golden turtle carried him away into the sea, never to be seen again. The five mountains are all that remain. But the five-petalled flowers can still be found in the area and it is said by some that they can be used as a cure for malaria. The local people call this beach Non Nuoc, which translates as Mountain Water. The mountains received their names during the reign of the second Nguyen emperor, Minh Mang, who in 1836 made a tour of the area and named the mountains after the five elements.

Another legend, told to me by my friend Tung in Hue, may suggest the conflict between the several religions that have competed for the devotion of the Vietnamese. According to this legend, Buddha wanted to punish a monkey god named Ton Ngo Khong, (there is a monkey king in the Hindu Ramayana). Because the monkey was stupid, he didn't want to follow the revolution (conversion)? The emperor of heaven (Confucian) wanted to punish him, but the monkey (Hindu) was very stubborn, so the emperor of heaven had to ask Buddha to help him. Buddha challenged the monkey to fly over his hand, knowing that the monkey couldn't fly. Then Buddha took the monkey in his hand and the monkey had to stay there, trapped inside for five hundred years. Later, to help the monkey to change, the Buddha set him free and ordered him to follow and to aid a Buddhist monk in bringing Buddhist scriptures from India to China. When the trip ended successfully, as a reward for having helped the monk to overcome the many difficulties of the journey, the monkey became a Buddha. People say that the Marble Mountains are the remains of the five fingers of Buddha.

This time approaching the Marble Mountains, I point-blank refuse to stagger up all those steps again, so I allow the first little girl who appears to lead me through the pines to a quiet part of China Beach, away from the shops selling stone statues and the attractive bracelets and necklaces. For the price of a cool bottle of water, she and an old crone selling seashells agree to watch my bags.

'No problem,' says the crone in an American accent.

167

She might have learned it from a marine, a quarter of a century ago. After a swim – surely it is a mistake that the human species ever left the sea – she leads me back through a quiet hamlet under the trees to her thatched wooden house, motioning that I may use her outdoor tap to wash the sand off my feet. Now this is kindness combined with thoughtful enterprise, so a very grateful guest rewards her with a few thousand *dong*.

But I have not come to Vietnam to loll on a beach, however agreeable. As the cruise did not include a visit to Myson, the most important Cham site in the area roughly forty miles (70 km) south-west of Danang, I am now hell bent on getting there and organise a four-wheel-drive taxi.

Driving anywhere in Vietnam can be something of an adventure, depending on the state of the road surface. You might be skimming along over freshly rolled tarmac for ten miles and then suddenly bump into the stone age – sharp stones, seemingly pointed intentionally at your tyres, or deep potholes, excavated during the last rainy season, if not by bombs. And that was the road to Myson.

The scenery, however, is lifted from those pale paintings on silk, or perhaps it is vice versa. We pass villages selling brass and watermelons. On a river, single figures under conical hats pole long slim boats, one foot on deck, one foot on the paddle. On both sides of the road, rice paddies look like soft strips of green, ranging from the electric green of seedling rice, through a palette of deeper greens to the pale hues of golden straw ripe for harvest.

Paddies are at every stage of growth. Ploughmen plod through mud behind buffaloes, women with their trouser-legs rolled up, toss out handfuls of rice seed into paddies already green with sprouting seedlings. Women lope along with bound bunches of seedling rice bouncing from shoulder poles en route to transplanting.

On one dyke beside a paddy, straw is being fed through a foot-peddled grinding machine to separate it from the grain.

In another place, straw is being tossed up in the air, then laid out on mats to dry beside the road or actually on the road surface. Basket trays beside the road hold unhusked rice and women are raking it to make sure that every grain receives a strong dose of sunshine. Along the roadside, women carry huge loads of straw suspended from shoulder poles to their homes where haystacks will be built in the courtyards. Apart from agricultural activities, outside nearly every house a tiny roadside kiosk displays jars of petrol, tinned drinks, strings of straw bonnets or clutches of long gloves. One woman triumphantly holds up a live frog for sale, doubtless just caught in a paddy or canal.

Inside the air-conditioned, four-wheel-drive vehicle, I cling to the handle above the door as we bounce and lurch along. Bicycle and scooter drivers pretend to be deaf to air horns behind them and eventually just beside them.

Motorized vehicles almost nudge them to the side of the road, like porpoises nudge swimmers towards shore. Surprisingly, the nudge rarely touches the bike or scooter, but when there is an accident, all on-coming traffic stops dead in the middle of the road and spectators stop to look and adjudicate, utterly oblivious to on-coming air horns.

Arriving at Myson around half past nine – we had started at eight to beat the heat – my brain is so scrambled from the ride that I am unsure on my feet. It is blistering hot, having reached a point for the superlative of superlatives: 'Heat that burns, boils, cooks, roasts, cremates.' In fact, that day at Myson in April was the hottest of my entire year in Vietnam.

I cannot imagine how the Chams managed to build even one tower. How long must it have taken them, working between dawn and nine in the morning – my considered recommendation if they valued their hides and sanity. To my joy and relief I am bundled into another four-wheel drive-vehicle, this one without air-conditioning, together with a Vietnamese mother and her small son clutching a packet of biscuits. To my chagrin, the vehicle stops on the bank of a shallow, wide stream over which stretches a long, sinewy bamboo footbridge. I snap a photograph of it, in case I survive. Somehow, I teeter across and fear subsides when my feet touch the far bank.

The sun beats down with a vengeance and heat waves waver on the horizon. Crickets chatter maniacally and yellow butterflies swoop like crazed vultures. There are two more bridges to cross, each consisting of two logs. Heat seems to rise from the dense green vegetation as well as pressing down from above. It is certainly 'heat to burst the heavens.' Finally rounding a bend in the path, the curved tips of the brick towers of Myson loom just above the treetops, silhouetted darkly against the sky. For a moment the sun slips behind a cloud – utter, total bliss. Low, broken brick walls form a square courtyard. Along one side lay the remnants of the statues of a bull, an elephant and a stone stele. Red wild flowers bloom just inside the

169

enclosure, and leaves and vines protrude from the cracks and the windows of the towers. Though it is doubtless unhealthy for the monuments, it is stirring to stumble upon ruins overtaken by nature, making one feel for just an instant, like a discoverer.

Myson is thought by some to have been the ceremonial burial place for Cham rulers and the first towers were built as early as the fourth century. Within the temple complex, carved stone pilasters and lintels lie strewn where they have fallen or sometimes where they have been lined up in front of their former openings by archaeologists from Europe and Vietnam, who in spite of under-funding, have worked hard to try to protect them from the ravages of nature – and earlier, from mines and bombs. The largest temple has carved stone windows with turned, stone balustrades, to the amateur eye, exactly like those of Angkor. The roof of the upper, smaller storey of one temple is sway-backed, the same curve as the roofs of the matriarchal Minangkabau of Sumatra. Two of the temples now serve as small museums, holding a few statues and large carved stone lintels. Several more temple complexes at Myson lie scattered over the hillsides. I have been warned not to venture off the paths because of possible undiscovered mines. The question is, where are the paths? Any path? I can see the tips of ruins above the trees, but whatever paths there are have now been completely overgrown. In the end, it is so oppressively hot that the tropics triumph over cultural curiosity and this temple tramp timorously retreats.

The Chams must have been one very tough race of people to have built brick and stone temples in this climate.

(Note: A new road and a bridge for vehicles have been built, paths laid, mines and the jungle cleared since my first visit and numerous tour buses arrive every morning from Hoi An.)

HOI AN – REFUGE OF THE FIRST BOAT PEOPLE

The swallow skims over the ground,
Rain will swell the pond,
The swallow flies high,
The shower will be short
– Vietnamese proverb

An easy half-hour from Danang, Hoi An is a very special old, three-street town, unlike any other in Vietnam. The oldest streets run parallel along the Hoi An river, a tributary of the Thu Bon river.

Used as a port by the Chams, rather surprisingly in the sixteenth century, Japanese traders established a colony here and sometime in the 1590s, built a covered, wooden bridge. In the late seventeenth century, successive waves of Chinese arrived, fleeing hostile regimes. Whenever a dynasty fell, the losers fled south. The first wave of Chinese boat people were members of the Ming dynasty, escaping persecution by the triumphant Qing.

Flourishing as an international trading port from the sixteenth to nineteenth centuries, Hoi An's heydays were contemporary with those of Macao and Malacca. Traders called in from as far away as China, Japan, Java, Siam and South India, and in Europe from Portugal and Spain, the Netherlands and France. Even the English stopped by, but didn't stay long. As late comers, the competition was already too well established.

Politically, in its heydays Hoi An was fairly autonomous. The settlement-minded Nguyen lords of Hue recognised the advantages of encouraging foreign trade and liberally allowed both the Chinese and Japanese colonies in Hoi An to appoint their own governors. Somewhat later in 1636, Japan introduced a Closed Door Policy and ordered the Japanese living in Hoi An back to Japan on pain of death or 'excommunication'. Hoi An proudly preserves a legacy of these early wealthy merchant houses, some of the finest domestic architecture in the country and in all of South East Asia.

But Hoi An as a port was doomed. In the nineteenth century, the river silted up and trading shifted to Danang, then variously called by the French, Tourane or Turon, leaving the town little more than a centre for Vietnam's ethnic-Chinese. Many still return annually to celebrate clan fetes, although nowadays, the Chinese have been fully assimilated, having married Vietnamese women generations back.

I am staying in a new air-conditioned mini-hotel on the far side of the Japanese Bridge. Walking into town in the midday sun, I pass two little girls, squatting beneath a tree, playing house with china teacups and saucers like little girls everywhere. At the Japanese Bridge, I follow as a young man lifts his bicycle over the door sills.

First called the Bridge of People From Afar, building the Japanese Bridge was based around the legend of a huge monster, so large that his head was in India, his body in Vietnam, his tail in China. Whenever this monster moved, there was a natural disaster: a drought, a flood or an earthquake. So to prevent these disasters, the bridge was built over the monster's weakest point – to pin him down. Local people believe that two sacred swords lie buried beneath the bridge, but no one can tell me how or why they got there, or how they fit into the story of the monster.

At each end of the bridge, small statues of a monkey and a dog commemorate the fact that the bridge was started in the Year of the Monkey and completed in the Year of the Dog. Midway across the bridge, hidden behind a pair of doors, a small shrine is dedicated to the god against floods and drought, both of which have afflicted the town over the centuries. The rainy season in Hoi An is sufficiently serious for the roof tiles to have grown velvety green moss and the last flood was recent enough to be pictured on colour postcards showing people in boats rowing through the streets, the water reaching half way up their doors. And no, it did not look like Venice.

Happily, the enlightened local authorities of Hoi An recognize the importance of their architectural heritage. In 1985 the town was declared a National Monument and in 1999, it became a UNESCO World Heritage Site. But 1990 was the real turning point with the opening of the town's first hostelry, the Hoi An Hotel, the colonial building a legacy of the French. During the Vietnam War it was occupied by the Americans and after 1975 by the Communists, who made it the town hall. In 1990, commercial wisdom prevailed and it became a hotel. The town's officials have also had the good sense to ban cars in the old part of town during certain hours, the only town in Vietnam so far to do so. Consequently, during business hours, visitors can stroll unmolested down the middle of Hoi An's oldest streets.

Many of the lovely old houses and the Chinese community assembly halls *(hoi quan)* are open to visitors, so Hoi An is a tourist

172

town. The oldest houses, many beautifully carved, afford a glimpse of life as it was lived a couple of centuries ago.

I start with Tanky House, a long, narrow, two-storey dwelling with an interior of dark wood, probably the oldest and grandest of the shop houses, its beams as ornately carved as furniture, its pillars inlaid with mother-of-pearl. The woods used are long lasting ironwood, mahogany and a local wood called *kim kieng*. In an age of high technology when theoretically, it is possible to produce anything, invariably it is skilfully hand-crafted objects that give us the deepest pleasure. I am invited to sit on the antique furniture and sip a tiny cup of green tea.

At the time Tanky House was built, the river came right up to the back door and a wooden pulley lifted cargo directly to the second floor warehouse. The current mistress of the house, a dignified matron wearing black silk pyjamas, sits at a desk. I am told later that the owners of the house, the umpteenth generation to occupy it, are very wealthy. This is not apparent in the simplicity of their lifestyle, unless they live elsewhere. They sleep on a straw mat on a wooden bed. Their kitchen has two clay pot 'burners' and well-seasoned pots piled on open shelves. The only concession to modernity is a small fridge. The lady of the house brings out the guest book and turns the pages to one holding the cards of English visitors. Here is the card of a travel writer from London's *Sunday Times*. Well, I couldn't expect to have been the first.

It was also in Hoi An where the first Christian missionaries, Portuguese and Italian priests, set foot on Vietnamese soil. Having been thrown out of Japan in 1614, the Jesuit priests fled to Hoi An, where they introduced Christianity to Vietnam.

The Jacques-come-lately French Jesuit, Alexandre de Rhodes, is much lauded by the French for having published the first Vietnamese dictionary in the Romanized *quoc ngu* script in 1651. However, according to scholars, who as proof point to the very un-French accents used in modern Vietnamese, it was Portuguese and Italian priests who actually developed the diacritical markings of the Romanized *quoc ngu,* which enabled the scriptures to be read in Vietnamese by the common people. Until then, the c*hu nom* ideograms could only be read by scholars. Although easier to print, *quoc ngu* was not popularised until the twentieth century when the French stopped the old mandarin examination system and with it, the use of *chu nom* ideographs for all official documents.

As I amble along the street, the unmistakable scents of a Chinese apothecary shop twitch at my nose. I slide past the jars holding snake wine.

The brightly-painted gate of Phuc Kien Assembly Hall belies its age, 1775. The painted monsters on the gate 'represent two vampires, who were so impressed by the pure goodness of a young girl seeking medicine for her sick mother in the terrifying dark mountain forests that they were converted into – good monsters.'

The gate conceals an older temple behind it, dating from 1697. Originally a Buddhist pagoda, the temple is dedicated to Thien Hau, goddess of the sea, who protected the first waves of Chinese refugees fleeing to Hoi An from China.

'Thien Hau's magical powers enable her to travel on a flying mat above the waves with her assistants to rescue sailors and fishermen, and particularly, the exodus of the Ming. Her assistant, Thien Ly Nhan, has the power to see for a thousand miles. Her second assistant, Thuan Phong Nhi, can hear for a thousand miles.'

And whenever the good goddess and her assistants get bored with flying around the South China Sea, saving sailors and boat people, they can stop to watch football on television with the friendly temple guardian.

Facing the courtyard stands yet another temple, 'popular with young couples.' A high threshold 'forces people to bow their heads reverently' – to keep from falling into the temple. Inside is a large wooden replica of a Chinese junk, exactly the kind of vessel that brought the waves of Chinese emigrants to Hoi An, the carp atop the mast, a good omen for seafarers.

'The central altar is dedicated to ancestors, the altar on the left to prosperity, the altar on the right to the birth fairy,' giving a fair indication of Chinese priorities. Religious people in Vietnam take the sensible, pragmatic attitude that one temple will do for the worship of several deities. Unlike Allah, their gods are not jealous gods.

A few steps away is one of Hoi An's oldest temples, Quan Cong, also known as Chua Ong, built in 1653. The Vietnamese have the disconcerting habit of changing the names of temples, pagodas, people and places altogether too frequently to suit the hapless foreigner, struggling with Vietnamese names. For instance, formerly a new baby would be given a rude nickname such as Ugly or Penis – to discourage the demons from carrying it away. Around the age of two, amidst much ceremony, the child would receive a proper name. But if the child later entered a monastery, this meant another name change. If a man became a poet, he adopted a pen name. In the past, if he were rewarded by the emperor, his name would change. Or if he became emperor, he would take a new name and when he died, of course, a brand new posthumous name.

Villages and towns, temples and streets have changed names often throughout the centuries. Yet oddly, while everyone else is changing names, Vietnamese women do not change their names, not when they marry, not ever, unless they became queen.

'Quan Cong temple is dedicated to a famous character in Chinese history, noted for his bravery, loyalty and benevolence.'

His statue stares out from the central altar, flanked left and right by one of his trusty generals and by his adopted son. The carved white horse that looks as if it has just leapt off a carousel was his steed 'until he was given the new red one to go into battle' – maybe to hide the blood. The temple serves as a mini-history museum and one exhibit points out that this area has been home to no fewer than three civilisations: Sa Huynh from 200 BC to 200 AD, which left behind burial jars containing treasures; Cham from 200 to 1500 AD and Dai Viet – the Nguyens – who came South in the sixteenth century.

An old wooden anchor leans against one wall. From what ship, through what seas and adventures has it travelled? No one knows. There is a framed nineteenth century drawing by one J. Barrow entitled *On the Hoi An River, Voyage to Dang Trong in 1792-1793,* stating that the book was published in London in 1806. I am told by a British academic that J. Barrow was the artist who accompanied Lord Macartney on his famous mission to China, where his request for trading rights was rejected because he refused to kow-tow to the emperor of China.

As an assemblage of exotica, the temple is a feast. In the next courtyard, painted dragons decorate the doors and a mynah bird chortles raucously from a cage beside a rock garden. It has to be said, in Vietnam a rock garden is quite something else from what a Brit or a Japanese might imagine, approaching dangerously close to kitsch and gnome-land.

It starts as a lump of rock or several rocks placed artfully together to form a mini-mountain range. Into the crevices all manner of small plants and orchids are introduced. So far so good. Unfortunately, this is never quite enough. Invariably, tiny plastic storks, frogs, a miniature temple, a tower, an arched bridge are added to produce an extravagant three-dimensional miniature fantasy land, a nursery play-table for adults, usually, the centrepiece of a courtyard.

With the sun beating down, I am glad to slip into the shade and darkness of the market just opposite the temples. A young man with alarmingly long, violet-painted fingernails does his best to impress me with his bolts of cloth. Is he gay or just an image-building entrepreneur? Hard to tell.

Behind the market along the quay, on both sides of the narrow passageway, wooden stalls hardly larger than kiosks display signs advertising massage, pedicures, manicures, head washes and head massage. I watch as without the benefit of running water, the procedure is to pour shampoo onto the dry hair, to work it in with the addition of a few drops of water, then when the head is foamy, to lay the client flat on a wooden bed, face up with the head extending off one end, the hair rinsed with water from a bucket. One step up in the consumer society from a shampoo in the river.

Beyond the market, the French Quarter is a one-block-long terrace of colonnaded, colonial houses lining Phan Boi Chau Street, faded cream paint still clinging to their facades. At number 25, a smiling Vietnamese gentleman graciously invites me into his French-style house. The house is not on the Hoi An house-visiting ticket, but the man has taken it upon himself to be hospitable, to invite visitors inside, to sit in his family's bentwood, thirties furniture and sip a cup of tea. As he runs his hand over the inlaid mother-of-pearl of the heirloom china cabinet, he explains that only old mother-of-pearl glints peach and green; new mother-of-pearl looks pearly white. He is especially proud of the enormous ebony bed measuring six by nine feet (2 x 3 m), which will sleep a family of four. He leads me through his house to the courtyard.

Most of the long narrow houses in Hoi An have courtyards for light and ventilation, he explains. 'When the light comes in, the doctor stays away,' doubtless a Vietnamese proverb.

The man has recently retired from a government job. His wife is still teaching. Upstairs, he keeps a small art gallery where he hopes that visitors will help with the upkeep of his home by purchasing a $3-landscape, painted by his architect son. I am pleased to oblige.

Without exception, I find the people of Hoi An, though thoroughly commercial, extremely friendly, mostly un-pushy, and the asking prices for their goods amongst the lowest in Vietnam. Perhaps the shopkeepers of Hoi An have learned that by and large, foreigners hate to bargain, and they have concluded that offering goods closer to the 'right' price is a quicker, pleasanter and possibly a more profitable way to do business.

Therefore, a stroll through the shops along Tran Phu Street is a pleasure, the shopkeepers happy to chat about this item or that, without pressure – although the tailors tout hard for business. Gallery after gallery displays paintings, shops offer ornate opium pipes, bamboo water pipes, chopsticks with inlaid mother-of-pearl, old coins. All cry out to be bought, in curiosity shop after curiosity shop. A pair of black-and-white metal balls, *ngoc ti,* that look like miniature footballs, are intended for fidgety worriers, or for those with arthritis to exercise their stiff hands. Carved circles of painted wood, 'door eyes', are for nailing up over an entrance to keep out evil spirits. I am still haunted by a mysterious genie, Datma, carved from a strange orange wood that stared from a shop window.

Outside another shop, a young woman sits, stabbing with a needle at a piece of fabric stretched over a frame. Her shop window holds elaborately embroidered table linen that would fetch a fortune in a Piccadilly arcade. To make a solidly embroidered landscape on a cushion cover ($10), it takes her ten days. A few doors away, a Siva with thirty-eight arms, carved from sandalwood, has removable arms for easy packing and reassembling – by number. The merchants of Hoi An think of everything.

I drop into the open-front Hoanh Thanh Restaurant in Nguyen Hue Street and the owner's daughter tells me that the restaurant has been in operation for forty-five years – that means during the Vietnam War – 'through several reincarnations.' Whenever you stop in an open-front restaurant, you are literally the sitting target for a band of smiling children, who zoom around the restaurant circuit on bicycles selling newspapers, chewing gum, cigarettes, postcards and greeting cards bearing delicate, miniature silk paintings. There is a woman selling tiny tins of Tiger Balm and a man hawking hammocks. After a few polite rejections, they desist.

Over a fresh lime juice, I gaze out at a picture-book sky of puffy white clouds against a brilliant blue sky. A flamboyant tree opposite is in riotous bloom. A young girl appears, a basket on her shoulder, tightly packed with clear plastic bags full of iced sugar cane juice, each sprouting a straw. Along the street, I follow the whir of looms and discover 'a cotton factory', each girl tending two mechanised looms. In a side street, I come across an old woman squatting on the pavement, laboriously untwisting rusted barbed wire so that it can be recycled to make wire baskets for carrying pigs. Waste not, want not.

Opposite, a young man is hanging out rice pancakes to dry. He invites me inside to watch his mother cutting them into noodles, having added a little peanut oil to keep them from sticking to her new electric noodle machine. His sister, working in another room by firelight, has the hot job of cooking the pancakes on a round, fabric-covered frame over a charcoal fire. She then carefully lifts each pancake onto a metal frame and when the frame is full, her brother carries it across the road to prop on a rack to dry in the sun.

In another street, two young men and a girl sit on the curb, painting comical *papier-mâché* masques. I remark on how quickly and with what skill they work and the girl explains that they do it every year.

From a restaurant alongside the market, I watch as a chicken vendor pushes her bicycle past, live chickens stowed in a double-deck basket on the back. A spice seller approaches my table selling packets of saffron, peppercorns and curry powder.

A few feet away, a young woman helps an older woman balance and tie a heavy basket on each side of her motorbike, steadying the load until the other starts the motor and speeds off. From a boat drawn up to the quay, a man unloads heavy hands of bananas into a cart attached to a bicycle. Just opposite, I watch as an itinerant cook wearing a conical hat, removes huge pots with lids from the baskets of her carrying pole and sets up a parasol and a low table with a checked tablecloth. From a low plastic stool – where has she stashed all that paraphernalia? – she serves a customer, who parks his motorbike beside her newly established restaurant. In the distance I hear the jangling sound of French pop music, evoking the South of France. The music grows louder and materializes as an ice cream *(kem)* vendor, his white foam cold box tied to the back of his bicycle – and the illusion shatters. When the sun has lost its burning fierceness, I wander towards the river. Halfway over the bridge, the elderly man from whom I bought the painting earlier, stops his bicycle to shake hands and say *bonjour.*

On the far side of the bridge, another mini-hotel is under construction. Western style wooden bedsteads are stacked against a tree on the riverbank beside a man, who sits sawing wood. For the new hotel, perhaps.

From an open doorway with a wooden fence across it, four beaming toddlers wave and shout hello – a day nursery for working mums. A little further on, two elderly men, one with a thin wisp of a beard, sit splitting bamboo to build a straw hut. Both stop and raise an arm in greeting.

As sunset cools to twilight, I sit on the quay watching a close-up of river life aboard four wooden boats tied up only a few feet away. The women cook supper on a single charcoal burner on the open bow of the boat or under the arched, thatched 'cabin'. I wonder how they keep the straw roof from catching fire. A father cuddles his toddler son on the prow of one boat to keep him out of the way while his wife cooks.

Another boat is so full of bananas, stacked from deck to canopy, that the family will surely have to sleep on the flat roof. There is simply nowhere else. Hopefully, they are peaceful sleepers. On the rail-less roof, if anyone rolls over, it will be into the river.

A thin, elderly Vietnamese man stops to chat in French, apologising for his lack of English, then continues to exchange pleasantries in very adequate English. Inscrutability is out. Hoi An charm is definitely in.

Along the quayside, excursion boats with red and yellow awnings float at their moorings, their bows alive with painted, slanting eyes to frighten off sea monsters. A huge flock of white ducks sail in a dizzy circle round the tip of a sandbar like meringue being slowly stirred.

At Tay Restaurant on the quay, I enjoy one of the best meals of many in Vietnam: grilled shrimp under crushed garlic, lime juice and freshly ground pepper, accompanied by a beer. Tay and her husband serve, her mother cooks.

A lethargic half moon rises in the indigo sky and Venus switches on. The limpid waters of the Hoi An river gleam between the dark hulls of the boats. There is a homely babble of voices as the boat people settle for the night. Savouring the moment, I store the scene away in my memory as one does the face of a dear friend. Yet despite the pleasure, suddenly, I feel very alone, gazing out at the cosy boat families. The detachment from one's social framework creates a kind of limbo, time becomes meaningless, one's identity slips away. I am torn by the desires to sustain this weightlessness, this detachedness, and the longing for a friend.

PART IV

HANOI IN WINTER

OLD HANOI

Sell distant relatives to buy near neighbours
– Vietnamese proverb

Having stayed in the former French quarter south of Hoan Kiem Lake during my first few months in Hanoi, now I head north to the Old Quarter of Thirty-Six Streets.

Despite arriving with the names of three recommended mini-hotels, all three are full. Seeing my crestfallen face, the manager of the third kindly escorts me to the Ngoc Minh Hotel, a few doors away. The large, second floor room with dark, carved traditional furniture has a new tiled bathroom with shower – and tub – no plastic slippers required. Best of all, the windows overlook the street life of Luong Ngoc Quyen and there is cable television – I can watch same-day CNN in English.

Once again I find myself on a street named after a military man; Luong Ngoc Quyen was a martyr in the resistance movement. Next door are two identikit mini-hotels, bulging with curved balconies and balustrades. Further along, older buildings open at street level as pavement cafes to sell rice cakes, grilled chicken feet and wings, noodle soup *(pho)* – chicken or beef – and *(banh cao)*, steamed rolls of rice paper stuffed with fried mushrooms and pork, topped with coriander and parsley. I am introduced to *banh cao,* a very hearty breakfast, by Hong, the Ngoc Minh's receptionist.

Across the street, a corrugated iron canopy attached to the wall with plaited straw nailed up as a backrest, serves as an impromptu pavement teashop, which I inwardly dub the gossip shop. Often, a cyclo, SMILING HANOI painted across the back of the seat, parks here while the driver sips tea. Each morning I look out to gauge the temperature. If the old ladies are wearing socks with their sandals and jackets, it is cold.

Beside the gossip shop is a six by six-foot (3 sq m) video shop, open to the street. A narrow lane leads to three-storey blocks of flats. Further along is a near as damn it, twenty-four-hour *pho* stall, its cauldron simmering over charcoal in the hollow of an open stairwell.

When I lived in the old French quarter, I thought that Hanoi curled up on its mat at nine o'clock. But Luong Ngoc Quyen and the surrounding streets are as lively until midnight as they are throughout the day. At dusk comes the thump of bass and the jangle of pop music from the video shop, adding to the carnival atmosphere. Later, as I lie down wearing wax ear plugs to dim the horns, the growl of motorbikes and clanging cyclos, children are still shouting as they chase one another along the busy street. Adults cry out as they sight friends and mothers screech at their offspring.

Sometimes, I am roused from sleep by the clatter of dishes in the small hours, to peer out and find the *pho* woman squatting beside a huge aluminium dish-pan, washing up in the middle of the street or stacking her tiny plastic stools. I always have to check the time to see if she is closing down at four, or opening up again at five. Eventually with the help of Hong, the receptionist, I learn that the *pho* shop is operated in shifts by a girl and her mother from a distant village, who came to Hanoi to find an easier way of earning a living than trying to farm on their own. They start boiling their cauldron of meat bones before dawn for the breakfast shift, adding noodles, vegetables, fresh herbs and more water as the day progresses, then start again around four in the afternoon. I can't imagine when they sleep. Their regular customers in the wee hours are taxi and cyclo drivers, who according to the daughter, arrive starving, as well as a fair number of young motor bikers about town, who roar in.

Next to the *pho* stall is the biscuit shop, boxes and boxes stacked to the ceiling. On the other side of the gossip shop slumps a row of old villas, their once elegant cornices decorated with swirls of plaster. The balconies, now choked with straggling pot plants and laundry, have lost their dignity, their once cream stucco, stained by the rains of many monsoons, the slats of their louvres sagging askew. Weary as they look, these villas are probably no more than a century old. Anything older would have been built of wood and there is still, here and there, braced between a sleek mini-hotel and an old stucco facade, a wonky, woebegone wooden structure that looks as if it were leaning on the shoulders of its neighbours. During the day, to the babble of the local inhabitants, add the calls of itinerant hawkers, women dangling heavy baskets from their carrying poles. Whenever it is warm, slices of watermelon appear on the bicycles. My favourites are the flower girls, selling bright pink chrysanthemums and red roses from baskets on the back of their bicycles, each rosebud tenderly wrapped in wet tissue to keep it from opening if the day is especially warm.

One afternoon I hear an almighty din, recognising what can only be a temple band: a sinewy oboe, a drum and a fiddle. I look out to find a procession leading a black hearse, its back door open to reveal a brass-bedecked coffin. Family members in white follow, several walking with their hands touching the back of the hearse as though they cannot bear to let go of the dearly departed. Hong tells me that it is the funeral of a very old man, bedridden for several years, who lived nearby in the street.

TV aerials, satellite dishes and laundry litter the skyline. One evening, I look out to see a young man at eye-level on a rooftop terrace, his elbows bent like a boxer, jabbing at his trousers, hanging on a clothes line. The jumble of rooftop towers and cubes has grown by creeping geometric accretion through the years, resulting in a vernacular hodgepodge, the lot festooned with illegal electricity and cable wires that would give a town planner nightmares. Surprisingly, most of the time it works. In the odd power stoppage, there is a knock at my door and a candle handed in.

My daily walk towards Hoan Kiem Lake takes me round the corner where invariably, a woman squats on the pavement, fanning her charcoal brassier, roasting ears of corn or strips of lean pork. The scent of the sizzling pork always sets my mouth watering, no matter what time of day.

The next street, Hang Bac, according to Hanoi's Research Institute for Architecture, 'is the oldest urban thoroughfare in Vietnam,' established in the thirteenth century as Silver Street. Jewellery shops still line the street. Strolling towards the lake along Ta Hien Street takes me to a bustling street market, past a shop selling carved bamboo water pipes and a bicycle mender where the feathery occupants of a row of cages sing a constant chorus of birdsong for the owners of broken bicycles while they wait.

Although people had told me that Hanoi winters were cold, I simply had not believed them. So in December when the temperature falls to 11 C (40 F) with humidity of 90 to 95 per cent, it is bone-piercingly cold and I pile on every polo neck, sweater and jacket I have and am still cold, indoors. The hotel owner kindly sends me an electric radiator. Towards the end of the month, the temperature soars to 27C (80 F) degrees.

Then in January, a few days before the Vietnamese New Year, *Tet,* the temperature drops again, colder than before, with the added joy of what the Scots call a fichy mist. One long-term Hanoi resident calls it dust rain, as the mist congeals to form an oily scum of mud on the streets.

The surfaces of Hanoi's Thirty-Six Streets are like an old frying pan, well seasoned. Although every evening female rubbish collectors in smart green and iridescent yellow uniforms, clang their bells for people to bring out their plastic bags of rubbish, and although they sweep the pavements and load the refuse into small hand-drawn carts, the streets always have a well lived on look.

Nappy-less babies are held bare-bottomed over the gutters to pee, older children pee openly into the gutters and household waste water is emptied into them.

Small piles of peelings are deposited along the gutters, sometimes in plastic bags, just as often, not. Together with the tantalising smells of cooking, a variety of scents assail the nostrils as one negotiates these crowded streets.

Hanoi has its share of beggars, small boys, the occasional little girl, a mother with a baby around Hoan Kiem Lake and a spindly-legged old country man, who I see every two or three days in a different part of the city, holding out his tattered conical hat for *dong.* But I am appalled one day to happen upon quite a young man, lying flat on his belly on the pavement, dragging his useless legs across a junction as he begs!

Another evening, incredibly loud amplified music – even drowning out the video shop opposite – seems to be increasing in volume. I look out to see an old blind man, being led by a young boy, playing an amplified guitar. Even the beggars are modernizing.

To stroll Hanoi's Thirty-Six Streets is like threading one's way through a bowl of noodles. Shopkeepers perch on low stools on the pavement with their fluffy little dogs (no, not everyone eats them). Motorbikes and bicycles park along the edge of the pavements. Shoppers meander slowly arm in arm, pausing on the pavement, blocking passage, whenever an Armani T-shirt catches their eye. There is nothing for it then but to step into the street, where would-be shoppers browse from the seats of their idling motorbikes, among the bicycles that have stopped to unload passengers and of course, the busy, moving traffic.

Even after a millennium, the Thirty-Six Streets remain an aggregation of villages. Each street has been settled by the inhabitants of a craft village and has been occupied in turn by their descendants, generation upon generation, living openly and communally. Therefore, the families not only know one another, they hold a collective memory of the heroes and black sheep of every family going back generations. It makes the curtain twitching of an English hamlet look innocent by comparison.

The Vietnamese have a difficult time trying to understand our nuclear families. Having no privacy, they find it impossible to understand the Western need for it. They even find it difficult to understand a Westerner choosing to travel alone, a state much to be lamented. They find it incomprehensible that anyone in the West should choose to sleep alone. In Vietnam, brothers sleep together, sisters sleep together and if a person has lost a spouse, two family members, two adult women or men share a bed to stave off the loneliness at night.

Yet despite this intimacy of street and family life, the streets of Hanoi have changed rapidly in the past few years and continue to change. Before the open market policy of 1986, *doi moi,* shopping was confined to the market or the dusty out-of-date goods from Eastern Bloc countries that stocked the shelves of the government-run department store. With the private enterprise that galloped in with *doi moi,* houses sprang open their fronts to become shops, pavement teashops and cafes. The intimacy of family-oriented street life will probably remain only until families are affluent enough to spread out. It is already happening. The *nouveaux riches,* are building narrow, vertical, French style villas as fast as they can around West Lake, sometimes leaving grandparents behind in the old family home.

HUNTING BUDDHAS

Chew carefully and the stomach is content,
Work well and the rice will grow thick
– Vietnamese proverb

The master sculptor, Tran The Koi, is a good man, very hard to find. Even two Vietnamese, one of whom lives in the hamlet, get lost trying to find him in the tucked away warren of workshops where he lives, around the corner from a neo-kulture centre, up an alley off Thanh Nhan Street.

At the back of his house, he leads me up steep steps to a partly open showroom, the shelves lined with 'old' statues of Buddha and new statues of water puppets. The 'old' statues only look that way. Tran The Koi is in the serious business of restoring or replicating old statues from temples, pagodas and village halls that have been lost or damaged during the war years, riddled by termites or crumbling from wet or dry rot. Most importantly, his new statues look identical to the old, having been carefully aged to look exactly like the antiques they are to replace.

A man who copies antiques naturally attracts suspicion and one wonders if the shops that sell Tran The Koi's work are always as scrupulous as he in declaring the statues and carvings as reproductions. Koi himself immediately dispels suspicion by showing me authentic pieces of sculpture and china alongside the astonishingly exact copies.

Koi points to a selection of blue and white china. I am drawn to a plump china elephant wine jug with a crazed glaze surface, the copy of a fifteenth century original. The replica of a large Ming dynasty vase worth maybe $3,500 (£2,300) in the antique market, sells for $20. The original of an opaque green celadon Tang vase would fetch $3,000 (£2,000); the exquisite copy, $15. Tran The Koi deals not only in sculpture, but in ceramics and basketry – Vietnamese crafts. And he collects much more.

A curious row of carved bamboo pipes with straps dangle beside the ceramics – 'scroll holders'. A nest of fine, tightly woven, round baskets with fitted lids about the size of a clinched fist have been copied by the Thai minority and sell for only $5 each.

Koi shows me a basket darkened by age that he estimates to be forty to sixty years old. 'Years ago these baskets were made using needles and fine rattan thread.'

Hanging from a beam is what I take to be a large, cylindrical rattan bird cage. Koi lifts it down with a twinkle in his eye and shows me that it also contains a second, inner cylindrical cage. This inner cage would considerably complicate the life style of any songbird. What is it? Koi reaches for a CD and shows me how each opening between the rattan bars is just wide enough to hold one cassette. The $22-bird cage, designed for export to the US, accommodates one hundred fifty cassettes and I can imagine it standing in a corner of my sitting room.

For some years Koi has been exporting to many countries, surprisingly, considering the earlier trade embargo, first to the US. Then came pottery, sculpture and the tightly woven rattan baskets to Japan, itself a country known for producing pottery and baskets, thereby testifying to the fine quality of Vietnamese workmanship. Later came France, Holland and Argentina, for which Koi produced woven rattan menu covers and the finest split bamboo place mats I have ever seen, the edges bound in raw silk.

There is so much to look at that it is impossible to take it all in. Every surface, even the ceiling, is covered with baskets, lamps, pottery and statues. Reluctantly, I follow Koi downstairs to a small dark room almost entirely filled by an openwork, reddish, lacquered altarpiece, topped by a ferocious dragon.

'The central figure is Buddha as a young baby, Sakyamuni, surrounded by many disciples.'

Koi points to the small statues representing the different stages of Sakyamuni's life: 'Stage one as a plump baby; stage two, seated cross-legged practising meditation, his thin ribs showing, during the period when he only ate one grain of rice each day; stage three, seated in the lotus position, having reached Nirvana; stage four standing, having become a teacher of disciples; stage five, reclining at the age of eighty.'

Like most craftsmen in Vietnam, Koi learnt to carve 'from my father and my uncle – my mother specialised in sedan chairs.'

In answer to my question as to whether he was allowed to continue carving during the war years, he replies flatly.

'I was in the army for seventeen years.'

On each side of the altarpiece stand two elegant life-sized, red lacquer and gilt cranes that I covet enormously, each wearing a price tag of $750 (£500). Perhaps in another life.

An assemblage of bronze Buddhas sit beneath the altarpiece and line the shelves along one wall, together with an assortment of smaller cranes. Shelves opposite display more tiny Buddhas, a boy riding a griffin, and the entire procession of a successful doctoral candidate returning in honour on horseback to his home village.

The next room holds larger statues of Buddha and in the open courtyard beyond stand several swashbuckling, larger than life-sized temple guardians and two multi-armed statues of Vietnam's goddess of mercy, Tien Nhan.

Long, narrow areca wood panels, black lacquered and inscribed with gold *chu nom* ideograms, hang on each side of the door frame. 'Parallel sentences, used as decorative embellishments at the entrances and gates of temples.' These two translate as:

An apricot tree in the moonlight is more beautiful than any painting.
No notes of any instrument are as beautiful as the sound of the wind
rustling through a copse of young bamboo.

In a nearby alcove, Koi points to a gilt, lacquered, horizontal panel, carved to resemble an unfurled scroll, that I can imagine hung heraldically above my headboard. It is about here that I ask Koi if he could make me a very special price for the lot, or alternatively, if I could simply move in.

Koi chuckles and leads me to an inner room where three large china statues of the goddess of mercy have been copied from Chinese antiques. He introduces me to one of his sons. Both of his two sons and a daughter, who studied at the College of International Trade, have all learned to carve.

At a workshop across the lane, eight young men busily carve wooden statues and bits of furniture. In the lacquer room, three women apply first, a black sealing coat, then silver, then gold, then red lacquer, after which the piece is fitted together and aged. In a small room adjoining, a statue has been placed on a cloth on a straw mat beneath a naked light bulb to dry. Such elegant, delicate work is accomplished in such simple surroundings.

Another red and gold panel, this one carved to resemble a folding screen, is mounted casually on the wall of 'the garage' – for motorbikes! An unclaimed order, perhaps?

187

Back in the showroom, Koi leads me up more wooden steps, saying, 'We are about to enter a wooden stilt house built by the Muong ethnic minority, which I had brought down from the hill country and reassembled.'

We drop our shoes at the door and step onto a mat made of pale, tiny wooden tiles, each branded with a flower. This is a wooden house with a straw roof. Light pierces the cracks between the wooden wall planks, air circulating through the fretwork beneath the ceiling – not an ideal house for Hanoi's chilly winter, I would have thought, much less for the colder hill country.

A large carved, lacquered bed serves as a display table for a dozen statues of Buddha in different styles. A huge bronze head of Buddha balances on a slim-legged, wooden stand.

Beside it, a low split-level, reddish lacquer table with two open shelves immediately takes my fancy. I can just see it, slightly larger, as a coffee table. To my delight, it only costs $100 (£66). Shipping would add another $300 (£200), plus handling, we discover after a phone call. Pity.

Sittting at a low table, we sip tea as Koi shows me his catalogues of pottery, rattan, sculpture and lacquer work. Two enormous, black and gilt mandarin hats from the seventeenth century that look as if they would virtually swallow any Vietnamese head, rest on top of glass-front cabinets, which hold Koi's collection of antique porcelain.

Koi brings down a tiny, uniquely Vietnamese, round china pot, which one day he thinks might become as rare and collectible as Japanese *netsuke*. These little pots, each with an ornate handle on top, a hole in one side, were used to store shell lime paste, one ingredient of the betel chew, now only practised by old ladies.

Koi hands me an enormous, round, woven rattan tray, a woven rattan knob on its openwork lid. It took four days to make. There is also a covered, woven rattan cake tray. So many finely crafted objects. I point to a gilt lantern just outside the door that I can envision hanging in my hallway. Mistaking what I have pointed to, delightedly, Koi lifts down a long cylindrical metal lamp.

'It is a peasant fisherman's lantern. The lamp in one hand, his fishing basket trap in the other, the fisherman goes out at night to search for the tiny fish that sleep around tree roots.'

Clearly, it is with as much pleasure that Koi has rescued this humble, antique peasant tool as it is for him to own the rare ceramics.

I ask what commission he is most proud to have accomplished. He doesn't quite understand the question. Is it the word 'commission', or 'proud', that causes the problem? I rephrase the question, asking what was the most difficult job of sculpture he has ever been asked to do?

'To replace the four most precious statues at the Con Son pagoda in Hai Hung Province. The statues were of Buddha, of a *bodhisattva,* and of the husband and wife who had made the donation to build the pagoda. Wooden statues do not last for a long time, five hundred years at the longest. These statues were from the Le dynasty in the fifteenth century and they could not be taken out for display.

'I have inherited the art and skill as a sculptor of statues and I am very interested in Buddhism. I have to have a good knowledge of religious sculpture. Every statue has a specific position, depending on the legend associated with the statue.'

In fact, scholars often consult Tran The Koi on matters relating to religious statues and carvings. He is currently writing an essay for a scholarly journal on the difference in the positioning of dragons and the moon in temples, compared to those decorating *dinh* (village halls). Koi opens a notebook containing drawings, layouts he has sketched for statues in pagodas and temples. One is very simple, having only a few statues; another seems to have legions of statues. From the wooden bed in the corner he lifts a statue of Matria, Buddha of the future, explaining that 'this aspect represents the aspirations of people, wishing for wealth, a better life and happiness.'

Another graceful statue just over two feet tall is Sakyamuni, standing on a lotus blossom, his hands folded in front of his black and gold gown, his puffy lidded, half-closed eyes looking down on earth. Although this position is known as 'sorrow', laugh lines play around the corners of this Buddha's smile, his lacquered face as pale as ivory. It is the only half-smiling Buddha I have ever seen apart from the roly-poly, laughing Buddhas sold in souvenir shops and the enormous golden Buddha in Thien Mieu pagoda in Hue. Koi then shows me dozens of photographs of Vietnamese costumes, ranging from ethnic minority and peasant dress to modern *ao dais,* which he is assembling for a collector in Australia. A computer sits between the display cupboards and the lacquered cabinet I so covet. Clearly, Tran The Koi is a man who has moved with the times. But he is first and last an artist who loves and respects the relics of the past and who in his own way, is helping to preserve the treasures of Vietnam's cultural heritage. I can only hope that he succeeds.

189

TRIPPING THE HANOI FANTASTIC

The old spiced hen is worth as much as the young chicken
– Vietnamese proverb

Hanoi is just possibly the last place on earth I thought I'd go dancing. After all, it is the conservative capital of a Communist government and Ho Chi Minh was known to have thought dancing to be frivolous.

Furthermore, I remember the complaint of a young Chinese man staying at The Gioi's guest-house, that there was no ballroom dancing in Hanoi's open spaces. In his home town, Kunming, there was dancing in the town square.

Some weeks later, I am therefore surprised to be invited to come dancing by my new friend, Barbara Cohen, who I met at Huu Ngoc's garden party. Her dancing partner is Vietnamese, she explains. They both simply love dancing and belong to a ballroom dancing club. The club holds competitions occasionally and Barbara and her partner compete. Barbara tells me to 'wear leather-soled shoes in case you are asked to dance.' From that, I should have been warned. Thinking to go along and watch, I agree to come.

Barbara's partner arrives for her on his motorbike, but considerately, she accompanies me in a taxi to direct the driver to the Tang Bat Ho Youth Club, a large round building with a sweeping external staircase leading to the ballroom. We buy 10,000-*dong* ($0.65) tickets and enter to a darkened circular dance floor surrounded by tables, coloured lights flashing *a la disco,* recorded pop music blasting out. Welcome to aural assault.

I order a mineral water and am surprised when my friends follow suit. A guitar player, a drummer and a keyboard player climb onto the stage and casually start to set up. The live music gets going with a quick foxtrot. Where my generation would have done a jitterbug to this music, these couples slice across the floor, both partners facing the same direction, dancing side by side – straight out of the thirties. Barbara and her partner are amongst the best dancers on the floor – they go in for competitions. Surprisingly, the ages of the Vietnamese couples range from early twenties to the retired.

190

Before I have time to watch the intricacy of the steps, a tiny Vietnamese of indeterminate age in a brown suit approaches, holding out his hand to invite me to dance. Oh dear, I have not danced – at all – for twenty years and he turns out, not to be the strong leader a woman of my uncertainty requires. Before I know it, I am hippity-hopping, trying to keep in step, just a fraction belatedly in starting the repeated twirl he indicates. After three twirls I am decidedly dizzy and nearly fall over as he gently pushes me in the opposite direction. The dance floor is on the slippery side, the kind of dance floor I would have relished in my youth because it required less effort. But at this juncture of unsteadiness, it is a distinct possibility that I might go feet up – splat.

As my partner marches me back to the table at the end of what seems a rather long set, to my dismay I am breathless. By now, I begin to appreciate that water is the drink of serious dancers, who get thirsty and have no desire to be tipsy. I gulp down a few swallows and the next dance begins, a *cha cha*. And here comes a fluffy grey-haired Vietnamese man wearing gold-rimmed glasses, very natty in a sports jacket, white trousers and white shoes. He, too, is another quick-stepping wonder.

Perhaps I should explain here that apart from having been taught at a tender age, the rudeness of rejecting an invitation to dance, in Vietnam it is exceedingly rude to say *no* in any form. The Vietnamese simply never use the word and will go through verbal cartwheels of euphemisms and positive expressions to avoid doing so, even saying *maybe,* when they most certainly mean *no.*

Now, once upon a time I could do a semblance of the *cha cha.* At least I knew the basic step. But I also knew that I didn't know anything else. So what does a nice, polite Western woman say to a non-English-speaking Vietnamese gentleman, who asks her to *cha cha* when she doesn't really know how? Answer: she tries.

Oh dear, my partner is thrilled that I know the basic step and proceeds with little flourishes. All around me, couples are doing fancy turns and quick little steps that look ever so Latin. Alas, I cannot watch how they are doing them and follow my partner at the same time. He, too, is either a master of the light-touch-lead or just plain shy at pushing an Amazon around the dance floor. This is a very uphill learning experience on a lights-flashing, slippery dance floor. Somehow, we manage to stay upright throughout the set and this time I am gasping as my partner leads me back to the table.

The next number is a tango. Now, I know when I'm beaten before I begin, so when Barbara's partner politely asks me to dance, I explain that I don't know how to tango.

'Never mind, he'll teach you,' says my so-called friend and before I know it, I am out of my chair and back on the dance floor, desperately trying to get a bite on the tricky rhythm. Not much teaching goes on. I can only claim to have remained upright, with the odd long-quick-quick, here and there. Of what happened in between, I know not.

All around us, svelte Oriental couples are whirling, snapping their heads to right or left, clicking their synchronised heels, motionless below the waist, sometimes a lady swept into a graceful low dip in her partner's arms.

This is becoming desperate. I had previously considered myself a reasonably good dancer, who found it easy to follow strange partners. Not any more.

Trying to dance is all too like climbing aboard a pair of ice skates after years of not setting foot on ice, except that with the ice skating, after half an hour my knees stopped trembling and my legs seemed to remember how to move. This is decidedly not happening on the dance floor.

The next dance is another two-step and my dapper, grey-haired partner reappears. Poor man, perhaps it is some kind of unspoken, polite generosity on the part of Vietnamese gentlemen, another facet of that overwhelming Vietnamese hospitality – and kindness to the honoured foreign guest – that no Western woman should be allowed to sit out a dance.

Genteel or whatever, I am frayed, dizzy, gasping for breath and more than a little worried about slipping and toppling heavily onto a delicate Vietnamese partner. Somehow, I don't think Vietnamese *sang froid* would stretch to a stretcher case. It also begins to dawn on me that these dandified gentlemen are simply not strong leaders. Moreover, I rather suspect that they have all learned to dance out of the same little textbook and expect their partners to know the same neat little diagrammed steps.

Attempting to glide around the floor of Hanoi's dance club with a highly choreographed partner is about as foolhardy as for a novice player to wander into a tennis club the week after Wimbledon, when all of the members are especially keen. Somehow, I have to get myself – out of here!

At the end of the tango, I take a deep swig of water and turn on Barbara, saying with acid sweetness, 'I'm sorry, I'm feeling rather dizzy. It must be the antibiotics' (I have just finished a course). 'If you don't mind, I think I had better go now.'

I would have preferred to stay and watch, but Barbara replies sweetly that 'Vietnamese men always like to dance with Western women, because they know how to dance.'

Well, some maybe. I make a very hasty exit.

After that, I go in for spectator sports. In the *What's On* section of *Heritage,* Vietnam Airlines' magazine, I had seen a tiny mention of performances of *cheo,* Vietnam's comic opera, performed at village festivals. Most of the dialogue is sung, there is dancing and slapstick buffoonery and as humour is international, never mind the words, I want to see it.

I set out one evening with a couple of *Viet kieu* (Vietnamese, who have emigrated to another country), staying at my hotel. We arrive at the Traditional Arts Theatre at 15 Nguyen Dinh Chieu Street, ten minutes late to find that the performance of the Cheo Circle is packed out. We had been told by the hotel receptionist, who inquired, that tickets would cost $4. Once again, although there is an overflow of people standing at the doorway peering in, as visitors from abroad we are kindly bustled inside, probably because it is late and my friends are Vietnamese and therefore admitted free.

My new friend Linh drops her shoes. I follow her example although it is freezing cold. We are motioned to sit on a straw mat in front of the rows of chairs with the children. The children are wearing leather jackets, woollen leggings, no socks and have kicked off their sandals to bare feet.

After some shifting to make sure that the children can see, the performance begins with the master of ceremonies, doubtless, saying what an auspicious occasion it is and how good it is to see so many interested people.

At centre stage, an altar under a red cloth holds two brass candlesticks and a large brass incense burner. Red lacquer candlesticks as tall as standard lamps stand to either side of the altar. On a lower altar, a handful of burning joss sticks has been stuck into a pyramid of mandarin oranges as an offering. The first performer is a female singer seated on a mat between a guitar player and a thin, elderly man with a tiny drum – I am sure I recognise them from the

193

Traditional Folk Music Club evening. This is decidedly not *cheo*. The song in a minor key, seems to be a gentle lament and the audience continues to chatter throughout. I am beginning to sympathise when my *Viet kieu* friend, Ang, whispers at the end of the song that the words are a poem written by an elderly poet, highly embarrassed at finding himself in love with a young girl.

Three musicians in silk mandarin costumes carrying a bamboo flute, a two-string fiddle and a moon-shaped guitar, seat themselves to one side of the stage. Four pretty girls in brightly coloured peasant costumes appear with two rouged clowns, waving paper torches. They sing and dance, using their large straw hats to form a synchronised, moving circle. Next comes a flirtatious female singer, who uses a fan to vivacious effect, followed by a male crooner, his tenor voice heavy with vibrato.

Then a grand personage in a scarlet velvet mandarin tunic, flashing gold and silver sequins, strides onto the stage. The embroidered dragon head spreading across his tummy is especially riveting, his ensemble completed by a pair of scroll-toed boots and a blue fabric head band. In each hand, he carries a red rod with yellow silk tassels and he stamps deliberately about the stage in his platform boots, singing gustily.

'Performing a ceremony,' whispers Ang. At one point, the mandarin balances precariously on one foot with the other held high, bent at the knee. Everyone claps, his balance, I assume.

Suddenly, the master of ceremonies, who is wearing a white business suit, breaks into song and takes on the character of 'an emperor,' says Ang.

The next number has us all shrieking with laughter. A beautiful princess has obviously set her sights on her humble lute teacher. The flamboyant princess, dressed in royal yellow, carries an ostrich-feather fan and flirts outrageously with the poor tutor, a strikingly handsome young man, who looks extremely discomforted by the whole procedure, as well he might be, not only in fear of losing his job, but rather more importantly, his head, if the emperor were to discover this highly dangerous game. At first, the princess sits on her red velvet stool, flirting demurely from behind her fan. The young man sings a sorrowful song and she gazes at him appealingly. He refuses even to glance at her. Her next ploy is to drop her fan, but he continues singing and doesn't pick it up, so rather irritably, she picks it up herself. Not to be rebuffed, she approaches him from behind and touches his shoulder. He leaps up as though he has been burnt and crosses the stage to another stool. The princess pursues him, throws her arms around him and tries to sit on his lap. Highly alarmed, he leaps up again and moves off, but the princess follows with her stool and places it very close to his.

Now the princess becomes more determined. She places her fan in her teeth to leave her hands free and approaches him from behind, touching his neck. He leaps away again. She twirls in front of him and ends by kneeling at his feet. Apprehensively, he moves off again and she lunges for him, finally catching him by the arm. Steadfastly throughout, he has never stopped singing.

Now she holds onto his arm and drags him to one side of the stage, then catches hold of him by the shoulders. Meekly, he holds up the last three fingers of one hand, one, two, three, as she curls her fingers over his in triumph.

In desperation, once more he tries to beat her off, this time with the lute. She wrests it away from him and in anger, flings the lute to the floor. With an anguished face, weeping, the tutor kneels to pick up his broken lute as the princess laughs bitterly. The audience adores every minute of it.

'Cheo,' whispers Ang.

The finale is a medley of folk songs, the stage full of singing peasants. I shall long remember the impassioned, frustrated princess.

195

THE VIETNAMESE DREAM

He who sows the wind will reap the whirlwind
– Vietnamese proverb

One must raise children to understand one's parents
– Vietnamese proverb

Think of football mad nations – Brazil, Britain, France, Italy – and Vietnam does not immediately spring to mind. But despite their fly-weight stature, the Vietnamese have taken to football with an enthusiasm that threatens to stop all but life-supporting activities whenever a match is being played. And not just their own football matches, either.

Whenever the satellite sports channel or Australian Television carry coverage of European games, the Vietnamese sit transfixed in front of their sets. Reception desks in hotels stand empty and television sets are installed in hotel dining rooms – so that waiters can watch. Cyclo drivers cease pedalling, students play truant and workers fail to turn up for work – unless there is a television set.

When European games are broadcast on short-wave radio in the wee hours, absenteeism soars the next day. I now know what they are talking about so animatedly in pavement cafes – their favourite European teams and players. A Vietnamese finds it incomprehensible to encounter a European, who doesn't care a tiddlywink for football. Even the girls are football mad, and not just because the boys are. Come a game between Vietnam and any team in the South East Asia League, offices might as well close. No phones are answered. You could starve to death except for the old women selling *pho* and oranges in the streets.

When Vietnam wins, Hanoi streets became a race track of celebrants hooting motorbike and car horns – even forbidden firecrackers are set alight – until long after midnight. It is like Bastille Day, the Fourth of July and New Year's Eve, rolled into one.

The story goes that back in the nineties when Vietnam won the bronze medal in the South East Asian championships, more than ten thousand fans in Hanoi converged ecstatically en masse at the airport to welcome home their victorious team, forcing the delay of all flights. That was when Colin Murphy – yes, Britain's Colin Murphy – was Vietnam's football coach. On landing, he was hoisted aloft on the shoulders of worshipful Lilliputian fans and born through the airport in probably the biggest celebration the country had witnessed since the end of what the Vietnamese call the American War in 1975. Mr Colin and his winning team had to take refuge in a police station until they could be smuggled out through the back door at three o'clock in the morning.

Mr Colin, disguised under a police helmet, was put in a police van travelling at ninety miles per hour – even at 3 a.m. that was brave! – through the still teeming streets of Hanoi, strung with victory banners. It is said, that of the few faces instantly recognisable to Vietnam's population at the time, one was the president's, one was the prime minister's, the third was bald-headed Mr Colin's.

After football, the second greatest passion of every young Vietnamese is his, particularly *his,* motorbike. Everyone who is anyone has to have one. It is the dashing macho, trendy image for the young Vietnamese male. For the girls, too, it is part of the image of today's modern miss about town, and girls are just as anxious to be chic and with it as their male counterparts.

Motorbikes and now scooters, are not a cheap fashion accessory. The top Honda SH scooter can cost as much as $6,000-7,000 (£ 4,000-4,650), a mid-range Honda Spacey between $3,000-5,000 (£ 2,000-3,300), a cheap Hondo Future $1,300 (£ 860). Even popular Co-Ops, a Vietnamese-Japanese joint-venture between the two countries, cost $1,000 (£ 660).

Used Chinese motorbikes cost around $750 (£ 500) – a little lacking in status, but nonetheless acceptable. Considering that most young workers, unless they are extremely well qualified, speak excellent English and work for multinational companies, rarely earn more than $600 or $700 (£ 400- 460) per year, one cannot help but wonder where they get the money from. They certainly don't peddle their bicycles for ten years until they save up. Banks, I am told, do not make loans for motorbikes, but parents and relatives do.

Doting grandparents, I suspect. But where do *they* get the money? It must be admitted that getting around the sprawl and traffic snarls of Hanoi is not easy. Hanoi has introduced a fleet of new buses and they always look full, but not nearly as crowded as the streets, growling with motorbikes. Me, I mostly take motorbike taxis *(xe om),* perched on the back, placing my faith in the zooming style of an unknown driver through the swirling traffic – best not to look! I do see the occasional Vietnamese using taxis, many take *xe oms,* but preferably, if at all possible, they buy a motorbike or scooter of their very own.

And not just the young. Sedate matrons sit high-heeled as they zoom, often quite viciously, towards their offices; dignified, ageing civil servants in dark suits, likewise. Aged grannies sit side saddle on the back of motorbikes, and of course, young families defy death by asphyxiation not to mention collision, by stuffing babies and toddlers in front of and between parents, often four, even five to a motorbike. Sometimes they toss a veil over the face of the baby to protect it from pollution.

I swear that the speed of traffic in Hanoi increased between July when I left Hanoi and November when I returned, thanks to an exponential cloning of wild-eyed young men, drunk on speed, cutting through streets crowded with bicycles and pedestrians. In the interest of lowering traffic accident statistics, the police are trying to discourage the lads' game of streaking through slowly moving traffic, weaving like skiers in a downhill slalom, the younger the rider, the more daring. I have come to think of them as hunter-killer motorbikes. Happily, Hanoi police have stopped the racing around Hoan Kiem Lake after midnight!

Television is another passion, and not just of the young. When I first came to Vietnam on the cruise, I was struck by how many people in the streets I saw sitting, reading books and newspapers: men touting cigarettes or raffle tickets, young children sitting on the pavement with their parents, old men and women.

In the space of six months, I have noticed the total disappearance of readers and how utterly addicted both the young and old have become to television – and now, internet shops. In Hanoi, the children sit square-eyed, clamped to the cable cartoon channel; teenagers ogle the pop music and movie channels or sit in internet shops playing computer games.

The women, young and old, are addicted to Vietnamese films and soap operas during the day, Chinese soap operas with voice-overs in the evening. The men, of course, watch football. In Hanoi, no one seems to sit on the street reading anymore. But it isn't quite all Western imports. VN-TV does its best to keep popular Vietnamese music alive. Every evening for an hour on VN-TV, meltingly beautiful young singers in *ao dai* glide around Hoan Kiem Lake, peering demurely through the wind-ruffled, weeping willows, singing ballads, sometimes joined by a shy tenor in a Palm Beach suit. But they are no match for the raucous popsters in bum-hugging trousers, who bare their belly buttons and jiggle their wobblies on the pop channel. The elegant and demure *ao dai* and romantic ballads seem to be sinking like Ophelia.

Of course, cable television, flaunting the lifestyle of the West – pop music, discos, upholstered sofas, beds with mattresses, modern kitchens – has contributed dramatically to a changing lifestyle in Vietnam. The most important item in any girl's wardrobe is an expensive pair of jeans, skinny black or faded blue, day and night, tank tops in summer, sometimes nippy little fitted jackets, bulky or velvety sweaters in winter.

However, T-shirts and blouses are always neatly tucked in. I met one European English teacher, who had been told that it was disrespectful to wear her blouses hanging loose in the torpor of Hanoi's summer.

Women wear dresses or suits, only if they work in air-conditioned international offices or hotels. If a hotel receptionist or a waitress is required to wear an *ao dai* at work, she wears jeans on her bike or motorbike en route and changes when she gets there.

Sadly, the only *ao dai* one sees floating behind a bicycle are those worn by high-school students – white *ao dai* remain the school uniform in the South. I hope they never change it. Once at university, it's jeans all the way.

For the lads, it's also trousers or jeans, white shirts neatly tucked in for office workers. For non-office workers, it's a T-shirt with Western writing on it and a bomber jacket, in cool weather made of parachute material, in winter of fake leather. In fact, nearly everyone in Hanoi wears a leather jacket in winter, woolly scarves and knitted or felt hats. A few men wear suits to the office, but when it's really hot, leave the jackets at home, unless their offices are air-conditioned. Naturally, Western fashions cost money and although a good many are manufactured in Vietnam, especially trainers, the Vietnamese covet imported fashions – or copies – for their status.

Footwear also apes the West, but the little black boots favoured by Hanoi girls in winter pay more tribute to French fashion than the clod-hopping Doc Martins of Britain. A large part of the population, it must be said, still wears plastic sandals – practical when it rains. In summer, girls and fashion-conscious women wear platform sandals or strappy sandals with heels. Men wear sandals with or without socks, or trainers, and men of a certain status and prosperity wear leather loafers.

It is astonishing just how fast things have changed in so short a time. In the mid-eighties, the country was virtually on its uppers. People were starving, not only in the remote hills, even in the cities. It is only natural for people who have been hungry, once they have enough to eat, to yearn for more and more consumer products.

Since *doi moi* in 1986 opened the doors to trade, the pent-up yearning for consumer goods has exploded. Vietnam desperately wants everything the West has, even before such basic needs as purified water and the infrastructure to produce or deliver these goods has been developed. Therefore, imports rush in like air into a vacuum, especially from China. But the Vietnamese have quickly learned that their own products are better quality than Chinese. The demand for gadgets, electrical appliances and Western style plumbing knows no bounds. The status-conscious *nouveau riche* have started drinking Johnny Walker and Hennessy – at $22 (£ 15) and $37 (£ 25) a bottle. Even monks have mobile phones. But Vietnam still remains a long way behind Thailand or Malaysia.

Given the fact that more than two-thirds of the population is under thirty and has no memory of the suffering of the war years, the stampede towards consumerism is threatening to trample traditional Vietnamese values, which held that wealth was of little consequence or importance compared to performing worthy acts to gain merit for the after-life (or lives). The young in Vietnam want it all and they want it now. And not only the young. So while in the West, many people have come to realize that the quality of life is more important than the rush to amass more wealth, in Vietnam the young, particularly, are money-mad – determined to make as much money as fast as possible. The country is a-changing, very, very fast.

SEEING IN THE NEW YEAR – *TET*

For old bamboo, new growth
– Vietnamese proverb

Having become accustomed to the kind hospitality of the owners of the Ngoc Minh Hotel, imagine my shock one morning to find a china bowl on the reception desk containing three fairly frantic fish, swimming in congested circles.

Hong, the receptionist, mutters 'kitchen gods' and all becomes clear. I should have known. For the past week, the back of nearly every bicycle trundling through Hanoi's streets has carried a small kumquat tree, the small orange fruit dangling like Christmas balls, the equivalent of Christmas trees for the Vietnamese lunar New Year, *Tet*. Coloured lights blink from shop canopies, the tall trees bordering Hoan Kiem Lake have donned twinkling electric jewellery for the festive season and long red banners wish passers-by Happy New Year in Vietnamese. Hanoi is all dressed up for *Tet*.

I had heard about the kitchen gods and the carp that transport them at the end of the lunar year to the palace of the heavenly jade emperor, so that the kitchen gods can report on the family's virtues and misdeeds throughout the year. The journey to heaven on the back of the carp begins on the twenty-third day of the twelfth lunar month and the kitchen gods return at midnight on the eve of *Tet*. While the kitchen gods are away, lights are left on and lots of noise is made – when isn't it? – to frighten away evil spirits from the household.

The fish on the reception desk, therefore, are none other than the heavenly steeds for my hosts' kitchen gods – three kitchen gods, three carp – and judging from their antics to leap out of the bowl, they are more than ready to start their celestial journey.

'What happens to the carp?' I ask Hong.

'Oh, they go back to the river,' which I should have guessed in a society deeply rooted in life-preserving Buddhism.

Of course, there is a legend surrounding the kitchen gods, in fact, two. According to one, a married couple quarrelled and during the quarrel, the husband struck the wife. So the wife left her husband and went to a village far away and remarried. The husband, having

201

repented, looked everywhere for his wife, but couldn't find her (this bit is the most difficult to believe in gossipy Vietnam). By the by, he went blind and became a beggar. One day, arriving at the home of his former wife, she recognised him and taking pity, offered him food. Fearful of what might happen when her new husband came home, she suggested that he sleep, hidden under the haystack. When her new husband returned, not seeing the man asleep, he set fire to the haystack to make compost. The blind man caught fire and burnt to death. His former wife felt so guilty and grief-stricken that she threw herself into the flames, followed by her second husband. All three of them perished.

In another version, the couple were happily married, but fell on hard times, so the husband decided to go away to seek work. In parting, the husband said to his wife, 'If I am not back in three years, it is because I am dead, so try to remarry.'

While he was away, the wife found a job in the house of a man who, although not rich, was full of pity. The grapefruit had flowered three times and the woman's husband had not returned when the employer asked his housekeeper to marry him. She replied that as her husband had promised to return after three years, she was certain that he must be dead.

'Therefore, let me do my duty and mourn for him for three years.' Another three years passed and still, the husband had not returned. So after performing a ceremony for the spirit of her dead husband, the woman agreed to marry her employer. Three months later, the woman's first husband returned, not rich but longing to see his wife again. Embarrassment, guilt and confusion ensued, but the first husband was forgiving.

'It's my fault. I stayed away too long. You were right to remarry,' he told his wife. 'Only I very much wanted to see you again. Now I will go away forever.'

Deeply saddened, in a fit of despair he hanged himself from the village banyan tree. His wife felt so guilty and grief-stricken over his death that she drowned herself. Her new husband, equally bereft at his new wife's death, poisoned himself. These three ill-fated victims of 'pure-hearted conjugal love' were transformed into Vietnam's kitchen gods, symbolised by the three bricks that traditionally hold the pot over the straw fire.

Other traditions surrounding *Tet* have to do with flowers. In addition to a kumquat tree (*quat* in Vietnamese), every Hanoi family must have a branch of pink peach blossoms stuck in a vase with *Tet* cards propped amongst the branches. In other parts of the country, it is apricot or plum blossoms that herald the arrival of spring and the New Year.

Just before *Tet,* the nurseries around the edges of West Lake are at their busiest and for the nurserymen, it is a very anxious time. What if the weather is too warm and the peach blossoms open too soon, or too cold and the buds refuse to open?

Choosing a *quat* for *Tet* is a subtle and serious business, nearly approaching in magnitude the decision of choosing a suitable boy. Huu Ngoc and Barbara Cohen co-authored a book on *Tet* that might well have been sub-titled, *A Suitable Quat.* They point out how the buyer must evaluate the symmetry of the tree, the bushiness, the shades of green of the leaves, the colour, shape and the arrangement of the fruit. A desirable *quat* should have thick, dark green leaves, yet with some light green leaves, still to ripen. The leaves will have been pruned very precisely to display deep orange, ripe fruit with smooth, clear skin, shining like golden coins or tiny suns on the first day of *Tet.* There must also be fruit tinged light green to ripen later, reflecting the wish that wealth should come to the family, both now and in the future. The ripe fruit represents the grandparents, the flowers the parents, the buds the children, the light green leaves, the grandchildren. A proper *quat* therefore symbolises four generations.

The ritual of visits on the first day of *Tet* includes discrete compliments or subtle, euphemistic criticisms regarding the choice of *quat* – its size, shape, condition and placement – by friends and family visitors.

Watching a programme on VN-TV, I deduce that the upwardly mobile Hanoi family must also have a flower arrangement for *Tet.* Any relationship to flower arrangement in the West, or the East for that matter – Japanese *ikebana,* for example – is utterly incidental.

Ideally, the Vietnamese start with a gnarled root. Then with a drill, they add a lot more gnarls, leaving a hollowed out hole for water and a plastic sponge into which the stems are secured. The mixture of colours, textures and contours of these arrangements seems haphazard in its diversity to the Western eye.

An arrangement might include delicate mauve wild flowers; heavy-headed, hand-nurtured red roses; tiny yellow chrysanthemums; an orange blossom or two; maybe even a cascade of purple orchids, set off by sprigs of dried grasses and a small jagged palm leaf. Sometimes unexpectedly, a floral conglomeration turns out to be quite fetching. More often, the Vietnamese aesthetic of flower arrangement eludes me entirely. In another VN-TV transmission, a procession of villagers thread their way along a dyke, a water buffalo pulling a wooden cart in which a saffron-robed monk is seated with a huge cardboard box. At the village hall, to much applause from the villagers, the box is unloaded and two villagers and the monk erect a television aerial. The item finishes with the villagers in the village hall, sitting cross-legged, worshipping television. Presumably, the television set was a *Tet* present – from the villagers, to the villagers.

Tet celebrations used to go on for an entire month, but Ho Chi Minh thought that a bit excessive for a poor nation, so now officially, *Tet* has been reduced to just one week off work. Nevertheless, *Tet* parties like Christmas parties in the West, start nearly a month before the holiday itself. Offices hold a series of *Tet* parties, a different party for each set of people with whom they have dealings and finally, a *Tet* party for themselves, usually the last day of work before the holiday.

If he or she possibly can, every Vietnamese in the world comes home for *Tet,* however far, be it across oceans and continents. On the eve of *Tet,* families gather for present giving and a feast of special *Tet* food, amongst which are the special square rice cakes called *banh chung*. Naturally, there is a legend about the origin of these cakes. A long time ago, during the reign of the sixth Hung king (pre-history BC), the old king decided to hand over the throne to a successor. But which of his heirs should he choose? In Vietnam, the line of succession is anything but direct and this seems to have been the case for a very long time. A genie suggested to the king that he set his sons a challenge.

'Go anywhere in the world and bring back to me the recipe for the best savoury dish you can find,' the king told his sons, which says something about the lengthy gourmet tradition of Vietnam.

The princes set out in all directions in greater or lesser state, depending upon age and rank. Sadly, the king's motherless sixteenth son, Lang Lieu, watched the departure of his wealthy brothers. Having neither servants nor advisers, what was he to do?

One night, a genie came to him in a dream.

'Nothing is more precious than rice,' said the genie. 'Therefore, take sticky rice, clean it in clear water and steam it, then make two loaves. One should be round, like heaven in gratitude for its help; the other square, as everyone knows, the shape of the earth. Inside, put mung beans ground with a mortar, lard and minced meat with green onions. Then stew it for a day and a night. Trust my words,' said the genie and disappeared.

When he awoke Prince Lang Lieu went to find his old nurse and told her his dream. Together, she helped him to make the cakes and after much practice, he learned to do it himself. When the long awaited day came for the brothers to put their dishes before the king, they brought exotic fruits, spices and strange, unknown fish from foreign lands. The old king tasted each of their dishes, taking the opinions of his courtiers – and chose the sticky rice cakes of the sixteenth son.

He not only approved of the symbolic shapes of the round and square cakes, but appreciated the far-sighted common sense the prince had demonstrated in having relied on foods that were easy to hand. When the king asked Lang Lieu how he had come to offer the rice cakes, the prince told him about the genie in the dream.

From this revelation, the king realised that Lang Lieu already had heavenly backing and felt happily confirmed in his choice of successor. As for the cakes, the king had the recipe distributed throughout the land and decreed that the round cake should be called *banh day,* the square cake *banh chung.*

I wonder if Prince Lang Lieu made a good king. He must have died a fat one.

The square cakes with which I have had two sticky encounters, are shaped in a wooden mould eight or nine inches square and wrapped in banana leaves to steam, which gives the rice a ghoulish, green tinge and does nothing for the taste – the least appealing Vietnamese food I ever eaten. Delectable, they are not. The first time I encountered *banh chung* was at the gathering of retired puppeteers. I cannot imagine how the Hung king found them to his taste, not even helped down with sips of strong rice wine.

The second time was at a *Tet* party at the Ngoc Minh Hotel for two of the staff, departing for their villages before the holidays. A thick wedge was placed in my bowl and my *Viet kieu* friend genially joshed, 'Go ahead, they are all waiting to laugh.' Put like that, how could I but comply?

Doubtless, watching me wrestle with chopsticks to cut off a bit of sticky *banh chung* was the funniest thing since Mickey Mouse, judging from the suppressed giggles round the table.

The other story about *banh chung* cakes is drawn from history. Towards the end of the Tay Son rebellion in the late eighteenth century, after both the Nguyen and Trinh clans had been defeated, the Tay Son army rushed north on the eve of *Tet* – so there is a tradition of *Tet* offensives – to defeat the Chinese Qing, who were attacking Hanoi. In their haste, they munched their *banh chung* cakes as they marched and defeat the Qing they did (1789).

I found the commemorative battlefield in the Dong Da area of Hanoi (corner of Thai Thinh and Tay Son Streets), where a mound of earth is said to cover the fallen Chinese soldiers. A megalithic statue of Nguyen Hue, leader of the Tay Son rebellion, has been erected in social-realism style.

These were the same Tay Son brothers from south of Hue – Nguyen Hue, who in victory became the Emperor Quang Trung, the liberal-minded ruler who having married the daughter of the old Le king, died only four years later, before his reforms could take hold and whose grief-stricken young widow wrote such a poignant love poem expressing her despair.

Behind the megalithic statue of the hero, in a crowded concrete *bas relief* tableau, foot soldiers of the Chinese army march to a drumbeat in strict formation as if passing on parade, their swords held high. Others advance on horseback, beneath flowering peach blossoms. Cannons menace the Tay Son peasant soldiers, armed with bows and arrows, signalled by a man blowing a curved buffalo horn. Nguyen Hue commands from the back of an elephant.

Following the tableau like a scroll, a little further along lies a scramble of fallen Chinese and a scene of grateful Tay Son soldiers, giving thanks for their victory, backed by a cluster of women, who no doubt supported the army by carrying baskets of the famous *banh chung* cakes.

On the fifth day after *Tet,* a festival is held here at Dong Da to commemorate this victory, as well as a somewhat magnanimous ceremony of absolution for the enemy soldiers killed in battle. The hero's palanquin is carried from Khuong Thuong communal house nearby to the temple beside the burial mound. Straw torches and a dragon dance remind observers of the army's use of torches during the battle, their bobbing motion alluding to the dragon's undulations.

Considering the thud of *banh chung* cakes in the pit of the stomach, I am surprised that Nguyen Hue's soldiers could eat them and march anywhere at all. It is also said that during recent wars, *banh chung* cakes hidden in village ponds fed many a hungry guerilla fighter. I wonder how they kept them dry?

For *Tet* lunch at the Ngoc Minh Hotel, the table is laden with numerous savoury dishes: a special chicken soup with lotus seeds, a dish containing thin slices of beef and stir-fried vegetables; a plate of chopped chunks of fried chicken; *nem chua* rolls made from chopped pork; a stew of young bamboo and of course, *banh chung* cakes.

The savoury courses are followed by watermelon, plates of pumpkin seeds, sun dried slivers of sweet potato rather like orange crisps (chips) and delicious sweet candied Chinese crab apples. As a *Tet* gift, my hostess hands me a tiny red envelope, decorated as prettily as an old fashioned valentine, containing a new 10,000-*dong* note – 'lucky money for the New Year.' I notice that not a soul eats a bite of *banh chung* during lunch, except me.

Tet is celebrated with first-footing, a bit like the Scottish New Year. However, as the first person to cross the threshold determines a family's luck for the entire year, a guest is especially invited to perform this honour.

To be lucky, the guest should preferably be rich, handsome or beautiful, and of good character. Anyone who is unlucky, who has lost a relative during the past year, who is poor, divorced or a scoundrel would be considered decidedly bad luck. That probably includes Tiger ladies (like me, reputedly cantankerous).

Accordingly, I am invited round to a Vietnamese friend's house on the third day after *Tet* – no point in taking chances.

The night of *Tet,* I take a taxi back from supper in a hotel – everything else is closed – through eerily empty streets, no cyclos, no bicycles, no motorbikes, not a soul on the pavements. The doors and grills of shops and houses are tightly closed. Only chinks of light here and there suggest that anyone is at home. *Tet* must be the only day of the year when Hanoi is quiet. And it's the only day of the entire year when I feel decidedly lonely.

IF YOU'VE SEEN ONE TEMPLE – OH NO, YOU HAVEN'T

Speak gently to reach the soul
– Vietnamese proverb

A gift from the heart is valuable
– Vietnamese proverb

Late one misty night walking back from a *Tet* party, on the spur of the moment Barbara Cohen asks if I have visited Vu Thach pagoda, hidden behind shops at the south end of Hoan Kiem Lake.

Ten o'clock at night seems an odd time to visit a pagoda, but before I know it, I am following her down a dark, narrow alley past the public toilets and bathhouse. We enter a large, open space with thick columns under a low ceiling, the red glow of an altar visible at the far end. An elderly, moon-faced nun in a brown knitted hat and habit greets Barbara like an old friend and invites us to drink tea. After tea, she leads us past stone memorial tablets, some etched with photographs, mounted in rows on the wall. Numbers have been scrawled in a few blank spaces – reservations. Although this is the ground floor of the pagoda, the memorial tablets give it the eerie feeling of a crypt.

We climb the stairs to the main entrance and slip out of our shoes into straw slippers. An elderly man – he turns out to be the head monk out of uniform – appears and turns on the lights. To my blinking amazement, this is an enormous pagoda. Thick, red lacquered columns, altars, and beyond, a dozen or so magnificent, red lacquered Buddhas rise in ranks progressively higher, who despite their benign expressions in the dark of night under the glare of electric lights, look far more like devils than saints. Individual statues, like an unmatched set of giant chessmen, sit along both sides of the pagoda.

'*Arhats* are monks who have not yet reached enlightenment,' Barbara explains, indicating the rows of statues. 'They appear in pagodas in many different styles, ideally in a band of eighteen, sometimes fewer. They may be elegant and distinguished, amazingly life-like, or pale, plump-faced primitives. They might be seated in a

208

variety of formal Buddhist postures or slouched as if they were lounging under the village banyan tree for a neighbourly chin-wag. Sometimes several are standing or the entire set can be riding buffaloes or a variety of beasts, sometimes mythical. They can be covered in gilt, lacquer, brightly painted or of natural wood.

'A pagoda's statues are one of the factors that contribute to its importance. A pagoda may be famous for its antiquity, for its architecture, its fine sculpture, for the distinguished monks who have presided over it – or who currently preside – or for the personages to whom the adjoining temples are dedicated. Temples, as opposed to pagodas, are dedicated to mortals elevated to 'sainthood' for their good work as heroes or heroines, though just occasionally, temples have even been dedicated to scoundrels, thieves or beggars!'

So, like the Catholic church, Buddhism has 'saints'.

Historically, the defeat of the Confucian Chinese in the tenth century heralded Vietnam's golden age of Buddhism – from the eleventh to fourteenth century – when there was a proliferation of pagoda-building. From the fifteenth century, Confucian ideology again dominated, although Buddhism continued concurrently.

The practical-minded Viets were originally animists, worshipping natural forces: the rain god (Phap Vu); the god of clouds (Phap Van); of lightening (Phap Dien) and thunder (Phap Loi), until Buddhism was introduced. Not to waste perfectly good gods, the Viets simply added Buddhist divinities to their indigenous deities. The same happened with Chinese Tao deities such as the emperor of heaven (Ngoc Hoang); and Nam Tao, who registers births; and Bac Dau, who registers deaths.

When I first arrived in Vietnam, as an inveterate temple tramp I wondered if the old religions would have survived the current political regime. I need not have worried. As Huu Ngoc so elegantly put it, 'Lying dormant in the subconscious Vietnamese mind is an inclination towards Buddhism, which has been the basis for religion in Vietnam for eighteen centuries. The Vietnamese are attracted by the preaching of universal compassion rather than karma, non-self and nirvana.' Uncle Ho has simply been added to the pantheon, and many a plaster bust of the nation's founder adorns a village community hall or temple. That he never married in a country where everyone marries, merely adds to his mystique, not only as a political, but also as a spiritual leader. (I am assured that he had girlfriends when he was young and certainly was not homosexual.)

209

So despite Communism, come the first and fifteenth of every lunar month, crowds still troop to pagodas and temples to light joss sticks and make offerings, they climb ridiculously high mountains on pilgrimages and burn votive 'pretend' paper money on the pavement in front of their houses in pursuit of prosperity and happiness. They overlook no holy opportunity to honour Buddha, the Taoist deities, sometimes the earlier goddesses, the dead monk patriarchs of the pagodas and any ancient or local personages deified in their temples. And of course, they make offerings to their ancestors at home. So, the Vietnamese reluctance to say *no* seems to have applied to incorporating religions as they came along, except for Catholicism, which remained determinedly separate. Formerly every Vietnamese school child was taught to recite:

'The pagoda of my village has a gabled roof. It stands by a pond, surrounded by a garden. A triple gate *(tam quan)* with a belfry on top leads to a court. Inside the pagoda, three gilded wooden Buddhas sit on pedestals. At the back are altars dedicated to deceased bonzes and the dwellings of the monks. Guest halls are found on each side. Inscribed on a stone stele in the middle of the court are the names of followers who have contributed to the construction and repairs of the pagoda. In the garden, stupas hold the ashes of the deceased monks.'

Different deities live in different kinds of religious buildings. The communal hall *(dinh)* is dedicated to the tutelary spirit(s) of the community. The pagoda *(chua)* is reserved for Buddhist worship, although sometimes Taoist statues creep in, especially since bombings, when a good many statues found their way into strictly speaking, inappropriate buildings.

To confuse things further, there are three different kinds of temples: *den* for the cult of heroes or genies; *dien* for the Taoist-tinged worship of spirits and immortals and *van tu* or *van chi* for the cult of Confucius. None of them have convenient signs out front to tell you which they are.

The rectangular hall of a pagoda is divided into two areas: the wide open space for worshippers, the hall of ceremonies, *bai duong;* and the area for altars and statues, *tam bao* or *chinh dien.*

Behind the pagoda, the separate temple is dedicated to the patriarchs of the pagoda and sometimes to early Buddhas. Many times when visiting pagodas and temples in Vietnam, I have longed for an introduction to the buildings, the statues and their stories, like the photocopied sheets that English churches sell for a few pence, telling visitors a bit about the church or cathedral. All too often, there is never a monk when you need one.

The old monk beckons us to follow, down a few steps in the dark and around a corner to where he switches on another light. An external alcove reveals a sunburst of gilt, a brand new golden statue of Quan Am Thien Thu Thien Nhan, to give her full name, she of the thousand arms. Two of her hands are in an almost prayerful *mudra* position, slightly open, like a child making a church with a steeple. In one of her many hands, this goddess grasps a spear.

Later, my Buddhist friend tells me that this statue is probably Tantric, a Tibetan talisman incarnation, 'because a Buddhist Quan Am would never hold a weapon.'

Several tiers of faces make up her crown, representing her thousand eyes to watch over everyone in this world. The slender fingers of her many hands curve in graceful postures and she sits in the lotus position, her eyes half closed in ecstasy. We pay tribute to the goddess with a joss stick apiece and return to the lower level for a chat with the old nun, the monk shutting off the lights behind us. She serves more tea and biscuits and insists that each of us take a plastic bag containing an orange, an apple and a small packet of biscuits as a kind of benediction.

These gifts called *lok* (pronounced luck), Barbara explains, would first have been blessed as offerings and remained on the altar at least the length of time it takes to burn a joss stick. I wonder if the street urchins who beg and sell postcards can avail themselves of such *lok.*

Next day, I return to the pagoda in daylight. This time I find another approach from Ba Trieu Street where a sign reads: *DI TICH* (historic relic), *DINH* (community hall), *DEN* (temple), *CHUA* (pagoda), *DA XEP HANG, CAM VI PHAM* (registered with the government). Happily, the government has recognised the value of the country's religious antiquities.

There seems to be no other way to reach the upper pagoda than passing the gaggle of old ladies drinking tea in the lower altar room. The nun is nowhere to be seen. Upstairs in the daylight, I encounter two giant, glaring, temple guardians and four lesser guardians, just inside the doors of the pagoda. So much for their guardianship if I hadn't noticed them the night before.

211

I remove my shoes and step into straw slippers.

Instead of writhing with gilt dragons, here the thick, red columns are hung with boards carved in gilt latticework, inscribed vertically with ideograms – poetic parallel sentences. The old monk is not helpful with the *chu nom* ideograms.

Propped against a statue is a sign reading: Duc Chua Ong. Sometimes I marvel at the obscurity of Vietnamese divinities. This chap, the monk says, was a very rich man, who had many charitable activities for the poor and orphans, not in this parish, but long, long ago – in India! He was brought to Vietnam as a 'saint' by the Chinese (sic)! The Vietnamese, as they seem to do with travelling deities, welcomed him, took him in, Vietnamised him and added him to their local deities.

In the opposite corner sits pale-faced Duc Thanh Hien, a disciple of Buddha, whose responsibility, apart from keeping his two tiny attendants apart – one righteously white-faced, the other black and evil-looking with glinting green glass eyes, – is 'to deal with the re-education of naughty children.' He also acts as a kind of fortune teller, so during *Tet,* people come to consult him about the New Year. The story goes that he once held a great feast and invited all the wandering souls, poor things, who were so hungry that some of them stuffed themselves fit to burst and a few did – burst! To keep more souls from dying – though I am a little unclear as to how a wandering soul between lives could die – he charged his tiny attendants to drive them out of the feast and perhaps in desolation at his good deed gone wrong, asked that he himself be transformed into a general.

In the light I examine the *arhats* along the right wall. The first is a curious tiny gilt statue, seated like a doll in a throne several sizes too big, the baby Sakyamuni Gaitama Buddha. The second is a bald-pated statue wearing a robe carved in graceful folds; the third, a thin, elderly *arhat* leaning forward in a posture reminiscent of Rodin's Thinker, but a particularly scrawny and sorrowful thinker. It was Koi the sculptor, who told me about the sad Buddha, who looks down and contemplates the earth's population, as sadly he might. The fourth, fifth, sixth and seventh are almost identikit *arhats* with pale faces, painted black hair and golden robes. With a total of fourteen, clearly four *arhats* have missed the roll call. The second altar holds bouquets of flowers and candlesticks. The first rank of statues behind the altar look like graduates, each wearing a tasselled mortarboard, no less personages than the kings of hell – ten of them – a hell to fit the crime, so to speak, and as might be expected, the hells are ranked, progressively worse and worse. When I ask the monk why such demons are allowed in a pagoda, he explains that in Buddhism, being a compassionate religion, it is the duty of the kings of hell to save the souls of errant sinners – not just to punish them.

It sounds like a remarkably benevolent penal code. Like the *arhats,* the kings usually appear in sets of ten; here there are only two.

The kings stand on either side of an openwork carved gilt grotto, a nine-dragon throne, popular in the North and unique to Vietnamese Buddhism, containing a statue of Buddha as a baby. The function of the nine dragons – always dragons – is to provide ablutions for the newborn babe.

The second tier of Buddhas sit on red-hot lotuses.

At the third level, a huge gilt Buddha daintily holds a lotus blossom in his right hand. My Buddhist friend enlightens me as to its significance. Buddha, during his teaching period, gathered a group of disciples around him. When he plucked the lotus and looked into their faces, one of them smiled knowingly – and Buddha recognised the follower who understood, the follower who would carry on his work.

The Buddhas of the fourth rank wear crowns – *bodhisattvas* – Buddhas who have reached enlightenment, Nirvana, but who have chosen to remain in this world to help others in their religious quest. The one on the right holds a thin-necked vase representing benevolence, 'water to save those who have been tortured'; the one on the left, a book, 'symbolising knowledge.'

Huu Ngoc, humorously acknowledging the simplistic Western mind, describes '*arhats* as undergraduates, *bodhisattvas* as having attained a Master's Degree and Buddhas as full-fledged PhDs.'

The fifth and largest Buddha sits hatless and crown-less, his hair rolled in tight curls with a bump on top. This pose of Buddha in a state of Nirvana is probably the image most common in Vietnamese pagodas. Above and behind him, seated side by side in the lotus position, are three more, only slightly smaller, red lacquered Buddhas: Buddhas of the past, present and future. This trinity of Buddhas appears in nearly every pagoda, usually at the top rank. Amongst the *arhats* lining the opposite wall are the fat and happy Buddha, Duc Phat Di Lac, also known as Maitraya. Believers rub his tummy, hoping for prosperity. But the first *arhat* in the line is a female *bodhisattva,* holding a baby on her knee. I can make no sense of the old monk's toothless French, but later learn that she must have been the Vietnamese Quan Am Thi Kinh, a reincarnation of the Chinese Kwan Yin. Her holding the baby has nothing to do with the birth of Buddha.

According to the story, the last trial of a good monk before reaching Nirvana is – to endure living one life as a woman. She married, but one night when she attempted to trim one whisker from her husband's chin while he slept, he woke and thinking she was about to slit his throat, beat her and banished her from his home.

The poor wife took refuge in a pagoda disguised as a male monk and was besieged by the unwanted attentions of the village belle, Thi Mau. Despite the monk's rejection, when Thi Mau fell pregnant through another liaison, out of spite she pointed to the monk, who obviously did nothing to support his/her innocence by agreeing to adopt the baby. When the monk(ess) finally died, it was discovered that he was a she, and much was made of the wrong that had been done to her. Not surprisingly, having endured this greatest of afflictions and mortifications – life as a woman – the monk(ess) attained Nirvana and has since been known as the Vietnamese Quan Am Thi Kinh. That is why she often appears, holding an infant. In another incarnation, she is the lady of a thousand arms and a thousand eyes, the Vietnamese goddess of mercy. Naturally, she is a very popular goddess, much in demand.

The old man, displaying more pride in a flowering Christmas cactus than in the statues, then leads me around the corner of the pagoda to an alcove where a statue wearing a crown sits holding a sceptre: the *bodhisattva*, Duc Dai Tang Vuong Bo Tat, who presides over the underworld. It is his duty to save the deceased – but only good Buddhist followers, the monk explains. Note: It takes ten kings of hell to look after the rest. I do a quick body count of statues: inside the pagoda, thirty-three, plus the two tucked in alcoves outside, and this is not even a particularly old nor famous pagoda.

Up a few steps behind the pagoda is the temple, which Barbara said was dedicated to worship of the mother goddesses. Three golden goddesses sit in regal state in glass cases: goddesses of heaven, forests and waters.

Five chaps in glass cases, 'subjects from the court' sit below, with two cherub-like attendants, minding the brass incense burner and red lacquer candlesticks. A pair of stilt-legged bronze cranes balance on the backs of turtles. The cranes represent the soul, wisdom and longevity and, more practically, operate a flying shuttle service between earth and heaven for the righteous (live carp carry the kitchen gods). According to the monk, this is a Tao temple. As I see it, open-mindedness exigency plays an important role in the intermingled religions of Vietnam. Beside the glass cases stand two large, painted statues, the first with a puce pink face labelled Ban Tran Trieu. The monk mutters 'General Tran Hung Dao' – he who defeated the Mongolian hordes – doubtless, after a very long march in the sun. On his right sits a pale faced lady, Ban Son Trang, the Tao goddess of the pure land. Perhaps we should start a Taoist revival to stop pollution.

In the opposite corner sits a colossal statue of a bearded monk, Bodhidharma, the Indian who founded the Zen sect in China, called Tsien in Vietnam, with two ancestral monks from this pagoda for company.

A double-row of pike-like weapons stand nearby. Originally, they represented the symbolic Taoist eight precious weapons, applied against the sins of deceit, envy, greed . . . but with the passage of time, they came to represent the symbols of royal power, my Buddhist friend explained. It is at this point that the old monk points to the donation box and when I drop in a 10,000-*dong* note, he takes it from me complaining, *'Tres peu, madame'* – which rather ruins the mood of the moment. It'll be some time, I suspect, before he becomes a *bodhisattva.*

'And this is the king of hell,' says the young monk, indicating a statue wearing a multi-pointed crown, the kind of crown that children draw in primary school. The young monk has such warm, friendly eyes in a such an open, handsome face beneath his brown woolly hat, that many a girl must have sighed at his becoming a monk.

'Are you sure? The king of hell?'

'Heaven – the king of heaven,' he corrects himself, laughing.

The king has a thin moustache and a straggly beard and sits beneath two ceremonial fringed umbrellas on a modest, dark wooden throne – not even gilt – though the arms have been carved as royal dragons. He holds a notebook.

The notebook gives me an idea. If this is the king of heaven, might he be the self-same Taoist celestial jade emperor to whom the kitchen gods from every Vietnamese household report just before *Tet?* The monk nods, delighted. Smoking joss sticks waft incense from an enormous porcelain urn at the feet of the king, around which two dragons frolic in a *bas relief.* According to the monk, the globe where the dragons meet, is the moon – with sun rays? I let it pass.

In the week following *Tet,* I decide to return to Quan Su pagoda, the ambassadors' pagoda that Huu Ngoc started to show me through. It is named after a famous Confucian, one of the master's most devoted disciples.

A bell tower crowns the entrance gate, characteristic of pagodas in Vietnam. But such variety. Some gates are plain yellow or white, others elaborately painted with flowers and dragons, some are one storey, others are two or three storeys, their tiled, hipped roofs turned up at the corners.

In the deep South, the colours are so exuberantly gaudy that it is sometimes difficult to take them seriously. Coming from a religious tradition where statues and architecture tend to be pale and sombre, one feels that any monk who ordered such garish decoration simply had to be joking.

Inside the gate, a line of women sit selling flowers, joss sticks and wooden rosary beads. Two very old ladies, wearing traditional round velvet headbands, sit together, reading scriptures. A third is counting money.

A sign near the steps informs me that this pagoda serves as the headquarters of the Buddhist Council of Vietnam and the Vietnamese School of Higher Buddhist Studies. So, the study of Buddhism continues, officially. Having said that, some people are still somewhat wary of flaunting their Buddhist faith, hence, I have not named my Buddhist friend. Inside the pagoda, two more old women in long brown tunics sit reading scriptures, one leaning against a column. Incense fills the air.

The ornately carved and lacquered beams bear the soot of centuries of smoke. There is much coming and going as people stand in front of the two successive altars, one behind the other, raising their hands three times above their heads in an attitude of prayer, with or without joss sticks.

I go in search of someone to show me around and find a monk, seated at a small table in a tiny room, surrounded by people. 'Just after *Tet* is a particularly busy time,' he says apologising, and asks me to ring for an appointment.

A few days later, I am met by the handsome young monk, Tien, who leads me to a classroom. He pours tea and starts to read in English from a page giving a brief history of the pagoda.

'Built at the village of An Tap in Tho Xuong district by the southern gate to Thang Long, the ancient capital. In the book, *Dai Nam Nhat Thong Chi,* the author stated that in the Le dynasty (1428-1788), Champa, Siam and Laos all sent their envoys to Vietnam to offer tributes. The king had a pagoda built beside the residence for these envoys.'

Struggling to decipher Tien's accent and seeing an idle photocopier nearby, I ask if possibly he could make a copy of the page from which he is reading. In addition to the potted history, he kindly gives me a photocopy of a diagram of the pagoda and a photocopied list of the names of the statues. Exactly what I wanted, the names of the statues of Quan Su pagoda – in Sanskrit!

The names on a separate list are in Roman script, sort of. Tien tells me that the diagram was worked out with the help of a Hungarian. Pity the Hungarian hadn't gone one step further and numbered the little circles that indicate the statues on the diagram. We set out to do just that.

After only a few minutes, I begin to appreciate the patience and diligence the Hungarian and presumably Tien, both must have exercised to get this far. It takes a very long time and many blank walls of complete incomprehension, followed by jubilant enlightenment as I pounce on the meaning of what Tien is trying to explain. Triumphant at last, I have numbered the circles and checked the numbered list against it. As a reward, Tien presents me with a small book entitled *Some Teachings of Lord Buddha on Peace, Harmony and Human Dignity.* Later, I mark a few passages, some reflecting the ethics underlying Christianity:

> Subdue anger with no anger,
> Subdue evil with good,
> Subdue stinginess with generosity,
> Subdue untruth with truth.
> – Turn the other cheek.

> My mind wanders in every direction in this world.
> But I cannot find anyone who is dearer than one's own self.
> If in everybody the self is so dear, so cherished,
> Those who have loved themselves,
> Please do not do harm to the self of others.
> – Do unto others as you would have others do unto you.

A few could only be Buddhist thoughts:

> There is no fire like the fire of lust,
> There is no grip like the grip of anger,
> There is no net like the net of delusion,
> There is no river like the river of craving.

> The sages do no harm to anybody,
> They are restrained in their bodily activities,
> They go to the deathless state,
> Going there they have no sorrow.

> One should take one's self as one's own refuge,
> Because there is no other refuge.
> By a self well tamed and restrained,
> One obtains a refuge that is very difficult to obtain.

> A person who sits alone, sleeps alone,
> Walks alone, industrious and active,
> Alone, he subdues himself.
> Such a person will take delight,
> In living deep in the forest.

Although I have no pretensions to sage-hood, I particularly liked:

> The sage leaves home,
> He wanders, homeless,
> With folk in the village,
> He has no intimacies.
> Empty of sensual desires,
> Devoid of any expectations,
> He wages no verbal quarrel with anyone!

Quat trees stand beside the main red lacquer and gilt altar, holding red lacquer candlesticks and offerings of fruit. The splendid bronze chandelier with marble panes could be *art nouveau,* except for the standing statue of Sakyamuni balanced in the centre. Carved, wooden lanterns – 'very old' – hang in the side aisles. Lamentably, these beautiful old lanterns are often replaced by bare fluorescent

218

bars. Perhaps the next incarnation will be electric lanterns. Staring quizzically at our diagrams, it is then that I discover that Quan Su pagoda seems to have far fewer statues than the diagram. Smiling, Tien tells me that the diagram is merely 'a layout for a typical Vietnamese Buddhist pagoda.'

Basically, we have to start all over again!

In one corner a gilt *bodhisattva* named Kehitigarbha sits wearing a multi-pointed crown. In the opposite alcove sits the figure of the thousand-armed gilt *bodhisattva,* Cundy, otherwise known as Quan Am. Tiny red Christmas lights border the tapestry pelmet, creating a festive spirit. Although many statues in pagodas and temples bear a serious mime, especially the older statues, some have plump, happy faces and many wear elaborate, colourful gear, particularly temple guardians.

Even statues of the most emaciated Buddha of the Himalayas, he who lived on only one grain of rice a day while he meditated, never look as pathetic as a Christian crucifix. Buddhism is essentially an optimistic, compassionate religion. It may entail renunciation, but renunciation in favour of an attainable peace and tranquillity now, not only in some never-never Nirvana.

Engraved stone tablets with etched photographs of the deceased line the walls, 'people of the neighbourhood.' The opposite wall has a list of names inscribed on granite. 'War dead,' says Tien. Just like the roll of honour in a Christian Church. From the French and American Wars?

'And the Chinese,' he replies, reminding me of the more recent border conflict with China in 1979.

The central altar space, lit by glowing red bulbs, holds five rising ranks of statues. Beside one altar stand a pair of larger than life carved cranes *(ha),* exactly like those I coveted in Koi's workshop.

Behind the altar is a small guardian with a pale face, streamers swirling from each side of his crown, 'part of his uniform,' says Tien. Usually larger than life, these guardians glare ferociously from their posts strategically placed at pagoda entrances. This one is guarding a carved openwork gilt grotto, a nine-dragon throne, only this time there is no baby Buddha, but a standing statue of Buddha, the prince as a young boy. Behind the grotto, Tien names the statues of two bald monks as the (Taoist) celestial emperor or the king of the sky – heaven? Yes, him again – and a celestial chess player. It seems that the gods enjoy a good game of chess. Looming above them is a

219

huge seated Buddha, his hair is in tight ringlets, 'Buddha having reached Nirvana – at the moment of enlightenment,' says Tien. Just behind him sits an even larger gilt Buddha flanked by two statues wearing crowns. Pointed, prickly crowns, Tien explains, indicate *bodhisattvas,* monks who have reached enlightenment. The uppermost rank of statues wearing halos at the back of the pagoda are the familiar Buddhas of the past, present and future.

Outside, Tien leads me up a few steps to a temple building 'dedicated to Buddhist ancestors.' The walls are colourfully painted with life-sized, very human portraits of famous monks who have attained Buddha-hood, dating from earliest Buddhist history, some wearing Indian beards. Amongst them is Phut Ma Dat Ma, 'the very first to become a Buddha.'

The central altar is dedicated to 'ancestor monks.' Framed photos of venerable deceased monks of this pagoda stand on altar tables, rather like family photographs displayed on the parlour piano.

But it is the attractive, colourful portrait frescoes that hold the eye. Suddenly, it occurs to me that these men, so commemorated after two thousand years, have possibly come as close to immortality as is humanly possible without actually attaining eternal life. How ironic, to have achieved this personal eminence and enduring fame within a religion that denies the importance of the self.

Later it strikes me, how sensible it would be if, like the Vietnamese, the rest of the world could simply amalgamate its religions, thus eliminating religious strife.

THE BALLAD OF THE SAD LITTLE THEATRE

It's easier to speak well than to act well
– Vietnamese proverb

Duc Thinh, a director and playwright of the Golden Bell troupe at the Cai Luong Theatre in Hanoi, is a man extremely worried about the future of his art form.

For several days I have watched as the small theatre around the corner at 71 Hang Bac Street, receives a face-lift. First, its faded wooden shutters get a fresh coat of brown enamel, then its plaster walls take on fresh cream paint.

A friendly *Viet kieu* from France, also staying at the Ngoc Minh Hotel, an engineer working for UNIDO, tells me he has met and become friendly with a director of the theatre, often having coffee with him at the gossip shop opposite. He offers to introduce us and act as translator. But it is some days before all three of us are at home at the same time, the director's home being directly across the street from the Ngoc Minh Hotel at bird-level in a nest of flats.

By late January, the temperature in Hanoi hovers around 60F (15 C), so when we finally meet, we adjourn to a relatively warmer, open-front cafe a couple of doors away where we sit shivering in low cane chairs sipping tea. The day I arrived at the Ngoc Minh, there had been a fire in the flats up the narrow lane where the director, Duc Thinh lives, and in the days to follow, forlorn piles of charred personal possessions were piled out front on the pavement for disposal. My first question, therefore, is whether he and his family suffered in the fire.

No, they had been lucky. Of eleven families, nine had been burnt out. Only his and one other flat had escaped damage.

Duc Thinh is a slim man with a fine permanent network of laugh lines around the corners of his thin lips and alert, blackcurrant eyes behind steel-rimmed glasses. He is wearing a black leather jacket and a dark, wide-brimmed felt hat. His parents had not been in the theatre, but all of his own family is, his wife and his two

221

daughters. A Hanoian, he had started as a musician, playing several traditional instruments. He then studied contemporary music, joined a group and little by little, turned professional, working first in another theatre now closed, a few doors down the street. When he tells me he has been a director of the Golden Bell troupe at the Cai Luong Theatre for forty years, at first I think he must mean fourteen. The man looks no more than a lean forty, even when he lifts his hat to show a few, very few, silver hairs.

He explains that as both a musician and a dramatist, he collaborates to create new productions – twenty productions to date. He is the recipient of three medals, one of which is a personal Medal of Distinction.

Cai luong, known as Reform Theatre, he explains, has nothing to do with politics, though some of the historical plots criticise feudalism in a general way. In this instance, reform merely means renovated theatre as opposed to *cheo,* the older popular, comic folk opera still performed in villages during festivals. Dating from the eleventh century, *cheo* matured in the fifteenth and sixteenth centuries, reaching its peak in the seventeenth and eighteenth. A recurrent theme is the sad fate of women under feudalism.

Historically, *cai luong* or Reform Theatre is an outgrowth of *cheo* and originated no more than a hundred years ago in the Mekong delta, borrowing a few lines of spoken dialogue from French drama, spliced between the singing. The result is more or less the Vietnamese equivalent of American musicals or German operettas.

'All aspects of the theatre are represented: satire, comedy, tragedy, domestic drama, literature,' Duc Thinh explains, saying that it would require a connoisseur to recognise the difference between *cheo* and *cai luong.* He then proceeds to demonstrate by drawing up a double list of musical notes, as in do, re, mi, and attempts to explain how the different scales are joined, altered and invented. The musician has some difficulty in meeting the engineering mind to explain exactly how this occurs.

Deducing incomprehension, he then tries to explain to me directly, by showing me the list of notes with the signs for sharps and flats beside some of them, but without an explanation in a common language, the list of notes might as well be algebra. All I can glean for certain is that the scales differ between *cheo* and *cai luong.*

Until recently, both *cheo* and *cai luong* were popular with the people and there used to be performances of *cai luong* every night.

But during the last few years, since television and videos brought pop music to Vietnam's young, the theatre has lost ground to discos and karaoke. Since the nineties, because of the fall-off in audiences, there have only been eight or nine performances a month, Saturday and Sunday nights only. Things have become so bad that rarely more than a third of the two hundred fifty seats are occupied for the performances of the Golden Bell troupe.

'Revenue from tickets is not enough to pay for the electricity,' Duc Thinh says sadly.

Having spent several months in Hanoi during the spring and summer and never once having heard nor read that *cai luong* was on offer, I ask why the theatre does not make its performances known in the English language press. Having seen excerpts from *cheo,* I feel sure that foreigners, residents and tourists alike, would be curious and delighted to attend an evening of Vietnamese musical theatre, whether or not they understand the dialogue. The music, dancing and costumes would suffice to provide a spectacle. After all, apart from the water puppets and the circus – and films in Vietnamese for the dedicated and determined – there is little else to do in Hanoi in the evening except stroll around the lake or sit in a cafe, unless you are a karaoke fan.

I ask Duc Thinh why notices of their performances don't appear in the English language press to which he replies that there is no money for advertising. Nor could they pay for translations of the advertising copy into English. Clearly, there are a few dark pockets that the entrepreneurial spirit of *doi moi* have yet to reach.

The theatre keeps going, just, on support from the city of Hanoi. The meagre salaries (not enough to live on, which seems to be the norm) of the fifty of so actors, musicians and theatre workers are paid by the government and the government also covers the cost of one new production each year.

Now, as I am a Tiger lady – and all Asians know that Tiger ladies are trouble – I rush in to say that surely we could find someone within the theatre who could help me to translate the ten to twenty words necessary to prepare a notice for the free *What's On* pages of the various English publications. My friend who is translating and who often summarises the lengthy answers to my questions rather than translating them, replies that perhaps it is more complicated than I realise, that outsiders often don't understand all of the implications. Well, Duc Thinh immediately makes it quite clear that he would be delighted if I could help them to prepare notices for the English language newspapers and magazines. So we get our heads together and do just that.

A few days earlier, I had been gently cajoled into joining the International Women's Club. It occurs to me that the international ladies probably might be as unaware of the theatre as I have been, despite spending several months seeking out such cultural events. When I ring their 'excursions person', she has never heard of *cai luong,* thinks 'it sounds great' and is pleased that I am willing to organise a night at the theatre.

'Come any night, there will be plenty of seats,' Duc Thinh says somberly. The date any production is performed is determined by which actors are available, dependent upon their other earning commitments. We agree a date and decide then and there that the international ladies should be treated to an adaptation of Vietnam's great epic poem, *The Tale of Kieu.* It was written by the country's most illustrious poet, Nguyen Du, who in Vietnam enjoys no less esteem and respect than Shakespeare in the West. Kieu scholars endlessly debate the Vietnamese concepts of *tai* (talents and gifts from the gods) and *menh* (fate) and how the latter thwarts the former, how the talented and gifted are doomed by fate.

Simplistically, *Kieu* is the Vietnamese *Romeo and Juliet,* the story of star-crossed lovers, so deeply embedded in the Vietnamese psyche that it has been said that no one can possibly understand the Vietnamese unless he or she understands *Kieu.* The poem has even come to be used rather like the Bible in that a Vietnamese will let the pages of *Kieu* fall open as a stroke of fate to guide him in decision-making. Naturally, with that kind of a commendation, I read the poem (in the English translation by Michael Counsell) and weep in sympathy with the sufferings of the pure hearted heroine, *Kieu* – as well as marvelling at the poetry. I had even gone so far as to suggest, only half in jest, to a member of the Writers' Association that they should make a movie of *Kieu* and export it to the West, after which, every romantic from Prague to Patagonia would have to visit Vietnam. A film of *Kieu* would leave *Indochine* sinking in a basket boat. From reading the poem, I also know that there is plenty of drama in the plot to make it easy to follow, with or without the poetic dialogue, unfortunate though it may be to miss the poetry.

Duc Thinh's wife had earlier played the character of Kieu, also his stunningly beautiful daughter, whose photograph he proudly shows me in a full-colour, expensively printed programme, produced during the theatre's heydays. Unfortunately for me, I am too late to see his daughter perform. She has married a Swiss, who has carried her off to the land of yodelling. Geneva, I learn, has been blessed with at least one performance of *Kieu.*

I am overjoyed when there is a strong response from the international ladies, their husbands and friends. The instant impresario, I write a plot synopses, make a calendar of future performances and provide a few pages of background on the poet, the poem and the part it has played in Vietnamese life, cribbed from the anthology of Vietnamese literature by scholars Nguyen Khac Vien and my friend Huu Ngoc, who confided that they had first started work on the anthology under exploding bombs.

By the night of the performance of *Kieu*, eighty-five people have reserved tickets and I have the satisfaction of knowing that if I accomplish nothing else in Vietnam, at least *cai luong* will have been introduced to a wider audience. My stress level, however, is soaring. What if a good many of them don't turn up – worse, what if those who do are disappointed? What I hadn't realised is that taking people to *Kieu* as an introduction to *cai luong* is tantamount to introducing a newcomer to opera with a performance of *Gotterdammerung,* which does rather go on – as does *Kieu* – for over three hours. Thankfully, I do not yet know this when the curtain goes up on a silky backdrop with a silhouette of weeping willows. Instant theatrical magic.

My heart goes slightly faint at the first sounds of music, an over-loud onslaught of flute and high-pitched, very Oriental soprano. The five-tone scale can strike terror in the ear of any Westerner on first impact and the smallish Cai Luong Theatre is awash with it, every nook and cranny. I can imagine the gut reaction of any red-blooded American, Australian, Hungarian or Swedish man in the audience – and I know they are there, I sold them the tickets – to the first character to appear on stage, a quintessentially Vietnamese hearth-throb in the form of a long-finger-nailed young man (to prove that he is a gentleman and does no physical work) wearing rouge, lipstick and false eyelashes, a rhinestone bedecked headdress and a green silk glittering tunic – a dress, for Chris sake – over flowing white trousers. To add to this seeming effeminacy from a Western point of view, he is not only a sugary tenor, but his voice register swoons into the counter-tenor range. Oh dear, will the chaps understand that this is the hero, the romantic lead?

225

To my relief, soon enough the girls come on, a bevy of beauties in white silk with blue scarves floating through a kind of formation dance. We are left with the lovers Kim and Kieu alone on stage. They sing their romantic duet and soon enough make their vow of eternal love, recording it on a scroll. The lights dim and the scenery is changed, as all the scenes are changed, without lowering the curtain, thus keeping the action moving.

In the next scene, the villain, a moneylender and four bad guys in black, turn up at Kieu's home. When Kieu's father can't pay, amidst the weeping of his dear wife and two daughters, he is led away to prison. Woe upon the family of Kieu. Much weeping and lamenting, the conclusion of which is that Kieu decides that somehow, she must save her father – the child's Confucian duty, first and foremost to the parent.

But the only precious thing she has to sell to raise money is – herself. Kieu is played by a sweet, innocent, sorrowful, dazzlingly beautiful young girl, of course, wearing white. There is a heart-rending scene with mother and daughter wrapped in one another's arms, which must have moved even the most unsentimental American, Australian, Hungarian and Swedish male in the audience to visions of heroism.

A couple of baddies play the next scene of haggling over the price of Kieu. We know they are baddies because they flick their fans angrily at one another (polite Vietnamese never show anger). The female go-between is fat, overly made-up and alternately simpering, charming and nastily ugly, making bad tempered asides. Her sparing partner in the bargaining, the pimp, looks equally vulgar. *Cai luong* is anything but subtle.

Kieu, of course, cannot leave without entrusting the precious scroll to her sister, beseeching her weeping sister to promise to honour her vow of love to Kim in her stead.

Another weeping scene – and people on both sides of me have wet eyes – as Kieu is dragged from her mother's and sister's arms. The acting is superb.

The audience is then given a chance to rein in emotions as the scene switches to the brothel. The lights go up on a grotesque queen of evil, sitting slouched on a couch as a young masseuse lightly pummels her shoulders. This is the madam of the brothel to which Kieu will be taken. When Kieu is brought in, the madam greets her gleefully, greedily gloating on the profits to come from such a prize.

Kieu in her humiliation and distress, draws a knife from within her tunic and stabs herself.

In the *cai luong* dramatization, thankfully, we have been spared Kieu's humiliation at being deflowered by the pimp she has been forced to 'marry'. *Cai luong* is rich in sexual innuendoes, but never explicit.

Presently, a man with a kind, open face, wearing a peach-coloured tunic, appears in the brothel. This is Thuc Sinh, who falls in love with Kieu and buys her out of the brothel, but when he takes her home, his jealous wife, Hoan Thu, humiliates Kieu even more, treating her as a servant, demanding that she play the lute and sing, even ordering her to compose poetry. The pain suffered by both Kieu and Thuc Sinh is evident.

So well known is this terrible wife in Vietnam, that the name of the character, Hoan Thu, has become synonymous with cunning, wicked wives. And in case you have a modicum of sympathy for the wife, whose husband brought home a second wife right under her nose, in feudal Vietnam husbands had as many wives as they liked, although often the first wife was allowed to choose the second. This guaranteed that the second would be biddable and easily dominated by the first and from the husband's point of view, that the two would get on. At one point in *Kieu,* the terrible wife laments, 'If only he had told me before,' suggesting that all might have been so very different.

Poor Kieu, as miserable in Thuc Sinh's house as she had been in the brothel, throws herself into the river, but is rescued by an abbess and taken to a pagoda where we next find her kneeling in the plain brown habit of a novice before an altar. But Thuc Sinh comes in search of her and tries to convince her to escape. He explains that there is nothing he can do, his wife is so cunning. Unbeknownst to him, his wife has followed him and stands listening from behind one of the pillars. In Confucian, male-dominated Vietnam, the only explanation for this hen pecking that I can imagine is that it must have been the wife who had the money or political connections.

From the pagoda, the drama takes an abrupt leap to a posturing general, resplendent in red and gold velvet, strutting about the stage as only an oriental general can. It is, however, a trifle difficult to take a general too seriously whose headdress is festooned with springy, red and yellow pompoms and trembling gold medallions. Vietnamese drama – perhaps one should say melodrama – is about as subtle as a silent movie. Feudal characters are held up to ridicule by over-dressing them in outrageously fine costumes and their make-up instantly tells the audience whether the character is good or evil. For this reason, it is easier for a foreigner to follow the plot in *cai luong* than say, certain Italian operas.

The victorious general, despite his ridiculous bobbing pompoms, is the good hero who rescues Kieu and marries her. In the next scene, Kieu is seated beside him, wearing a glittering gold headdress, yellow and white silk, and all those who have made her suffer in the past are brought before her for punishment. The cowering pimp, the madam and the go-between kneel, all begging for mercy. They are quickly dispatched. Only Thuc Sinh, the kind but weak man, who pleads for mercy for his wicked wife, is magnanimously pardoned by Kieu, along with his jealous wife.

At that point the general receives a message from an enemy feudal lord, asking him to negotiate peace. Kieu, longing for peace, pleads with him to negotiate rather than to continue fighting. To please her, the general agrees to meet the feudal lord. But it is a trap. He is ambushed, first by four soldiers bearing pikes. These he kicks aside in a fine display of *kung fu,* but the nasty feudal lord laughs and the poor brave, betrayed general is no match for the feudal lord's archers. He dies, standing on one leg, frozen in an attitude of rage in a brilliant theatrical convention, the position in which Kieu finds him.

Naturally, she is distraught and the lament she sings is no less heart-rending than the *Liebestrod* of Isolde in the last act of *Tristan* – if one's ear has adjusted to the five-tone scale. Once again, poor Kieu is in despair and goes once more to the river. Briefly, all of the characters parade before her as if she were reliving a flashback of her life. Then dancers in white appear waving white silk streamers to artfully create rippling waves. Gradually, Kieu sinks beneath the waves, one last delicate hand remaining, then only a flower . . .

There cannot be a dry eye in the house.

To celebrate *Tet* while waiting for the performance of *Kieu,* I had gone to the new production, a play created through a collaboration between Duc Thinh and his friend Phan Van Quy. The title translates as *The Strange Doctor.* Hong, the receptionist at the hotel, comes with me and fills me in as the plot thickens, but the exaggerated characters and their antics would have been funny and easy enough to follow with no translation whatsoever. This is fall-about farce, somewhere between British pantomime and Gilbert and Sullivan. The music –

two electronic keyboards, an electronic guitar and drums – although based on the traditional scale, sound more or less modern and the knock-about male and female chorus lines of singers and dancers in glittering costumes are captivating.

Inspired by Moliere, revised to set it in feudal times, the plot is about a peasant farmer who is mistaken for a doctor and taken to the palace of the king to cure a princess who cannot speak. By accident, he does cure her, but along the way, there is much mickey-taking of lesser officials, mandarins, puffed-up medics of assorted nationalities, lecherous philanderers and husbands who beat their wives. In this sort of company, naturally, the wives have to win. The hero and heroine, of course, are the farmer and his wife, who predictably decide that they far prefer to live the hard, simple life in their village rather than the complicated life of the palace. The audience loves it and we all tumble out of the theatre, our faces aching from non-stop smiling for over two hours.

All the world loves a lover, but even more, all the world loves a jolly good laugh.

Just as I am packing up to leave, Huu Ngoc invites me to come along with him to interview a Vietnamese painter.

WITH THESE HANDS

Qualities of the wife are shown by her cooking
— Vietnamese proverb

Artist Dong Thi Khue is waiting for us in the roadway outside her atelier or we would never have found it. She leads Huu Ngoc and me into a typical suburban Hanoi apartment block, laundry vying with pot plants for balcony space, up and up. The concrete stairs are divided by a narrow ramp for hauling motorbikes up from floor to floor, two, three, four. Finally, at the fifth floor, she unlocks a metal grill – all doors have grills – and we are inside a two-room workshop.

As a Vietnamese artist, Dong Thi Khue now is in a very enviable position. She has her own workspace, rare for artists in Hanoi where families of several generations often occupy one room. She has received a grant to produce a solo exhibition. Formerly, artists were only allowed to share exhibitions. For only the past few years she has been free to work and work she has, with the pent-up passion of an artist long deprived of the time and freedom to work.

During her early career, Khue was a peripatetic art teacher, travelling from village to village, up and down the northern half of the country. However, during the years of the Vietnam War, the Viet Minh propaganda effort consisted of two-person teams: in Dong Thi Khue's case, the artist herself and a photographer. She explains how they worked. After a battle, she and the photographer would move in, take photographs, then mount slide shows, travelling from village to village in a grass roots propaganda effort to keep the people involved in the war. On arriving in a village, she would sing folk songs to draw the attention of the villagers, then show them the slide show. I dread to think of the sights she has seen.

From 1978 until only a few years ago, Dong Thi Khue served as secretary general of the Vietnam Association of Plastic Arts, recently re-dubbed the Association of Fine Arts, while simultaneously serving as a deputy in the National Assembly of the government. Clearly, Dong Thi Khue is a patriotic artist, who has devoted all of her energies throughout most of her life to serving her country's cause. Now at least, she is reaping the benefits. At last free from administrative duties, she can express herself as the artist she always wanted to be. And such an artistic explosion. Her friends tell her that she needs three lives and from the variety of work in her tiny studio, that seems about right. She thinks of herself primarily as a painter and shows us photographs of her paintings, stored elsewhere for lack of space. Working with oil on canvas, she has used the traditional fabric designs of Vietnamese hill people as inspiration; she has painted headless female nudes. Many of her paintings are abstracts or surreal, often borrowing objects from everyday Vietnamese life, blending the shapes into an always colourful fantasy.

The studio is stuffed to the ceiling with works in progress. A forest of elongated, carved wooden female arms lie about, detached, some leaning against the walls, each hand in either a graceful position reminiscent of the Buddhist goddess of mercy, Quan Am, or in the gestures of a dancer. A few arms have been attached to deep notches cut into slim tree trunks still bearing their bark. Khue is much concerned with the role of women, with the placidity and smiles with which they greet life and with their deep, hidden passions, pain and turmoil. The arms in the tree trunks will form a forest to show how closely women are bound to the land. Perhaps it is no accident that her husband works in forestry. Two arms with the hands in an attitude of prayer will be hung from threads to float freely, occasionally coming together. Two more arms will be crossed, one hand holding a purple fan, a reference to a sensuous poem composed by the famously irreverent, eighteenth century Vietnamese woman poet, Ho Xuan Huong, who despite living in a period of rigid Confucianism, by subtly employing the *double entendres* made possible by the tonal Vietnamese language, wrote quite sensuous poetry. In one poem, she compares the demure fan behind which Vietnamese women shyly hide their faces to female private parts. The pair of wooden arms holding the fan will rest lightly on a slim, open, wooden Vietnamese plant stand with gracefully curved legs, echoing the lower part of the female body. Huu Ngoc warns me that translations of Vietnamese poetry, particularly the poetry of Ho Xuan Huong, are fraught with lost nuances, that in translation only one meaning is possible, rendering it altogether too direct and rather brash.

Nevertheless, here is his translation of *The Fan.*

231

Seventeen, eighteen* . . . what is the proper number?
Never mind, one loves it and will not let it go.
One loves it thin, splayed in a triangle
Or when gathered in ten, held in the grip of the tenon (sic)
The hotter one feels, the greater the delight in its coolness.
One is not weary of it at night and loves it still the day.
The persimmon paste puts a red glow in the cheeks,
Kings and lords, all cherish this little thing.
(tr Huu Ngoc)

*(The number of bamboo staves that make up a fan.)

Propped high on a shelf are kites with singing bamboo flutes attached, waiting to be painted. The three-sided frame of a bamboo screen stands on one side of the room. Long, fringed swatches of raw silk in strong, deep colours – vibrant green, purple, gold, red, blue, brown for earth, orange for bricks – have been attached, four colours to each frame. Beneath each segment of the frame, a pair of carved, wooden, traditional Vietnamese 'clogs' – similar to the platform base of the brocade boots worn by emperors – have been placed in whimsical 'sitting' positions, conveying an astonishing variety of moods! The open frames will have wind blowing through them to make the long swatches of silk float in the breeze like the North Vietnamese peasant woman's sash and the loose-hanging tunic she wears when working in the paddies.

Outside on the balcony, a typical woven bamboo wall from a village house leans propped against the railings, the lower sections tightly woven for privacy, the section above more open to allow air to pass through. Khue shows us a basket full of carved wooden birds, the same birds I have seen flitting through brocades and carvings in village halls. These unpainted, gracefully carved birds will be attached to the bamboo wall. Then she brings out the leaves, each more than a meter long, shaped like palm or banana leaves, each leaf stem wrapped in long, thin, grassy fronds of bamboo and painted a different bright colour. More than a hundred of these leaves will form an installation in the exhibition. Having long been a primary teacher, Khue feels very strongly that children and adults visiting the exhibition should be allowed to touch the wooden hands, the carved birds, the leaves, and to feel the swatches of silk, to experience her work not only with their eyes but with their other senses.

232

In this artificial world of inhuman, manufactured products and plastics, she hopes to keep the Vietnamese literally in touch with their heritage as well as with their traditional village environment, by simultaneously using natural materials and the deep well of Vietnamese culture to manipulate those materials and find new ways of expressing them as an artist.

Perhaps this is the moment to admit that I am not an enthusiast of modern art. People who stack bricks, make circles of stones, weld enormous shiny bits of metal together that you can walk through and much of twentieth century painting – not to mention the sick minds who cut preserved beasts in half – leave me cold, if not outraged. I have been annoyed at pop art and op art and most of what followed. So, you may be a little surprised that I found anything in Dong Thi Khue's bits and pieces that spoke to me. But I did, not because I have been gazing more than casually at the pleasant, souvenir landscape paintings in the many galleries that line the streets of Hanoi, but because I have been looking in a diffused sort of way at Vietnam's visual cultural history. What I see in Dong Thi Khue's work are allusions, reflections, echoes, memories, even her fears, that those traditions, styles and skills will soon be lost forever. Her fears are mine. What's more, her creations are attractive, even beautiful.

So, having set out with the underlying suspicion that I was about to visit a politically acceptable artist whose work would probably hark back to boring social-realism, I have the agreeable surprise of meeting an artist whose fomenting creativity, having been stifled by other work for many years, is at last free to fly.

As we walk to lunch, she shows us the pavement beside a children's playground where she worked while carving the wooden arms. When the children's mothers came to collect them, the children were always crowded around Khue, watching and talking, climbing frame and swings forgotten. At lunch over a bowl of *pho,* Huu Ngoc is bold enough to urge her to sing for us, one of the folk songs she used to sing to draw in the villagers during the war. In the back room of the small neighbourhood restaurant, she composes herself and begins. She has such a sweet voice, a much sweeter voice than any professional singer I have heard, that I am not at all surprised that she and her photographer colleague formed an effective propaganda team.

No wonder Vietnam won the war.

LOVE, DEATH AND LAUGHTER

His wife first, heaven afterwards
– Vietnamese proverb

Once in Hue, I saw a bride in a fluffy white gown, settling herself on the back of a motorbike beside Ngo Mon (gate), where she had been posing for wedding photographs. Many shop windows display wedding gowns and dresses in a rainbow of colours, which I assumed were for bridesmaids.

It isn't until Thanh, the handyman at Ngoc Minh Hotel, returns from his village wedding, proudly passing round the photograph sealed in plastic of his pretty bride wearing a frilly white wedding dress, that I learn that even village brides rent at least one dress – not always for the big day. His bride has remained in the village, having moved in with his family to help his mother, according to tradition. Only then do I learn that the well-dressed bride rents as many dresses as her family can possibly afford to change into, not for her wedding – but just for the photographs, sometimes days before.

In Ha Bac province of North Vietnam, traditional courtship used to be conducted in groups. A singing team of boys would visit a singing team of girls in a neighbouring village and the teams would challenge one another in a song contest. Tradition held that if a member of one team married a member of another, it was bad luck and they wouldn't be happy. A great incentive for not joining a singing team, I would have thought.

Members of competing teams were supposed to bond as brothers and sisters. Considering that Vietnamese poetry is littered with allusions to the beloved as 'little sister' or 'big brother', it is little wonder that sometimes tradition broke down and there were romances between members of opposing teams. Of course, this visiting from village to village gave ample opportunity for flirtation with eligible prospects. These *quan ho* songs of which there are more than three hundred, form one genre of folk music. The subject is romance and the words may be shyly flirtatious or full of caustic wit. With the *double entendres* offered by tonal Vietnamese, the words might be quite suggestive, much to the amusement of the matrons and grandmothers of a village, who sometimes shouted bawdy remarks. I am indebted to Barbara Cohen for the following. The boys might try to find out if the girls were free by singing:

> *Let me ask the apricot flower,*
> *Is there a path leading to the garden*
> *where you are growing?*

The girls might reply provocatively by singing:

> *The path to the apricot blossoms*
> *is marked with bamboo hedges,*
> *so bees can easily find their way.*

Or they might tease the boys' team:

> *Men! How much are they worth?*
> *Just three pennies a dozen*
> *One puts them in a cage*
> *and plays with them* (like a cricket).

    Another traditional custom associated with courtship and marriage in village life is the offering of the betel quid – a leaf from the betal vine that grows on the areca palm, wrapped around an areca nut – offered to the girl herself as a proposal of marriage, then to her mother to ask permission. The legend of the betel leaf and areca nut goes back to the time of the fourth Hung king in Viet pre-history –

    Two young brothers, perhaps twins they looked so much alike, were orphaned and taken in by a kindly scholar with a young daughter. As the three youngsters grew up together, naturally the girl became very attached to the brothers and wanted to marry one of them, but which? Knowing that she should marry the eldest, she set out to determine which brother it was. Finally, by observing them together, she deduced that Tan must be the elder as his brother deferred to him in offering him chopsticks at a meal. Accordingly, her decision was made to marry Tan. The parents joyfully agreed to the marriage and Lang rejoiced at his brother's happiness. However, as time passed and the newly-weds drew closer, naturally excluding Lang, Lang felt rejected and lonely. However, all went well until one day when Lang returned home first and his sister-in-law, mistaking him for her husband, embraced him warmly. Her husband Tan arrived just in time to see the two embrace and suspected the worst.

Lang knew that no matter what he said, his brother would always have doubts. So with a heavy heart, he decided to leave the only home he knew and one dawn he set out. He walked for days, through paddies and jungles, over mountains and streams. Exhausted and hungry, he reached a river where he collapsed and died. The spirits, who observe the sorrows and joys of man, knew that he had died from brotherly love and changed him into a rock for eternity.

After a time when Lang did not return, Tan set out to search for his brother. He questioned peasants as he went, wandering through paddies and jungles, up and down mountains, finally reaching the same river as his brother before him. Feeling much guilt and anguish at what his brother must have suffered, he too collapsed and died and the spirits changed him into a slender areca tree with fan-shaped leaves, growing from the rock.

Back in the village, Tan's wife became so distressed at the absence of her husband that she finally set off to find him. Perhaps guided by fate, she too eventually came to the same riverbank and sank down in exhaustion and grief to die, seated on the rock, embracing the trunk of the areca palm. The kindly spirits transformed her into a climbing vine that entwined itself around the palm, the leaves in which the betel nut are wrapped. In villages, old women still chew betel, colouring their lips red with the juice and a proverb runs, 'The betel quid starts the conversation.'

This is another Viet legend about a woman and two husbands – remember the kitchen gods? Certain ethnologists suggest that these legends may reflect a conflict or painful transition in early Viet society from polyandrous marriage under matriarchy to monogamous marriage under patriarchy – monogamous for women, that is. Men were allowed to have many wives.

These days, shyness is not what it used to be and courtship is conducted in a somewhat less gregarious manner than *quan ho* teams. Although privacy is a word and concept barely recognised in Vietnam – to be alone is considered to be miserable – I find it difficult to imagine how such a Vietnamese proverb as, 'A quick wedding stops evil tongues' ever came into being, except to borrow another proverb from the West: 'Love (and lust) always finds a way.'

On the subject of privacy, when the old man in Hoi An told me that his wife always liked to sleep with their children in their

236

over-sized bed, I remember wondering how, after the first child, the couple ever had any privacy. When you consider that extended families of several generations often sleep in one room with only a curtain as partition and even during the day, grannies, aunts and uncles, adolescent children and toddlers wander through endlessly, it is little wonder that in Hanoi, sometimes married couples rent a hotel room in order to be alone. There is even a joke in Hanoi about Lenin being the father of the nation, because so many babies have been conceived in Lenin Park! Another recent innovation in Hanoi is the popular *cafe vuons,* cafes with seats in a garden amongst dense foliage that provide discretion for couples to become better acquainted. Some of these *cafe vuons* are said to have tiny cottages of wood or bamboo, so small that only an enterprising couple might make 'full use' of them.

In an essay in which Huu Ngoc sets out to explain the Vietnamese concepts of love, he explains that the Vietnamese language is far richer than English in its choice of words to describe love. The word *ngia,* most often translated for the word love, is a phonetic Vietnamisation of the Chinese character that translates as justice, an important concept in Confucianism. But the Confucians laid even greater stress on humanism, *nhan,* than on justice. *Nghia* goes back several thousand years, Huu Ngoc explains. Mencius, a relative and disciple of Confucius, insisted that *nghia* meant doing the right thing, even at the expense of one's own interests. In his essay on the subject, Huu Ngoc quotes a passage from *The Tale of Kieu.*

> *Our love is lost and it is bitterly regretted,*
> *But our hearts, like a broken lotus stem*
> *remain bound by the straggling filaments.*

Huu Ngoc believes that only a Vietnamese can truly appreciate the beauty and poignancy of this verse, and more particularly, the full meaning of the word *nghia.* The concept is much larger than romantic love, drawing in 'a traditional Vietnamese ethical concept that can be understood as moral obligation, justice, duty, a debt of gratitude and mutual attachment based on duty.

'*Nghia* has to do with both the heart and the mind, which are closely linked in such terms as *nghia bung* (think in the belly) or *nghia trong long* (think in the bowels).' Traditionally, the belly and bowels (guts) were considered to be the centre or source of all emotions. Huu Ngoc goes on to set out three components of *nghia:* 'First, duration in time. A proverb says that one ferry trip across the river is (long) enough for passengers to feel bound together by *nghia.'* So simplistically, it might be concluded that the Vietnamese believe in what Westerners might call love at first sight.

'Second, the mind, as symbolised by the stem of the lotus: when the stem is snapped, the two ends are still linked by the tenuous filaments inside.' Though love may die in the mind . . .

'Third, the heart as represented by the filaments.' Once having loved, some slender threads of that emotional attachment always remain in the heart, no matter what may have happened to the rest of the relationship.

'In brief, far from being merely a dictate of conscience, *nghia* is a mixture of reason and feeling, mutual moral and sentimental obligation born out of human contacts, however brief.

'Moreover, *nghia* governs all relationships a person may have with other people, with his family, his village, his country.'

In Vietnam, romantic love generally leads to marriage and family. 'Conjugal love, based on affection and loyalty is expressed by *heu thuong* – a compound word very difficult to translate in all its shades of meaning.

'*Heu* implies passion, desire, affection and fondness. *Thuong* (with the exception of some southern and central dialects) means to have compassion, understanding or pity. *Thuong* also implies care, even tolerance.'

Huu Ngoc also translates conjugal love as *tinh nghia,* with *tinh* for love and *nghia* for 'mutual moral and sentimental obligation born out of love.' It is this *nghia* that keeps a married couple together late in life, long after passion has died and affection has become little more than a domestic habit. But even then, *nghia* is that part of the conjugal relationship that refuses to be governed by reason. A husband and wife remain together because they are bound by *nghia.*

'*Nghia* explains why so many couples remain physically faithful despite long absences, most especially in times of war.' This idea of *nghia* as a bond is expressed by the words of a Hue love song:

> *When there's no more water in the Song Nai canal,*
> *When only ruins remain of the Thien Mu pagoda,*
> *Only then will our pledge be broken.*

Vietnamese poetry concerning romantic love was not always peach blossoms and tendrils of the lotus. Sometimes it could be quite saucy, witness the lines written by eighteenth century poetess, Ho Xuan Huong, who not only subtly ridiculed the religious life, pagodas and monks, but dared to express through her suggestive poetry for the first time, a woman's feelings about physical love. In the hands of Ho Xuan Huong, the puns and double meanings of tonal Vietnamese were always witty, never vulgar, but very, very irreverent. Translation, perforce, tends to be less allusive, more explicit and blatantly direct, of necessity having to choose one meaning when there may be a choice or echoes of several. In regard to the poem below, the jack fruit is a huge roundish fruit with rough, nubbly skin that grows directly from the tree trunk and its bright yellow pulp has thick, sticky juice.

> *My body is like the jack fruit, prickly skin, thick pulp,*
> *dear friend, if you like it, drive a wedge into it,*
> *don't touch it, your hands will be slimed all over.*

Even Buddhist poetry can admonish people to make the most of fleeting hours:

> *The body is like an inhalation when one breathes,*
> *Life is like a cloud flying as the wind blows*
> *in the far away mountains*
> *The moor hen ceaselessly cries for months on end,*
> *We should not let spring pass uselessly.*

This is not to say that adultery and divorce do not exist in Vietnam. In feudal times, polygamous and adulterous relationships existed. For men it was one thing, for a wife the cost was high. If she were caught in an adulterous affair, she would be tied to a raft under the boiling sun and set adrift down river! Even an 'adulterous widow' could be punished.

In modern Vietnam, divorce is on the increase as women begin to become more economically independent. The reasons sited for divorce most often are: incompatibility of character (40%), adultery (18%), bad treatment of the wife (16%), family dissensions (11%), one of the partners drinking or gambling (11%), economic difficulties (3%), illness or infertility (2%).

In the West one often hears that life is held cheaply in the East. Otherwise, why would so many millions of young Asian lives have been sacrificed in Korea, in the French Indo-China and the Vietnam Wars. In Vietnam, this view ignores how hard the Vietnamese were pressed, by starvation, to rise up against the French, and eventually, whatever one's political persuasion, against the Americans, in an effort to free themselves as they saw it, from foreign domination.

The Vietnamese do have a different attitude towards life. Huu Ngoc explains that the Vietnamese take the view that life is temporary, but death is eternal. What he means is that 'living is only a moment; the one real abode is death, so we have nothing to fear. But life is not held cheaply, life is very dear to us. But we consider that life is temporary.'

Even after a short time in Vietnam, I too, would refute the Western notion that life is held cheaply in the East. Vietnamese short stories, films, television dramas, even the choreography of modern ballets, constantly express extreme grief at the loss of dear ones: husbands, sons and lovers, wives, mothers and daughters – a good many women were militarily active in recent wars. However, Westerners may not always see or understand grief in the East.

To the Westerner, a funeral may appear to be almost a festive occasion, as mourners in white headbands accompanied by a band, march through the streets behind the coffin. Later, a marquee is set up and food is laid out like a wedding feast. In Buddhist theory, those in the East believe that the soul of the departed has merely moved on into another, happier existence. However consoling that theory may be, it does not prevent a mother, daughter, wife, son, father, husband, sister, brother, lover or friend from grieving deeply. The traditional period for a spouse is three years. In reality, in the heart of the aggrieved, it may be for the remainder of a lifetime.

The grief is far worse if the body of the dead cannot be ceremonially laid to rest in the family tomb and is therefore, according to Vietnamese beliefs, condemned to wander, lost in the empire of darkness, venerated by no one – the fate of many who died in the wars of this century.

There is even a special day, the fifteenth of the seventh lunar month, when Buddhists dedicate ceremonies to the deliverance of these poor wandering souls; rice porridge is offered so that they can eat their fill to gain enough strength to be reincarnated!

The Vietnamese have had much pain and suffering to bear through the centuries, nearly a thousand years under Chinese domination, more recently in wars against the Japanese, French, Americans, and again in 1979 against the Chinese, added to the sufferings of feudalism and frequent natural disasters such as typhoons, droughts, floods and pests. Life at the best of times has been precarious.

They have survived their suffering by developing extraordinary resilience and strength – physical, emotional and spiritual. One day while waiting for a ferry, I stood beside a peasant woman who had removed her carrying pole from her shoulder. On impulse, I placed my shoulder under her bamboo pole and tried to lift her baskets of rice and vegetables. Now I consider myself to be reasonably strong and fit, but I could not lift her baskets off the ground, not even one inch! And this was a wiry little woman who just about reached my shoulder! She smiled at me wryly.

Humour is one thing that has kept the people going. The Vietnamese have transformed humour into a powerful weapon in their survival kit against horrific odds. *Cheo,* the peasant folk drama, is rich in irony and mickey-taking. Jokes, anecdotes and proverbs poke fun at anyone in authority, turning kow-towing reverence inside out.

The late Vietnamese writer, Nguyen Tuan, made a list of some one hundred and fifty different kinds of Vietnamese humour. He explains how anecdotes can make a laughing stock of anyone: the monk who had his lips caught in the claws of a crab, hidden in the cleavage of a well endowed woman; a miser who apologised for not being able to treat his friend to a meal, to which the retort was: 'Oh, it doesn't matter, we'll eat my horse. To go home I'll ride one of your fattened geese.'

Another anecdote concerns a doctor, summoned to heal the daughter of a king of hell, because of his excellent record, having lost only one patient.

'Oh, that's because I just set up shop this very morning,' replies the ingenuous doctor.

Another pokes fun at hen-pecked husbands, a group of whom decided to rebel. When one of the wives appears, they all flee except for one man, who hides in a corner. After she has gone, the scattered husbands reassemble and decide to make 'the brave one' in the corner their leader, only to discover that he has died of fright. There is also a strong strain of whimsical, innocent humour displayed in the sketches of the water puppet theatre, when a peasant chases a fox up a tree, or a fisherman is attacked by a fish. And there is more than an element of irony in many Vietnamese proverbs:

A too beautiful woman, backache

Tea too strong, no more voice

Too strong tobacco, a raw throat

Stupidity runs in front, wisdom behind

Long ago, it seems, the Vietnamese settled on their version of happiness. The ideogram for happiness is often associated with the image of a bat because the Vietnamese word for bat is pronounced the same way, *phuc,* and a good many people are named Phuc.

Besides happiness, *phuc* also carries the connotations of wealth, longevity, honours, peace, tranquillity, love of virtue and a natural, painless death. According to Sino-Vietnamese philosophy, the three abundances are: happiness, defined as carrying a child in his arms, the latest-born in his long line of descendants; wealth, described as a mandarin onto whom favours are poured by the king and gifts presented from the people; and longevity, as an old man with a healthy complexion and a white beard, holding the peach of the immortals in his palm. No definition is made of a woman's three abundances, a project, perhaps, awaiting a gender specialist. In Confucianism, the word happiness took on moral connotations: doing good brings happiness, not only to one's self but also to one's descendants. Buddhists say, 'to do happiness' to express the idea of charity. A beggar will beseech people 'to do happiness.'

The humour of the Vietnamese, his ability to make light of his woes, results in a healthy, resilient, almost irrepressible optimism. In Vietnam, even now, those who still have very little, light their faces with smiles. Their warmth of spirit springs from within and foreigners are greeted with such friendliness and generosity that one wonders at first whether it can possibly be genuine – it is – and conversely, one wonders at the sourness and unfriendliness often encountered in the West. It is tempting to conclude that the Vietnamese *au fond,* are a happy people. That would be far too simplistic. There are many for whom the struggle of daily life remains still, extremely hard, but the vast majority seem to be revelling in their achievements of peace and independence. Although great strides have been made, the country remains poor. Yet Vietnam is a very proud nation. The people have, after all, defeated two major world powers. And whatever one's own political persuasion, it must be said – and I am a committed democrat – that at last, the Vietnamese are being left to live under a government of their own creation.

The year I lived among them was deeply enriching. I enjoyed delving into the deep well of their culture and could happily have gone on for another year, maybe for a lifetime. I have been astonished and heartened by their warmth and kindness, by their open friendliness and humour, by their sensitivity, by their highly refined courtesy and civility, by the sophistication of their arts, by their sense of style and by their scholarship. I only hope that they will not allow the superficiality of materialism to swamp their rich traditional values and their sweetness of character. Their gifts to me were the realizations of how very little we need, that things are unimportant, unless they are beautiful; that sensitive consideration and courtesy, kindness and generosity are the gold of human relationships; and that humour and irony are the best weapons for survival. During my year in Vietnam, deprived of what we in the West would call a normal social life, the Vietnamese open-heartedly extended their welcome and rarely, only fleetingly, did I ever feel lonely.

Pleasant hours fly past
– Vietnamese proverb

HISTORIC APPENDIX

PREHISTORY

Earliest human habitation north Vietnam, 500,000-300,000 years ago
> In 1965 archaeologists discovered teeth of an early anthropoid at Lang Son, near the Vietnam-China border.

Epipaleolithic Son Vi culture 20,000-10,000 BC
> A subsequent discovery in the hills of Vinh Phu, 33 miles (55 km) north-west of Hanoi, provides a link to Mesolithic finds.

Two Mesolithic cultures 11,000-8,000 BC, when humans began to domesticate tuber vegetables:
> Hoa Binh Mesolithic 11,000-10,000 BC
> Bac Son 10,000-6,000 BC

Many regionally varied Neolithic and Bronze Age cultures
c. 4,000-600 BC

The Hung kings of the Viet kingdom, 7th C. BC-179 BC
> The pre-history of the Viets is a blend of the myths of the Hung kings, legendary descendants of a union of the Dragon of the Seas and the Fairy of the Mountains. One legend describes the eternal struggle against the devastating floods of the Red river delta as the conflict between the Spirit of the Mountain and the Spirit of the Waters for the hand of a beautiful princess.
> Van Lang, the 7th C BC embryonic state of the Hung kings, was made up of a federation of 15 Viet tribes called the Lac Viet. By the middle of the 3rd C BC, Lac Viet had been annexed by An Duong Vuong, chief of the neighbouring mountainous Viet kingdom called Au Viet. The new kingdom combining Au Viet and Lac Viet became known as Au Lac. Its capital was at Co Loa, north of Hanoi. An Duong Vuong was the first of 13 Hung kings.
> The culture of the Viets covered the entire Bronze Age and the beginning of the Iron Age, up to the beginning of recorded history. It is the Viets, also known as Kinh, who were the forebears of the 85 per cent, majority of the ethnic Vietnamese today.
> In 179 BC the Chinese warlord, Trieu Da (Chao To) conquered the Viet kingdom of Au Lac and became king of what he

called Nam Viet, the Chinese name for southern China. This was a prelude to Chinese colonization by the Han dynasty in 111 AD, which was to dominate what has become North Vietnam for more than a thousand years.

Vietnam's present-day minorities still number 54 distinct ethnic groups, made up of a mixture of Mongoloids, who came from the north and the original Malayo-Polynesian inhabitants of the central coast and mountains.

VIETNAMESE HISTORY IN SIX EASY STEPS

Vietnamese scholar Huu Ngoc simplifies Vietnam's convoluted and complicated history into five easy periods:

$$1000 + 1000 + 900 + 80 + 30 \text{ years}$$

1)   Somewhat less than 1000 years BC, represented the formative period of Viet national identity, the civilisation of the Viets in the Red river basin, the Bronze Age.

2)   More than 1000 years of Chinese domination, 179BC to 938 AD, during which there were numerous insurrections against the Chinese.

3)   Roughly 900 years of national independence from 938 to 1858, several national dynasties and territorial expansion to the south, cultural influence but resistance to invasion from China.

4)   Approximately 80 years of French colonization from 1862 to 1945, the first French conquests date from 1858, the French-Japanese occupation from 1940 to 1945.

5)   Then 30 years of war, the Wars of Independence from 1945-1975: resistance against the French 1945-1954, ending at Dien Bien Phu; resistance against the Americans, 1965-1975, ending at Saigon.

6)   Since 1975, efforts to overcome social and economic crisis, the politics of renovation, *doi moi* begun in 1986.

RECORDED HISTORY

Chinese domination 179 BC-938 AD
Brief rule by Trung sisters 40-43 AD
Uprisings in the 3rd and 6th centuries
Defeat of Chinese in 938 by Ngo Quyen at Bach Dang river
Hindu kingdom of Champa around Hue, late 2nd C AD

Champa

Included four ethnic groups, all belonging to the Austronesian race and was first recorded in Chinese records as the nation of Lin Yi. It ranged along the coastline from the Ngang Pass, (272 m, 439 km south of Hanoi), south to the province of Phan Rang. The Chams cultivated wet-rice and left traces of sophisticated irrigation systems as well as splendidly carved statues and numerous brick temple complexes dedicated at various times from the 7th to 14th centuries to their possibly matrilinear, Buddhist and Hindu gods. They were active traders from their ports at Hoi An near Danang and Thi Nai in Binh Dinh province, trading with India, Java, Arab countries, China and Japan.

Funan

Indianised kingdom in southern Vietnam, 1st-6th C. AD. Its capital port city, Oc-Eo, was in present-day Kien Giang province.

Chenla

Khmer kingdom that attacked Funan mid-6th C. and absorbed Funan.

VIETNAMESE DYNASTIES AND RULE

Ngo	939-965
Twelve Lords	965-968
Dinh	968-980
Early Le	980-1009
Ly	1010-1225

Tran	1225-1400
Ho	1400-1407
Post Tran	1407-1413
Chinese rule	1414-1427
Later Le	1428-1527 (nominally to 1788)
Mac	1527-1592
Trinh Lords	1545-1778 (North)
Nguyen Lords	1558-1778 (South)
Tay Son	1778-1802
Nguyen	1802-1945 (nominally after 1884)
French rule	188401945 (South a colony from 1867)
Japanese occupation	1940-1945
Nominal independence	1945-1954 (Indo-Chinese War)
Communist (North)	1954-1975 (VN War 1965-1975)
Republic of Vietnam (South)	1954-1975 (Diem 1954-1963)
Communist Reunification	1975

NGUYEN EMPERORS

Gia Long	1802-1819, dynasty founder
Minh Mang	1820-1840, Citadel builder
Thieu Tri	1841-1847, poet
Tu Duc	1848-1883, longest rule
Duc Duc	1883, ruled 3 days
Hiep Hoa	1883, 4 months, poisoned
Ham Nghi	1884-1885, exiled

Dong Khanh	1885-1889, French puppet
Thanh Thai	1889-1907, exiled
Duy Tan	1907-1916, exiled
Khai Dinh	1916-1925, French puppet
Bao Dai	1925-1945, died Paris 1997

BIOGRAPHY

Borton, Lady, *After Sorrow, An American Among the Vietnamese,* Viking, New York, 1995

Cohen, Barbara, *The Vietnam Guidebook,* Harper & Row, New York, 1990

Do Phuong Quynh, *The Ha Long Bay and Quang Ninh Province,* The Gioi Publishers, Hanoi, 1992

Do Phuong Quynh, *Traditional Festivals of Vietnam,* The Gioi Publishers, Hanoi, 1995

Ellis, Claire, *Culture Shock Vietnam, A Guide to Customs and Etiquette,* Graphic Arts Center Publishing Co, Portland, Oregon, 1995

Fox, Diane Niblack & Taylor, Nora A, *The Temple of Literature,* The Gioi Publishers, Hanoi, 1994

Hoang Kim Dang, (Introduction by Nguyen Khac Vien), *Vietnam Album,* The Gioi Publishers, Hanoi, 1991

Huard, Pierre and Durand, Maurice, *Viet Nam, Civilization and Culture,* l'Ecole Française d'Extrême Orient, Hanoi, 2nd ed 1994

(No author credited), *Hue,* Culture and Information Office of Thua Thien-Hue Province, Hue, 1993

Huu Ngoc, *Sketches for a Portrait of Vietnamese Culture,* The Gioi Publishers, Hanoi, 1997

Huu Ngoc and Cohen, Barbara, *Tet,* The Gioi Publishers, Hanoi, 1997

Jamieson, Neil L., *Understanding Vietnam,* University of California Press, Oakland, California, 1995

Lewis, Norman, *Omnibus: The Dragon Apparent, Golden Earth, A Goddess in the Stones,* Picador/Macmillan General Books, London, 1996

Mai Khac Ung, *Emperor Minh Mang's Mausoleum,* Societe des Historiens du Vietnam, Hanoi, 1993

Mai Ung and Dao Hung, *Hue, Monuments of an Ancient Capital,* The Gioi Publishers, Hanoi, 1993

Minh Chi, Ha Van Tan, Nguyen Tai Thu, *Buddhism in Vietnam,* The Gioi Publishers, Hanoi, 1993

Various contributors, National Committee for the International Symposium on the Ancient Town of Hoi An, *Ancient Town of Hoi An,* The Gioi Publishers, Hanoi, 2006

Nguyen Du, (tr Counsell, Michael), *Kieu,* The Gioi Publishers, Hanoi, 1995

Nguyen Huu Thong, *Hue, Its Traditional Handicrafts and Trade Guilds,* Nha Xuat Ban Publishing House, Hue, 1994

Nguyen Huy Hong, *Vietnamese Traditional Water Puppetry,* The Gioi Publishers, Hanoi, 1996

Nguyen Khac Vien and Le Huy Van, *Arts and Handicrafts of Vietnam,* The Gioi Publishers, Hanoi, 1992

Nguyen Khac Vien and Huu Ngoc, *Vietnamese Literature,* Red River, Hanoi, 1981

Nguyen Vinh Phuc, *Hanoi Past and Present,* The Gioi Publishers, Hanoi, 1995

Phan Huy Le, Nguyen Dinh Chien, Nguyen Quang Ngoc, *Bat Trang Ceramics 14th-19 th Centuries,* The Gioi Publishers, Hanoi, 1995

Phan Thuan An, *Monuments of Hue,* Nha Xuat Ban Thuan Hoa, Hue, 1996

Pham Hoang Hai, *Hanoi, Practical Guide Book,* The Gioi Publishers, Hanoi, 1996

(No author credited), *Saigon 20 Years After Liberation,* The Gioi Publishers, Hanoi (undated)

(No author credited) *Silk Paintings of Vietnam,* The Gioi Publishers, Hanoi, 1991

(No author credited), *Stone Stelae at the Temple of Literature,* The Gioi Publishers, Hanoi (undated)

To Hoai, *Diary of a Cricket,* The Gioi Publishers, Hanoi, 1991

Tran Duc Anh Son and Le Hoa Chi, *Hue Flavours,* Thuan Hoa Publishing House, Hue, 1993

Tran Ky Phuong, *Cham Ruins, A Journey in Search of an Ancient Civilization,* The Gioi Publishers, Hanoi, 1993

Tran Viet Anh, *Hanoi Atlas,* The Gioi Publishers, Hanoi, 1997

Trong Cung Nguyen, *Anything Novel in the Royal Palace of the Nguyen Dynasty?* Thuan Hoa Publishing House, Hue, 1991

Tu Hue, Den Quang and Cadiere, Leopold, *Le Sacrifice du Nam Giao,* Nha Xuat Ban, Da Nang, 1995

(No author credited), *Van Mieu Quoc Tu Giam, The Temple of Literature, School for the Sons of the Nation, A Walking Tour,* The Gioi Publishers, Hanoi, 1994

(No author credited), *Vietnamese Folk Tales,* The Gioi Publishers, Hanoi, 1992

(No author credited), *Vietnamese Legends and Folk Tales,* The Gioi Publishers, Hanoi, 1997

Vo Van Thang and Lawson, Jim, *Vietnamese Folktales,* Nha Xuat Ban, DaNang, 1996

Vu Cong Hau, *Fruit Trees in Vietnam,* The Gioi Publishers, Hanoi, 1995

Wintle, Justin, *Romancing Vietnam, Inside the Boat Country,* Viking 1991, Penguin 1992

33194362R00141

Printed in Poland
by Amazon Fulfillment
Poland Sp. z o.o., Wrocław